ECONOMICS FOR POLICY MAKERS

A Guide for Non-Economists

Gustavo Rinaldi

LONDON AND NEW YORK

First published 2019
by Routledge
2 Park Square, Milton Park, Abingdon, Oxon, OX14 4RN

and by Routledge
52 Vanderbilt Avenue, New York, NY 10017

Routledge is an imprint of the Taylor & Francis Group, an informa business

The designations employed in publications of the International Training
Centre of the ILO, which are in conformity with United Nations practice,
and the presentation of material therein do not imply the expression of
any opinion whatsoever on the part of the Centre concerning i.a. the legal
status of any country, area or territory or of its authorities, or concerning
the delimitation of its frontiers.

The responsibility for opinions expressed in signed articles, studies and
other contributions rests solely with their authors, and publication does not
constitute an endorsement by the Centre of the opinions expressed in them.

Reference to names of firms and commercial products and processes does
not imply their endorsement by the International Labour Office, and any
failure to mention a particular firm, commercial product or process is not a
sign of disapproval.

Trademark notice: Product or corporate names may be trademarks or
registered trademarks, and are used only for identification and explanation
without intent to infringe.

British Library Cataloguing-in-Publication Data
A catalogue record for this book is available from the British Library

Library of Congress Cataloging-in-Publication Data
A catalog record for this book has been requested

ISBN: 978-1-138-38880-2 (hbk)
ISBN: 978-1-138-38881-9 (pbk)
ISBN: 978-0-429-42432-8 (ebk)

Typeset in Bembo
by Apex CoVantage, LLC
Printed by CPI Group (UK) Ltd, Croydon CR0 4YY

CONTENTS

Microeconomics

Macroeconomics

FIGURES

TABLES

FOREWORD

Effective participation in bipartite and tripartite dialogues at national and sub-regional forums is one of the key roles that employers' organizations and trade unions are mandated to play.

In carrying out this role, the social partners participate by representing the interests and views of their constituents in various economic and social panels. Macroeconomics concepts often underpin the discussion. It is therefore essential that employers' organizations and trade union representatives have the capacity to apply fundamental economic concepts and tools in formulating and articulating their arguments and positions. Poor mastery of fundamental economic concepts has a multiplicity of negative effects, both direct and indirect. These effects include unequal and ineffective participation in consultations and negotiations, inability to influence the direction of debates and an incorrect interpretation and misunderstanding of economic facts and trends.

In this context, in 2016, the Programme for Employers' Activities of the International Training Centre of the ILO (ITCILO) launched a specific blended course on macroeconomics for social negotiators which has been rolled out in four continents at national, sub-regional and international level. Banking from this experience and in close collaboration with professors and practitioners, the Programme for Employers' Activities of the International Training Centre launched the idea of consolidating the training materials used in the course into a comprehensive manual not only for the benefit of social partners, but also of a wider audience to raise awareness of the importance of performing at all levels by means of evidence-based advocacy and substantiating policy proposals or advocacy campaigns with research, data and facts.

The originality of the manual derives from its being designed for non-economists, and also by its including, together with clear and solid explanations, references to cases and applications of the concepts of economics theory in real life situations.

The views expressed in this book are those of the author and do not represent the official view of the ITCILO or that of the (ILO).

Jorge Illingworth, Programme Manager,
Programme for Employers' Activities, ITCILO

ACKNOWLEDGEMENTS

The preparation of this manual entailed a long preparation and rich debate between the Employers' Activities Programme and the Employment Policy and Analysis Programme of the ITCILO.

Through the different drafts that led to the finalization of the manual, we are extremely grateful for the extraordinary work realized by the main author, Professor Gustavo Rinaldi, Faculty of Economics at Turin University: his technical expertise, endless efforts and openness in taking into account feedback by reputed academic reviewers and ILO officers needs to be emphasized.

We extend our appreciation to the two academic reviewers, Carlos Casas, main Professor in the Academic Department of Economics at *Universidad del Pacífico* Lima-Perú, Errol D'Souza, Professor of Economics & Dean, Indian Institute of Management Ahmedabad, David Chambers, Emeritus Professor of Management, London Business School and two anonymous referees.

Internally in the ITCILO, Paolo Salvai, Senior Programme Officer in the Programme Employers' Activities, and Samuel Asfaha, former Head of Employment Policy and Analysis Programme, followed up on the original concept and development of the manual providing key technical inputs and were the first internal reviewers.

Additional specialists and young researchers contributed to the manual development, including Masanneh Landing Ceesay, Gambian Institute of Statistics, and the external consultant Andrea Vinelli. Simon Robbins contributed with his excellent proofreading of the manuscript. Michele McClure and Tersilla Garella contributed by editing the different drafts of the book and Stefano Ceresa with graphical work.

In closing, we wish to acknowledge and thank employers' representatives from all over the world that attended the first blended courses on "Economics for social negotiators" in 2016 and 2017, tested the training material and provided critical information and reflections for the finalization of the manual.

Jorge Illingworth, Programme Manager,
Programme for Employers' Activities, ITCILO

AUTHOR'S NOTE

Economics for Policy Makers presents economic reasoning for those who face economic decisions whether in a company boardroom or in a negotiation between trade unions and employers, in the conduct of a country's government or in the running of a household. Most of those who are decision makers will probably not be economists, nor will they have the option of delaying making a decision in order to take a course in academic economics. Typical texts of economics make frequent use of formulas, equations and technical jargon which can deter the non-specialist reader and which this book avoids.

Many economic decisions concern policies which affect the whole of society. Many actors are involved in their formulation: citizens, elected representatives, governments, political parties, trade unions, representatives of the employers, business associations, corporations, the media, think tanks, lobbies, committees, associations, groups of citizens. But many of those involved in the process of defining policies or in negotiating contracts are uncomfortable with using the economic terminology in which the debates are often framed. Worse still, the decision maker may be unaware that he or that he or she is misusing terms he or she has not understood.

Economics for Policy Makers introduces and explains the relatively small number of basic concepts and definitions, which the decision maker needs in order to make use of the economic pages of newspapers and economic reports and to locate relevant information within the vast store of publicly available economic data. The text is grounded on the real-world problems which the reader will have encountered at work, or in reading reports from expert organizations or in newspaper reports. It makes direct reference to representative articles and reports covering current and recent economic debates and published in different parts of the world.

The reader will be helped to analyse such sources critically in order to formulate his/her own positions and conclusions.

I will be very grateful to those readers who contact me with comments, criticism, additional information and suggestions.

Special thanks to the publishers of many newspapers which have authorized the reproduction of their articles for this book. I have tried to contact all the copyright holders of all material reproduced in this book. If anyone has been inadvertently omitted, I apologize and I remain at their disposal.

Any errors or omissions are entirely due to the author.

Gustavo Rinaldi, Turin, December 2018

gustavo.rinaldi@unito.it

Microeconomics

Any serious negotiation and policy making must be based on solid information and good analysis. Well-managed firms can distribute wealth to employers and employees and pay substantial taxes.

Here we consider a business from the economic point of view.

First we consider its objectives, then we analyse what a firm produces, how it can be efficient, and how size can influence its performance; and then we consider the relationship between a business and its customers, and its relationship with competitors.

PART I

Introduction

Before analysing how business creates jobs and finds the resources to pay for them, we consider some concepts, which underpin many parts of this text: economic profit and value added. Economic profit must, at least in some measure, be the objective of any business that aims to be sustainable. Value added gives a measure of what the firm can share between employers and employees.

1

ECONOMIC PROFIT

In order to survive, firms should create value which, in private business, is synonymous with profit; however, the economic concept of profit is different from the accounting concept of profit. The former takes into account opportunity costs and sunk costs. In this unit we therefore present these concepts, showing inter alia, that firms may have different objectives and that profit maximization is just one of them.

1.1 The value of the best foregone alternative[1]: the opportunity cost

Economics as a discipline is about how people make choices under conditions of scarcity. Scarcity compels individuals to take into account trade-offs between different alternatives. When we consider the capital or the time available to a person, we should consider the alternative uses which that person could make with those resources.

Even if a resource, my work or my capital does not cost me anything, I should take into account the opportunities that I miss through using that resource to pursue a specific project instead of other projects.

The working hours of an entrepreneur could be sold to a different firm where they could go to work as an employee and earn a monthly wage.

Entrepreneur's opportunity cost[2]= Best possible net salary as an employee[3]

The capital of the entrepreneur could be invested with minimal risk in some safe bond and it could give a safe return. Otherwise this capital could be invested in a different project with the same risk as in this project, but with a higher return.

If the firm uses capital which belongs to the entrepreneur, to partners or to shareholders, that capital may not appear as a cost in the income statement of the firm because the firm uses this production factor at zero cost. It will receive some remuneration in the eventual presence of profits. In some cases, the entrepreneur, their family or some shareholders lend money to the firm at a rate below the market rate. In both cases the opportunity cost of capital must be considered.

Opportunity Cost of Capital = Potential remuneration in the next best alternative project[4]

Read

The first recommended text is Indian. It is an interesting way to analyze our choices about such things as buying a mobile phone, having holidays or buying a car. Too often we choose something without taking into account what we have to give up in order to follow that path. The consideration of the alternative choices may help us to decide better.

Costly phone or a holiday? Look at opportunity cost

Vivek Kaul,[5] *DNA*, August 26, 2018. www.dnaindia.com/personal-finance/column-costly-phone-or-a-holiday-look-at-opportunity-cost-2655174

Questions

- What is the main objection of the author to the purchase of a mobile phone for 65,000rupees?
- What is the experiment suggested by the author?
- What happens when we spend money on one thing?
- What was the experiment of Dan Ariely?
- What was the point that few people could get?
- What is the effect on our decisions?

Analysis

The author observes that a mobile phone does not do much besides making and receiving calls and logging onto the internet. The experiment that he suggests consists of thinking about what he can do if he does not spend 65,000 rupees on a mobile phone. He could instead buy a motorbike or have a good holiday in Goa or Bali. "When we spend money on one thing, we are basically deciding not to spend money on other things, given that we don't have an unlimited amount of money." There is an opportunity cost.

The experiment of Dan Ariely consisted of asking potential buyers of Toyota cars what else they could do with the amount of money corresponding to the cost of the car. Few people were actually able to realize that the purchase of that car was sometimes alternative to providing their children with a better education, having better health treatment, improving their house, buying a piece of land to grow an orchard, attending some concerts, contributing to a charity, having dinners in certain restaurants, inviting friends for parties, or something else. We do not consider the opportunity cost of our actions, and probably our decisions are not going to be in our best interests.

1.2 Sunk costs vs recoverable costs

Sometimes companies spend money on something such as a piece of equipment, a building, or the acquisition of knowledge through training or a patent. Afterwards, the same piece of equipment, the same building, the same knowledge, commands a much lower price on the market. This lower value does not reflect the annual loss of value accruing to the capital of a firm or country because of wear, obsolescence or accidents. We call that loss of value "depreciation" and it has nothing to do with sunk costs. Here, the problem is that there is an asset which is designed to cater for specific activities and cannot easily be diverted to an alternative use. The second-hand market for such assets is limited. Examples can be found in certain training, advertizing or R&D expenditures.

The company could only sell that asset at a loss. A large part of the initial cost cannot be recovered; that part would remain even if the company stopped producing. For this reason, we can say that the part of a cost that cannot be recovered has little to do with the firm's future projects. It will be there both with and without them. Economists have introduced the concept of "sunk cost" to describe this type of cost. A sunk cost is an "expenditure that has been made and cannot be recovered. (. . .) A sunk cost is usually visible, but after it has been incurred it should always be ignored, when making future economic decisions. Because a sunk cost cannot be recovered, it should not influence the firm's decisions".[6]

Is a sunk cost the same as a fixed cost? It is not: a fixed cost could sometimes be recovered in the long run, for example, if or when the firm completely abandons its industry. A sunk cost can never be recovered, neither in the short or long run. All sunk costs are fixed costs, but not all fixed costs are sunk costs.

Short run vs long run

We often say that firms use labour and capital.

Any firm obviously uses far more than two inputs in its production process. The level of some of these inputs may be changed on rather short notice. Firms may ask workers to work overtime, hire part-time replacement from an employment agency, or rent equipment (such as power tools or automobiles) from some other firm. Other types of inputs may take somewhat longer to be adjusted; for example, to hire new, full-time workers is a relatively time-consuming (and costly) process, and ordering new machines designed to unique specifications may involve a considerable time lag. At the most lengthy extreme, entirely new factories can be built, new managers may be recruited and trained, and new raw material suppliers can be developed. (Nicholson, 1994:241)

The short run and long run denote the length of time over which a firm may make a decision. This distinction is quite useful when studying market responses to changed conditions.

> For example if only the short run is considered, the firm may treat some of its inputs as fixed, because it may be technically impossible to change those inputs on short notice. If a time interval of only one week is involved, the size of a firm's factory would have to be treated as absolutely fixed. Similarly, an entrepreneur who is committed to a particular business in the short run would find it impossible (or extremely costly) to change jobs – in the short run, the entrepreneur's input to the production process is essentially fixed. Over the long run, however, neither of those inputs needs to be considered fixed, since a firm's plant size can be altered and the entrepreneur can indeed quit the business.
>
> *(Nicholson, 1994:238)*

In the short run, at least one production input, for example a piece of equipment, is used in a fixed quantity which cannot be changed. In the long run, the quantities of all input factors can be changed. For example, the locomotive or engine of a train of a railway company is a fixed cost for the company, whether it travels and pulls a train or not; its cost does not change and must be paid. However, one day the railway company may decide to sell that engine and recover its value. The engine in the short term is a fixed cost, but in the long run it is a recoverable cost. If the same railway company trains its staff to do very specific operations which nobody else in the industry undertakes, the company will probably never be able to recover the money spent on that training. There is no way that the company can recover its money, regardless of whether or not the staff that received the training work for the company and produce something. That cost is sunk.

"Suppose that you have decided to lease an office for a year. The monthly rent that you have committed to pay is a fixed cost, since you are obligated to pay it regardless of the amount of output you produce. Now suppose that you decide to refurbish the office by painting it and buying furniture. The cost for paint is a fixed cost, but it is also a sunk cost since it is a payment that is made and cannot be recovered. The cost of buying the furniture, on the other hand, is not entirely sunk, since you can resell the furniture when you are done with it. It's only the difference between the cost of the new and used furniture that is sunk."[7]

Incumbents are those companies which have operated in a certain industry for some time with some success. They have already spent money on something, for example a plant, the acquisition of a certain technology or of certain skills. Sometimes they cannot recover that money for one reason or another. If they spent €100 to acquire certain capabilities and now their market value – i.e., the price they can get in the market today – is €10, then most of their cost, €90, is now non-recoverable or "sunk". We say that those companies have "sunk costs".[8] This is true whenever the market value, the price, which could be obtained on the market, is lower than the book value, that is the value written in account-ing books. Sunk costs are the effects of past choices and one can do nothing to eliminate them.

Sometimes understanding the behaviour of a company may be difficult if we do not realize that its costs are different from those of its competitors. Outsiders may consider challenging this company by entering its market. They still have to face certain costs. For the challenger, entering the industry implies bearing the full cost, while not entering means saving the money and using it elsewhere. For the incum-bent firm, this alternative does not exist because it cannot recover the money which it spent on unrecoverable expenses (sunk costs); so any decision on whether or not to stay in the industry should be made taking into account the fact that sunk costs will not be recovered, even if the firm's operations are terminated. Sunk costs will have to be paid in any event. In this option (remaining in the industry) as much as any alternative option (leaving this industry), it has to be paid. For this reason, sunk costs, **once incurred**, should not be considered a cost that the incumbent faces as a consequence of **its continuous commitment** – to remain in the industry. We cannot say the same for an outside challenger; the outsider may save money if it simply decides not to enter the industry. In this case incumbents and challengers may face substantially different costs even if they use the same technology. In this sense, sunk costs may constitute barriers to the entry of new firms (challengers) into the industry. Therefore, one should not be surprised if incumbents and challengers behave in different ways.

Spending money on non-recoverable costs sometimes constitutes a message that a firm transmits to the world: it shows its commitment to a certain field. This is the case with a tenant who spends money on refurbishing their rented prop-erty: they show their intention to rent it for a certain period, not just in the short term. Spending on sunk costs is like destroying the bridge you have just crossed. If you enter an industry with major sunk costs, you declare that you intend to stay there. The money you spend on recoverable costs can still be recovered. Choice is still available. Incumbents usually have greater sunk cost than new entrants, because they have spent money on specific plants, equipment, knowl-edge or training. In many cases these specific assets can only be resold to third parties at a price much lower than the price recorded in the company books. In some cases, the assets cannot be sold at all. Companies know that if they dispose of these assets, they should acknowledge the loss incurred by selling something at a price below the cost of acquiring it, even after duly taking depreciation into account. Incumbents have to pay eventual debts on these assets anyway, whether or not they remain in the industry. Therefore, if we say that these assets are a consequence of their present choice of remaining in the industry, we are mistaken. Now, assume that we have to decide whether this company should remain in or leave this industry. We calculate the company's future revenues and costs if it stays. Should we include in this calculation those costs that the company pays now, but which it would also pay if it left the industry? The answer is no, for if we did, we would not be calculating the value of the economic choice expressed by the company's decision to remain in the industry and we would be making the decision in the wrong way. Sunk costs strengthen the position of a company in its industry but can also limit its desire to do new things. Established companies in an industry are often resistant to disruptive innovation which threatens their existing capabilities and cannibalizes their existing products. Imagine a company which has invested huge sums in being a leader in fossil energy. Would it be willing to see renewable energies triumph? The answer is probably not; if renewable energies become cheap, most of the company's assets (mines, oil wells, knowhow, pipelines, etc) will lose much of their value. The company owners know that the introduction of certain innovations may reduce or completely destroy the market value of their assets. They also know that the market value of their assets may become much lower than the value recorded in their balance sheet for those same assets. In such a case they would record losses. The value of those assets would then be "sunk" or non-recoverable; the sum originally spent would become a "sunk" or "unrecoverable" cost. Sunk costs not only explain companies' choices but are also a key consideration when appraising the sustainability of a business.

Examples

- A company builds a plant which is very specific to a certain production process and which could just be bought by competitors at a low price in order to shut it down.
- A person has acquired skills in a specific field which cannot be used in other fields.
- A company has developed a brand which cannot easily be sold to others.
- A company has spent money on R&D to acquire knowledge that is difficult to sell on the market.
- What was the advantage of developing railways for those established in the horse-and-carriage business?
- Can you guess why Kodak was unable to become the leader in digital photography?

In the development of a firm's or country's business plan, sunk costs should not be treated as part of overall costs. The decision maker will bear their burden anyway, with or without the planned business.

When we discuss whether we can save a plant in which 100 employees work, the fact that the book value of the plant is $50m is irrelevant; this is true even if the plant has a market value much lower than $50m and cannot be sold anyway. In the business plan we could only include the present market value of the plant, provided that we would in fact be ready to sell it.

Read

The disadvantage of those who are leaders in one technology

Sony dominated the world's consumer electronics market for several decades. One of its most successful products was the Walkman, the first hand-held, portable record-player. Sony's leaders correctly perceived that devices and content could be integrated, and that a single hand-held device could ultimately provide any service that could be delivered electronically, such as radio, TV, photography.

So why did Apple beat Sony to invent the hugely successful iPod? Apple had no prior experience in the music industry.

Clayton Christensen (2016)[9] suggests an answer in terms of what he calls the Innovator's Dilemma.

Sony's leaders chose the acquisition route, focussing on music-producers (e.g. CBS Records) and movie-makers (e.g. Columbia Pictures). Its strategy was to assemble the capabilities needed to manage change.

If you try to assemble together the capabilities for making major change, you may end up with precisely the people who have an incentive to resist change. They may see the technological innovations as threats to their own well-established ways of doing business and perhaps cannibalizing their current products. They have invested time and other resources to become the best in one field. The innovation destroys the market value of this investment.

Innovation may be achieved instead by companies (like Apple) where there are no such vested interests in opposing change. Advantage rests with the shrewd outsider.

Read

John Kay, "Why Sony Did Not Invent the iPod," *Financial Times*, 4 September 2012. www.ft.com/content/7558a99e-f5ed-11e1-a6c2-00144feabdc0.

Questions

- Did Sony foresee the convergence of several tools into one?
- Why wasn't Sony the leader of the iPod revolution?
- What had Sony to gain in such a process?
- What had Sony to lose?
- Why may established companies in an industry be naturally resistant to disruptive innovation?
- Can you give examples of other industries where this occurred?
- What are the effects of having industrial policy heavily influenced by incumbents?

Analysis

Sony foresaw the convergence of several tools into one. It developed a vision of integration of devices and content long before Apple dreamed of going into the music business. Sony failed to implement its vision probably because, as John Kay writes,

> established companies in an industry are naturally resistant to disruptive innovation, which threatens their existing capabilities and cannibalizes their existing products. A collection of all the businesses which might be transformed by disruptive innovation might at first sight appear to be a means of assembling the capabilities needed to manage change. In practice, it is a means of gathering together everyone who has an incentive to resist change.

Sony could have become the new leader in electronics, but it was too scared of losing its previous achievements. Sony had important sunk costs. Any company with substantial sunk costs may make the mistake of focussing on them and giving up future opportunities. According to John Kay, financial services and education are industries with similar blocks. We can also cite producers of fossil energy and their approach to renewable energies. When industrial policy is heavily influenced by incumbents, there is the risk that it will look more at past rather than future technologies.

THE SUNK COST FALLACY

"Once you have bought something, the amount you paid is 'sunk' or no longer recoverable. So future behaviour should not be influenced by sunk costs. But, alas, real people tend to care about how much they paid for something. Researchers have found that the price at which owners listed[10] condominiums in Boston was highly correlated with the buying price.[11] As pointed out earlier, owners of stock are very reluctant to realize losses, even when it would be advantageous for tax reasons.

The fact that ordinary people are subject to the sunk cost fallacy is interesting, but perhaps it is even more interesting that professionals are less susceptible to this problem. For example, the authors of the condominium example mentioned above found that individuals who bought condos for investment purposes were less likely to be influenced by sunk costs than individuals who lived in the condos. (. . .) It appears that one reason to hire professional advisers is to draw on their dispassionate analysis of decisions."[12]

THE ITCILO MOVES ITS CAMPUS

The ITCILO has decided to move its campus. One month ago, the Director found a perfect new location. Its price is €5,750,000. The Director could not buy the place on the spot because of the need for authorization by the Board which would only convene in one month. The seller asked for a €500,000 deposit to keep the property blocked for one month.

A few days before the board meeting, a new property is offered to the Centre. It is as good as the other but its price is lower, the seller asking only €5,500,000. What should the Centre do?

The first property has an accounting cost of €5,750,000, but €500,000 is already a sunk cost, as deposits usually cannot be recovered. Today the economic cost of the first option is

€5,750,000 − €500,000 = €5,250,000

For the second option, the Centre should pay €5,500,000. In this case, the accounting costs corresponds with the economic cost.

€5,250,000 < €5,500,000. For this reason, the Board should choose the first option. You could also consider the problem in an alternative way:

Total payments to make in the first option: €500,000 + €5,250,000 = €5,750,000 Total payments to make in the second option: €500,000 + €5,500,000 = €6,000,000.
Under the present conditions, the second option entails greater payments.

1.3 Accounting profit

The accountants' objective is an accurate measurement of costs and benefits that accrue profits or losses to the firm, with the aim of reporting them to shareholders, creditors and tax authorities. They can take a static picture of the firm at a given

TABLE 1.1 Calculating the accounting profit

+ Revenues (price X quantity)
- cost of raw materials, partly finished goods, utilities and labour costs
- depreciation
= OPERATING PROFIT
- interest or financial costs
= PRE-TAX ACCOUNTING PROFIT
- tax
= **AFTER TAX ACCOUNTING PROFIT**
- dividends
= **RETAINED EARNINGS**

moment in terms of assets and liabilities (balance sheet) or they can show what the firm has achieved over a certain period in terms of what it earned and what costs it had to pay (income statement or P&L, see Table 1.1). They pay attention to written and unwritten contracts which generate rights and duties. They always have a legal basis. They pay attention to historical facts: "we bought this at a certain price on March 15th 2009". Costs and revenues are explicit: they derive from an invoice, a debt or a payment. In accounting terms, the cost of capital is the sum of interest + depreciation. The wage bill represents the cost of labour. The wage bill sometimes includes a salary for the entrepreneur who works in the company; sometimes it does not. Profits are the basis for corporate taxes, dividends or retained earnings.

The accounting profit is used to report to shareholders, pay taxes and obtain credit from banks.

1.4 The economic profit: comparing two scenarios

In essence, the economic profit of a project derives from the comparison of a scenario which includes that project with the best alternative scenario that excludes it (Table 1.2). In the first scenario you have the project (the firm) as it is. In the second scenario you consider the situation of the entrepreneur and shareholder if they did not carry out this project (or did not invest in this company) but chose the best from

TABLE 1.2 Two alternative scenarios

Scenario with this project	*Scenario without this project*
The entrepreneur works for this project or this company.	The entrepreneur works for some alternative project or company and receives a salary.
The entrepreneur invests their money in this project or in this company.	Their capital is invested in an investment with no greater risk and generates a return.
Sunk Costs, for example old debts on non- recoverable expenses, must be paid (there is no way of avoiding them).	Sunk Costs, for example old debts on non-recoverable expenses, must be paid (there is no way of avoiding them).

TABLE 1.3 Calculating the earnings of the owner in the alternative scenario (without this project)

\+ best possible alternative after-tax labour income of the owner (**opportunity cost of the labour** of the owner)

\+ best possible alternative after-tax return on the invested capital (**opportunity cost of capital**)

\- Costs to pay anyway, even when not following this project (**sunk costs**)

= **Net earnings of the owner in the alternative scenario** [1]

---

[1]See Cabral and Backus (2001)

the available alternative projects carrying approximately the same level of risk as this one. In that case, eventual sunk costs would also be paid since they do not depend on the project under consideration.

The sunk costs are thus a common feature of both scenarios.

For the entrepreneur this project makes sense (and an economic profit) if the entrepreneur is better off in a scenario with this project than in a scenario without it.

If the after-tax accounting profit of a firm (or a project) is greater than the net earnings of the owner in an alternative scenario (Table 1.3), the firm (or project) makes an economic profit.

Economic Profit		After Tax Accounting Profit		Net earnings of the owner in the alternative scenario
20,000	=	100,000	−	80,000

In some cases, we encounter firms which operate with zero economic profit.[13] This sounds odd only if we ignore the meaning of economic profit. In reality these firms remunerate the work and capital of the owner as much as in their best alternative uses.

An example

In 2008 a small software house had a revenue of €1,000,000. Expenses for employees were €500,000. It paid €300,000 in other invoices (non-durable goods). It also paid €50,000 for the participation fee in a research consortium. Two years earlier the company committed itself to participating in the consortium and paying €50,000 every year for three years. The owner who invested €2m in the business often receives job offers from Google, Microsoft and Facebook. The latter offered her a net salary of €100,000 per year. Risk-free bonds offer a 1.5 per cent tax-free interest. The owner now needs to understand whether the business was creating value this year or not.

Firstly, we must calculate the accounting profit (Table 1.4) of this firm.

Next we must calculate the net earnings of the owner in the alternative scenario (Table 1.5).

TABLE 1.4 The accounting profit in a small software house

Revenues	+€1,000,000
Expenses for employees	−€500,000
Invoices for non-durable goods	−€300,000
Consortium fee	−€50,000
Pre-tax profit	*+€150,000*
Taxes (33%)	−€50,000
After-tax accounting profit	**=€100,000**

TABLE 1.5 The net earnings (accounting profit) of the owner of a small software house in the alternative scenario

+	best possible alternative after-tax labour income of the owner (**opportunity cost of the labour** of the owner)	+ €100,000 Salary the owner could earn outside as an employee.
+	best possible alternative after-tax return on the invested capital (**opportunity cost of capital**)	+€30,000 1.5% of 2,000,000 Earnings of capital invested in risk-free bonds
−	Costs to pay anyway, even not following this project (**sunk costs**)	−€50,000 Consortium fee
=	**Net earnings of the owner in the alternative scenario**	+ €80,000

Therefore:

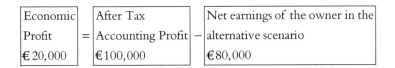

The accounting profit is €100,000, but the owner's labour and capital can generate earnings. This year the economic profit of the owner – the benefit deriving from carrying out this activity rather than being in the best alternative scenario – is €20,000.

The owner is financially better off in this scenario than in the alternative scenario.

1.5 Different objectives of the firms

Is economic profit the only possible goal that a firm may have? A firm can actually choose from many alternative goals, *viz.*:

1 Revenue maximization can be part of a strategy of maximizing long-term profits; you secure a market share, and eliminate competitors so as to behave as a monopolist (see Section 6.3) in the future; as a monopolist you will be able to exploit consumers. In other cases, this strategy is simply a way of satisfying the

managers' desire for power. In this perspective you can explain much merger and acquisition activity.

2   Maximization of the utility of the owner and of their family is very frequent in family-based systems, as for example in Italy. The final objective is not firm growth but family welfare. Possible expressions of this strategy are the renunciation of using the managerial market (preference for many family members as managers and directors) or limited growth so as not to share control with strangers or become accountable to third parties.

3   Employment maximization and welfare maximization sometimes characterize public administrations and charities. You can pursue them if some external source supplies resources (subsidies) for survival. Otherwise they must be complemented with some goal of minimal profitability in order to guarantee the survival of the organization.

4   Long-term profit maximization is the objective more linked with the firm's growth.

5   Short-term profit maximization is used as a proxy for '4' and it is particularly used by firms which are under strict scrutiny by financial markets. Sometimes it leads to some distortions. For example, firms avoid certain investments because they could negatively affect short-term profits, even if they would be beneficial for their long-term sustainability.

Watch

www.khanacademy.org/economics-finance-domain/microeconomics/firm-economic-profit/economic-profit-tutorial/v/economic-profit-vs-accounting-profit.

NB: This video calls "Explicit Opportunity Costs" those costs which are included in both the economic and the accounting analysis. It calls "Implicit Opportunity Costs" those which we call "Opportunity Costs".

Questions

*   If the accounting profit of a company is a positive number, does it mean that this company is creating value?
*   Did you ever think that if you were in a partially or totally different business you could actually earn more than you earn now?
*   Would you be surprised discovering that many businesses operate for long periods without generating substantial economic profits?

TABLE 1.6 Economic profit for selected US food and beverage chains, 1997–2004 ($m)

Company	2004	2003	2002	2001	2000	1999	1998	1997
McDonald's	551	172	−124	30	240	407	452	250
Starbucks	151	71	30	19	10	−8	−4	−1
Outback Steakhouse	68	90	113	90	104	96	73	61
Brinker Int'l	58	47	47	44	31	22	3	−16
Wendy's	15	31	36	17	10	−1	−22	7
Jack in the Box	7	6	23	22	26	39	18	−1
The Cheesecake Factory	12	10	11	7	4	2	−3	−3
Applebee's	48	48	36	35	32	25	27	16

Source: Besanko et al. (2007) quoting Stern Stewart Performance 1000.

Analysis

The video presents some concepts presented in this unit. The fact that accounting profit is positive does not mean that the business creates value. If opportunity costs are added, a profit may become a loss. Many businesses may operate for long periods without generating economic profit; they basically survive and remunerate intermediate consumption, capital and labour, but do not add any further value. This is the frequent case with many small businesses.

A company can have economic losses while it is posting accounting profits. An example: in 2002, McDonald's posted accounting profits of $893m but if investors put their money into an investment with similar or lower risk projects, they earned an additional $124m (Table 1.6).

Glossary

accounting profit   Profit calculated according to accounting criteria; it includes only explicit costs. It is the basis for paying taxes and dividends and for obtaining credit from banks.

capital   A firm's capital is the sum total of (1) financial assets including cash and funds held in deposit accounts at banks, (2) tangible equipment and machinery used in the firm's production operations, (3) buildings used in the production or storage of the firm's goods. The materials consumed in the course of the production process are not classified as capital.

depreciation   The annual loss of value accruing to the capital of a firm or country due to wear, obsolescence and accidents.

economic profit   Profit calculated according to economic criteria: it is an instrument for deciding whether or not to pursue a project. It indicates that a project or a firm creates value, i.e. that the value of the output is greater than the value of all inputs used. If positive, it indicates that the value obtained with this use of resources in one project or firm is greater than the value achievable with the best alternative use of the same resources.

financial costs   Interest and other costs that an entity incurs in connection with the borrowing of funds.[14]

interest on the debts of the company   The money charged by a bank, other financial organization or private individual for borrowing money. Also known as financial costs.

long run   A period long enough for a firm to completely adjust all its inputs to a change in conditions.[15] One could even decide to abandon the business.

opportunity cost   The value of the best foregone alternative.[16]

production factor   An economic term to describe the inputs used in the production of goods or services in the attempt to make an economic profit. The factors of production include land, labour, capital and entrepreneurship.[17] For simplicity here we usually refer just to capital and labour.

profit maximization   The action or the objective of achieving the maximum possible profit.

recession   Period during which the country's production (its GDP, see Section 8.1) decreases.

short run   A period during which the firm can make some, but not complete, adjustment of inputs to a change in conditions.

sunk costs   A sunk cost is incurred regardless of decisions and thus cannot be avoided.[17] When weighing the cost of a decision, the decision maker should ignore sunk costs and consider only avoidable costs.[17]

Notes

1 This is the definition by Besanko (2007:587). Varian (2006:201) and Baumol and Blinder (1997:51) give definitions which are similar to this, even if, in the case of Baumol and Blinder (1997:226) their definition must be interpreted as that of Pindyck and Rubinfeld, "Opportunity cost is the cost associated with opportunities that are foregone by not putting the firm's resources to their best alternative use" Pindyck and Rubinfeld (2015:244), which is similar to that of Bernheim and Whinston (2008:66) and to that of Sinclair (2000:1092). According to Baumol and Blinder (1997:226) "Economic profit equals net earnings, in the accountant's sense, minus the opportunity costs of capital and of any other inputs supplied by the firm's owners." Since the accounting profit is a balance, only if they add another balance, the difference between the value of the best alternative use of the factor and it actual compensation, can they obtain the economic profit. Both approaches are acceptable, here we follow the first.
2 By focussing on opportunity costs, we are then considering the value of the next best alternative that must be foregone in order to undertake an activity.
3 For consistency with what follows, here we consider the post-tax salary.
4 For consistency with what follows, here we consider the post-tax compensation.
5 Vivek Kaul is the author of the Easy Money trilogy.
6 Pindyck and Rubinfeld (2015:245–246); see also (Besanko, 2007:18), Varian (2006:363), and Bernheim and Whinston (2008:81 and 251) and for a different interpretation, see Baumol and Blinder (1997:159).
7 Varian (2006:362).
8 Baumol and Willig (1981).

9 Christensen (2016).
10 Listed here means "advertised for sale".
11 Genovese and Mayer (2001).
12 Varian (2006:556).
13 This is the case of firms operating in perfect competition.
14 Adaptation of the author from http://dictionary.cambridge.org/dictionary/english/interest.
15 See Fischer and Dornbusch (1983:162).
16 See note 1.
17 Besanko (2007:18).

Bibliography

Baumol, W. J. and Blinder, A. S. (1997). *Economics, principles, and policy*. New York: Harcourt Brace Jovanovich.

Baumol, W. J. and Willig, R. D. (1981). "Fixed Costs, Sunk Costs, Entry Barriers, and Sustainability of Monopoly," *The Quarterly Journal of Economics*, 96(3): 405–431.

Bernheim, B. and Whinston, M. (2008). *Microeconomics*. New York: McGraw-Hill Higher Education.

Besanko, D. (2007). *Economics of strategy*. Hoboken, NJ: Wiley & Sons.

Cabral, L. and Backus, D. (2001). "Economic Costs: The Ones That Matter," Firms and Markets lecture notes, NYU STERN. http://people.stern.nyu.edu/dbackus/1303/notes_costs.pdf.

Christensen, C. M. (2016). *The Innovator's Dilemma: When new technologies cause great firms to fail. Harvard Business Review Press*, January 5.

Fischer, S. and Dornbusch, R. (1983). *Introduction to microeconomics*. New York: McGraw-Hill Higher Education.

Genovese, D. and Mayer, C. (2001). "Loss Aversion and Seller Behaviour: Evidence from the Housing Market," *Quarterly Journal of Economics*, 116(4): 1233–1260.

Nicholson, W. (1994). "Intermediate Microeconomics and Its Application, Dryden Press, Fort Worth, Texas. OECD, 2007," in *OECD system of unit labour cost indicators*. Paris: OECD.

Pindyck, R. and Rubinfeld, D. (2015). *Microeconomics*. Harlow [u.a.]: Pearson.

Sinclair, J. (2000). *Collins English dictionary*. London: Harper-Collins.

Varian, H. (2006). *Intermediate microeconomics*. New York: W. W. Norton & Company.

Vivek, K. (2018). "Costly Phone or a Holiday? Look at Opportunity Cost," *DNA*, 26 August. www.dnaindia.com/personal-finance/column-costly-phone-or-a-holiday-look-at-opportunity-cost-2655174.

2

VALUE ADDED

An economy creates wealth and employment only if it is able to create value added. Substantially the value added is a "cake" shared between those that provide labour, namely the workers, and those that provide different forms of capital and land (business owners, banks, landlords and the state).

If there is no value added, there is nothing to share. For this reason, it is important that one analyses this concept which, moreover, is also very useful when analysing processes of industrial restructuring. To introduce the concept of value added, we start by describing costs which are *not* value added, intermediate consumption, and then we can present the concept of value added and its business implications.

2.1 Intermediate consumption and value added

Non-durable[1] goods and services (inputs) that the firm buys from external sources are termed intermediate consumption (IC). This definition treats the work of the firm's employees as not bought outside the firm.[2]

Intermediate consumption includes the cost of raw materials, partly finished goods, outsourcers and banking services. It corresponds approximately to the value of the sum of all received invoices, excluding those concerning the purchase of properties, equipment and other assets, for example, intellectual property, which are used by the firm over more than one period and which do not disappear into the final product. The latter are referred to as "fixed capital".

Intermediate consumption does not include:

1   Wages and salaries of employees and managers.
2   Pre-tax remuneration of risk capital (dividends and profits to owners).
3   Rents of real estate belonging to families (rents paid to real estate firms are included).

4   Interest.[3]
5   Indirect taxes (taxes on production and imports minus subsidies).[4]
6   Depreciation or consumption of fixed capital.
7   Material and non-material investments.

The net value added is the sum of items 1 to 5 above. Items 3 to 5 play a relatively lesser role, so attention is usually concentrated on the first two items. If one pays rent to a company, that is intermediate consumption; by the same token if one pays interest to a bank, that too is intermediate consumption. To obtain gross value added one adds item 6 to the net value added. In Figure 2.1 data of sales and intermediate consumption in the South African gold mining industry.

Read

The House of Commons inquiry on value added

What is a higher value-added economy?

The need to create a higher value-added economy is widely taken as a given in public policy debate – but what exactly does this apparent platitude mean? Just as policy interventions can only be considered appropriately with an

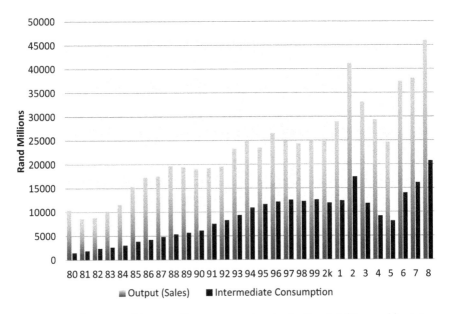

FIGURE 2.1   Output and intermediate consumption in the South African gold mining industry

The intermediate consumption of the gold mining industry includes power and chemicals.

Source: Data: Statistics South Africa (2011) elaboration by the author.

understanding of the real context, so it is necessary to understand exactly what the desired outcome, in this case a higher value-added economy, might be. As NESTA said, "A high value-added economy focusses on those activities that generate a large margin between the final price of a good or service and the cost of the inputs used to produce it, and thus create higher profits for businesses and higher wages for workers".

There are some sectors which are clearly higher value added, such as pharmaceutical development and advanced engineering. However, a higher value-added economy may encompass a far wider range of activity. The Committee received a large amount of evidence exploring the concept. Here we reproduce some of the most eloquent submissions.

The CBI gave the following explanation:

> The term "value added" refers to the differential that can be achieved between the cost of a service/product/process, etc and the price that can be charged for it. In turn, "higher value added" concerns maximizing that differential, be it through reducing input costs (e.g. reducing material, labour or process costs, etc) or increasing the price that can be realized (e.g. through brand association, improved quality, innovative features, faster delivery, higher specification, etc), or some combination of the two.
> . . . The global accessibility of inexpensive labour means that UK-based businesses cannot compete in markets for internationally traded goods and services on the basis of low labour costs alone. Thus our economy naturally tends to focus on higher value and higher value-added activity where investment in skills, knowledge, technology and innovation more broadly are important factors.

25 September 2009, The House of Commons: Business and Enterprise Committee – Eleventh Report. Risk and Reward: sustaining a higher value-added economy

Contains Parliamentary information licensed under the **Open Parliament Licence v3.0.**

Questions

- What is the NESTA definition of value added?
- What is the CBI definition of value added?
- Are the NESTA and CBI definitions of value added compatible?
- Should we pursue the production of high value-added products?
- Why?

TABLE 2.1 Value added according to the United Nations System of National Accounts

Gross output
- intermediate consumption
= **Gross value added**
- consumption of fixed capital (or depreciation charges)
= Net value added
Net value added =
gross wages
+ pre-tax profits net of depreciation
+ rents of real estate belonging to families
+ interest
+ indirect taxes
- public subsidies to companies

Analysis

The Nesta definition of value added is the standard definition of value added as it includes both salaries and profits. It therefore corresponds to the definition given in the UN System of National Accounts (Table 2.1). The CBI definition includes the cost of labour among the items, which reduces value added. In this way value added becomes a synonym for accounting profit (see Section 4.4). The two definitions are of course not compatible. A definition of value added identical to the definition of accounting profit would be redundant. The production of high value-added goods leaves firms with a good margin for remunerating both entrepreneurs and workers. Only in the presence of some value added can good jobs become possible. That is why several countries seek to develop value-added activities with the objective of generating better salaries for their workers and profits for their investors. They give incentives to industries or sectors with high value added.

★

It might seem that "intermediate consumption" is important for managers, supply managers in particular, and accountants, and not to those who decide policies at national level. But in fact, the way intermediate consumption is handled within a multinational company, and the way it chooses to fix the related levels of internal transfer prices, is an important determinant of financial well-being, or fragility, at a national level. Some firms are able to arrange operations by buying the intermediate consumption goods at the location where they are produced, and then transferring them to one of their subsidiaries in a country where their onward sale will incur low or zero corporate taxes. The subsidiary company may then add some further components to the intermediate goods (though often this need not happen) and will then send the goods on to the parent company at a much higher price. This price will appear, in the parent company's accounts, as the "cost" of its final product, so that the profit on which the parent pays tax in its own country (i.e. profit as the difference between the final price to the consumer and the company's apparent "cost" of bringing the product to market) will have been greatly reduced. The bulk of the profit earned on this product by the group as a whole, will have showed up in a low- or zero-tax part of the supply chain. There is a kind of triangle: the true supplier, the controlled company and the parent company. Thanks to these operations, some big multinational enterprises pay extremely low taxes. In this way several countries see the biggest business operating in their territory pay little or no taxes to them. They eventually try to balance the books by taxing more small businesses and local residents and cutting public services.

2.2 Value added and vertical integration

If we compare value added with turnover, we understand how much a firm is directly undertaking the production of the output and how much it is relying on external sources. This ratio depends in some degree on the type of business of the firm, for example, in a petrol station this ratio is usually very low while in a management consulting firm, it is usually high.

The vertical chain is "the process that begins with the acquisition of raw materials and ends with the distribution and sale of finished goods".[5] So, for example, in the footwear industry the vertical chain starts from the cultivation of animal feedstuffs, passing through breeding, slaughtering, tanning, shoe-making and distribution, finishing with sales to consumers. Vertically integrated[6] firms are those directly concerned with many links in the vertical chain; for them the ratio between value added and sales is usually higher than those of their competitors. In firms which only undertake a final operation and outsource every other aspect, the ratio between value added and sales may be lower. An analysis of the ratio of value added to sales is a way of understanding the relationship between the firm and the vertical chain. It indicates how far the firm is autonomous and relatively rigid or flexible and dependent on the outside world. This is indispensable for an understanding of processes of vertical integration, splitting, mergers and acquisitions. If one is in a very efficient market where buying and selling is cheap and easy, one will probably opt for a low degree of vertical integration and one will largely rely upon external suppliers.[7] If one is in a much less efficient market – an underdeveloped market in which any purchase entails many additional costs (high transaction costs, see Section 4.5), one will move as many functions as possible into the firm. A large part of the vertical chain will be within the firm. If suppliers cannot be trusted, for example, power suppliers, the firm may start producing its own inputs, becoming vertically integrated. Firms with high ratios between value added and turnover are relatively less dependent on suppliers and clients, but are at risk of becoming more rigid and encountering greater problems in reorganizing their production at short notice in the event of sector crises. At the same time, they are fully in control of the overall quality and scheduling of their production process.

Serious criteria for declaring a good "made in a country" should include one prescribing that a minimal proportion of the total value of the goods should be added in the location where the goods are produced.

In many countries, value added is the base of an important tax: VAT, or Value Added Tax. As value added implies generation of new value, the tax system only collects revenues imposed on this new element and does not take into account intermediate consumption because the producers of these goods have already paid taxes on them.

Today it is very frequently the case that firms have international supply chains with different phases of production carried out in different countries. Industrialized countries usually retain those phases which generate higher added value while very often, firms in developing countries handle lower value phases, this of course affecting the profits of their firms and the salaries of their workers. Only the availability of qualified workforces and good infrastructures will allow countries to retain phases of higher added value.

VERTICAL INTEGRATION OF POWER SUPPLY IN SUB-SAHARAN AFRICA

Overall, internal generation by firms – which has been on the rise in recent years – accounts for about 6 per cent of installed generation capacity in sub-Saharan Africa (equivalent to at least 4,000 MW of installed capacity). However, this share doubles to around 12 per cent in low-income countries, post-conflict countries, and more generally on the western side of the continent. In a handful of countries (including DRC and Nigeria) internal generation represents more than 20 per cent of capacity. Sub-Saharan firms which export to industrialized countries have a higher probability of producing their own power, probably because in this way firms can better guarantee the quality of their product and become less dependent on external suppliers.

Foster and Steinbuks (2008)

Glossary

capacity   The maximum or optimum amount that can be produced by a machine, a plant, a firm, an industry or a country.

capacity utilization   The average share of utilization of the plants of a firm, industry or country. "For a given industry, the capacity utilization rate is equal to an output index divided by a capacity index. (The) [. . .] capacity indexes attempt to capture the concept of sustainable maximum output – the greatest level of output a plant can maintain within the framework of a realistic work schedule, after factoring in normal downtime and assuming sufficient availability of inputs to operate the capital in place."[8]

degree of vertical integration   This can be measured by the ratio between value added and sales.[9]

gross value added   The difference between the value of the sales of a company and the value of its intermediate consumption. It is mainly made up of wages and profits.

intermediate consumption   Non-durable goods that are used to produce other goods. More precisely "it consists of goods and services consumed as inputs by a process of production, excluding fixed assets whose consumption is recorded as consumption of fixed capital. The goods and services are either transformed or used up by the production process."[10]

vertical chain   The process that begins with the acquisition of raw materials, (passes through their transformation) and ends with the distribution and sale of finished goods.

vertically integrated firm   A hierarchical firm that performs many of the steps in the vertical chain itself.[11]

Notes

1 There are exceptions:

> Expenditures on durable producer goods that are small, inexpensive and used to perform relatively simple operations may be treated as intermediate consumption when such expenditures are made regularly and are very small compared with expenditures on machinery and equipment. Examples of such goods are hand tools such as saws, spades, knives, axes, hammers, screwdrivers, and so on. However, in countries where such tools account for a significant part of the stock of producers' durable goods, they may be treated as fixed assets.
>
> (United Nations Statistics Division, 2009)

2 Labour is not an intermediate input and is considered a primary factor of production like others such as capital and natural resources (land).

3 According to the UN System of National Accounts the matter is rather complex, in theory, banks are suppliers of services as any other supplier of services and their services should therefore be considered intermediate consumption. However, commissions often represent only a minor part of their revenue. Much of their revenue derives from interests. Therefore, part of their revenue from interests is considered as their value added. See UN-DESA (2015:55–56). These implicit financial services are known in the SNA as financial intermediation services indirectly measured, or FISIM.

4

> The value added of an industry, also referred to as gross domestic product (GDP) by industry, is the contribution of a private industry or government sector to overall GDP. The components of value added consist of compensation of employees, taxes on production and imports less subsidies, and gross operating surplus. Value added equals the difference between an industry's gross output (consisting of sales or receipts and other operating income, commodity taxes, and inventory change) and the cost of its intermediate inputs (including energy, raw materials, semi-finished goods, and services that are purchased from all sources).
>
> (US Department of Commerce Bureau of Economic Analysis)

See more at: www.bea.gov/faq/index. cfm?faq_id=184#sthash.9dyOBhe1.dpuf. The gross operating surplus is: value derived as a residual for most industries after subtracting total intermediate inputs, compensation of employees, and taxes on production and imports less subsidies from total industry output. Gross operating surplus includes consumption of fixed capital (CFC), proprietors' income, corporate profits, and business current transfer payments (net). Prior to 2003, it was referred to as other value added or property-type income. The topic is quite complex and is presented in full in System of National Accounts (2009:103–104) available here: http://unstats.un.org/unsd/nationalaccount/sna2008.asp.

5 Besanko (2007:591).
6 Ibid.
7 Scherer and Ross (1994).
8 www.federalreserve.gov/releases/g17/CapNotes.htm.
9 See Tucker and Wilder (1977); Adelman (1955); Laffer (1969).
10 European Commission (2013:68). See also United Nations Statistics Division (2009:120).
11 Besanko (2007:591).

Bibliography

Adelman, M. A. (1955). "Concept and Statistical Measurement of Vertical Integration," in *Business Concentration and Price Policy*, edited by G. J. Stigler, 281–322. NBER-Princeton University Press.

Besanko, D. (2007). *Economics of Strategy*. Hoboken, NJ: Wiley & Sons.

European Commission (2013). *European System of Accounts — ESA 2010*. Luxembourg: Publications Office of the European Union.

Foster, V. and Steinbuks, J. (2008). *Paying the price for unreliable power supplies: In-house generation of electricity by firms in Africa*. Africa Infrastructure Country Diagnostic, Working Paper No. 2. Washington, DC: World Bank.

Parliament. House of Commons (2009). *Business and Enterprise Committee Risk and Reward: Sustaining a Higher Value-Added Economy (HC 2008–2009)*. London: The Stationery Office.

Laffer, A. B. (1969). "Vertical Integration by Corporations, 1929–1965," *Review of Economics and Statistics*, (February): 91–93.

Scherer, F. M. and Ross, D. (1994). *Industrial market structure and economic performance*. Boston: Houghton Mifflin Co.

Tucker, I. B. and Wilder, R. P. (1977). "Trends in Vertical Integration in the U.S. Manufacturing Sector," *Journal of Industrial Economics*, XXVI(September): 81–94.

UN DESA (Department of Economic and Social Affairs), Statistics Division. (2015). *Studies in methods*, Series F No.113 Handbook on National Accounting, Financial Production, Flows and Stocks in the System of National Accounts, United Nations, New York.

United Nations Statistics Division. (2009). "System of National Account, 2008," European Commission, International Monetary Fund, Organisation for Economic Cooperation and Development, United Nations, World Bank. https://unstats.un.org/unsd/nationalaccount/sna2008.asp.

PART II
Production and costs

In this part, we consider how firms produce. The manner in which they produce affects their productivity and therefore their costs. Only productive firms can prosper, make profits and pay good salaries. More generally the costs of a firm – whether they are fixed or variable, are increasing more and more, less and less, or at a constant rate – affect the behaviour of firms and the prices that make it possible for them to sell and operate.

Then we go on to consider how in some cases firms derive important advantages from being large: the so-called economies of scale. We also consider how large size can create disadvantages. Finally, we consider how a few large firms, thanks to their size advantage, account for most of the production sold in a given market.

3

PRODUCTION AND PRODUCTIVITY

The characteristics of production play a key role in determining the destiny of firms and employees. The ability of a firm to transform limited amounts of scarce resources into competitively saleable output is what determines that firm's survival. Efficiency can be analysed in terms of productivity, a concept that we present in this section. In particular, the concepts of productivity of labour and of unit labour cost, a concept linked to labour productivity, are key elements in the definition of salaries and therefore are staples for those concerned with industrial relations and social dialogue. Before directly analysing these topics we should first reflect on different ways of organizing production with rigid or flexible technologies, because they have important implications for productivity.

3.1 Rigid and flexible production techniques

Firms and organizations combine different production factors (see Section 1.1) or inputs, that is various types of capital and labour, technology, land and entrepreneurial initiative. In this way, they produce certain products. The relationship between the quantities of production factors (labour, capital and components) and the output is called the "production function".

Some technologies entail extensive use of labour and limited use of capital, for example, hand-made production and much farming in many developing countries; these are called **labour-intensive** technologies. In contrast, other technologies entail extensive use of capital and limited use of labour. Examples can be found in plants with a high degree of automation and in such industries as oil production, refining, telecommunications, railways and airlines. They are known as **capital-intensive** technologies.

In certain cases, the mix that firms choose permits no substitution between inputs. An example can be found in surgical theatres. There, every person has a specific role: surgeon, anaesthetist, theatre nurse, operating department practitioner, theatre support worker, cardiographer and radiographer. It is usually difficult or impossible to use individual staff in roles that are not theirs. A surgeon can rarely perform the functions of an anaesthetist and *vice versa*. One input cannot be easily substituted for another. It may be the case that a man cannot be replaced by a machine, that a certain specialist cannot be replaced by another specialist, or that a machine cannot be replaced with another machine, or with a human. A process can lead to a certain product and nothing else. We define this type of processes as "processes without input substitution"[1] or "technologies with fixed proportions".[2]

The quantities of every input are specified and in very rigid technologies, adding to one input, but not to the others, brings no increase in total output and may even reduce it. Inputs are "perfect complements".[3]

In this sense, these technologies can be considered "rigid technologies".

Why do firms potentially accept this form of rigidity, the constraints of the absence of input substitution? In certain circumstances, the explanation can be that these technologies are the most efficient and create the most value. Surgical operations are often very rigid processes in which substituting input factors is very difficult, but they often create much value; few people would advocate greater flexibility, using surgeons in the roles of anaesthetists and *vice versa*!

Other processes or technologies permit a much higher degree of substitution between input factors. Think about the employees of a fast food chain. Usually they are staff with a very short period of training. In many cases, others can easily be substituted for them. Those who work at the tills are potentially moved to frying potatoes and *vice versa*.

In fact, those restaurants have very high labour turnover. This is only possible thanks to the high degree of substitution between the people employed in this type of business. Does that mean that the technology is ideal? Not necessarily. Sometimes these technologies may entail production with low value added. In some cases, a technology involving input substitution is the only one available.

Read

Choosing production processes

When Henry Ford joked that he had offered his customers a car "in any colour – so long as it's black!" his remark accurately encapsulated key choices he had previously made about the market he would serve and the production regime he would adopt. He would sell to a mass market and not try to compete for customers able to afford custom-built models or Ferraris or Rolls-Royces. The cars would be assembled from standardized components, manufactured in large batches so as to minimize set-up costs. Factory jobs previously undertaken by engineers with craft skills would be split up into small components so as to be performed by relatively unskilled, low-paid workers. Car buyers were offered little choice ("low product variety") but benefitted from car prices spectacularly lower than any seen before. As for the workforce, it was easy to recruit people for the low-skilled, repetitive jobs in a period of widespread unemployment, and Henry Ford notoriously used bully-boy tactics to make sure that trade unions did not gain a foothold in his plants.

How have these same choices been faced in other firms, in other industries, at different times and with different available technologies; and what changes are happening today?

Historians have found examples of Ford-like practice in ancient societies such as Egypt and China. In Europe, Venice's great Arsenal, operating in the years around 1500, employed some 16,000 workers to produce both armaments and wooden-hulled ships and was a pioneer in the use of standardized parts produced in large batches. Using such parts, it could construct a substantial wooden ship in a matter of days.

Following the phenomenal success of Ford's Model T car, and then in the 1930s, of Germany's low-cost Volkswagen ("the people's car"), these and other car makers each pursued their own solution to the old dilemma: how to balance product variety and flexibility on the one hand, with production efficiency and low production cost on the other. Case studies in many car companies of the 1960s and 1970s reveal production managers struggling to meet the promises made by their sales departments, with production lines stopping and starting to accommodate product variants and with smooth flows interrupted to meet orders from priority customers. They were often operating, it was said, in "fire-fighting mode".

This time the breakthrough came from Japan, from Toyota's car plants and from the rare organizational genius of Toyota's leader, Kiichiro Toyoda. Under the Toyota system of "high-volume customization", a specified number of variants to the basic product is defined in advance and offered to customers (the "customer" will often be a retail agent). Customer orders are then bunched into uniform batches. A forward production programme is then composed (for example for two months ahead) and is strictly adhered to. As well as the cost benefits from a smooth production flow, there are further advantages because when the production schedule is fixed, it becomes possible to construct just-in-time supply chains for components (whether bought-in or produced in-house). Here, the savings come from not having to tie up money in large inventories of parts.

The most recent chapter in the story of product-variety versus product-cost comes in the emergence of so-called "personalised manufacturing" or "additive manufacturing". Using computerized design with 3-D printing, firms are now able to make complicated parts on demand. The batches can be small as the set-up costs in changing batches can be negligible. Many long-established companies have been developing the technologies (GE, EADS, Siemens, Rolls-Royce, Honda) as have a host of new ventures. Some writers believe that these technologies will make it easier for nations in the early stages of economic development to leapfrog the normal route to building up production capabilities. The relative advantage of 3D printing is its virtual low cost compared with the variety of components that it can produce. A bicycle part, a heart valve or a vacuum cleaner part can all be printed the same day. This flexibility can be particularly valuable in places where the scarcity of capital may be a major problem. Others suggest that the new methods will open a way for a new kind of small-scale craftworker to emerge and flourish.

Read

"Production Processes: A Lightbulb Moment," Peter Marsh, *Financial Times*, 28 December 2011. https://www.ft.com/content/b59678b4-313b-11e1-a62a-00144feabdc0.

Questions

- If you want a speedy and efficient production process, what should you usually sacrifice?
- What did standardization allow?
- Could additive manufacturing (3D printing) bring any benefit to countries at early stages of industrial development? Which can be their advantages for countries in the early phases of industrialization?
- What did Henry Ford create? What benefits did it bring?
- Could Toyota's manufacturing system provide useful lessons to manufacturers in developing countries?

Analysis

Peter Marsh reports on one of the first examples of standardized part production which has been behind the development of the modern factory with fast and efficient production. Standardization entailed giving up personalized products, that is those involving flexible results and flexible techniques.

This was the case of high volume standardization by Henry Ford, which produced highly standardized cars of low cost and good quality, but also with a very uniform design.

Toyota has been able to balance standardization and customization.

Such new techniques as 3D printing or additive manufacturing may eliminate the contradiction between efficiency and flexibility. This new technique may also help developing countries leapfrog the conventional route to building manufacturing capabilities since they require much less conventional infrastructure.

3.2 The measurement of efficiency

Productivity is a measure of efficiency. It indicates the ability to transform small quantities of production factors into large quantities of valuable output. One measure of efficiency consists of dividing the total output of a company by the total number of its employees to obtain so-called "average productivity".

$$\text{Average Productivity} = \frac{\text{Product}}{\text{Production Factor}} = \frac{\text{Output}}{\text{Input}}$$

These are average measures of productivity.

If Q is the quantity of output that a company produces and L is the number of workers who work for that company, Q/L is the **average productivity of labour**.

Output may be measured in physical units (e.g. number of cars or kilos of potatoes), or in terms of sales or of value added[4] ($, £ or other currency). Labour may be expressed in terms of the number of employed individuals or alternatively, the number of hours worked, which is a more accurate measurement and therefore to be preferred.[5] In Figure 3.1 an example with different measurements of labour.

Or we may be interested in knowing the output per dollar of invested capital. This is called the average productivity of capital. An investor is usually more interested in investing in industries in which output (Q) per capital invested (K), that is average productivity of capital, is higher. Q/K is the **average productivity of capital**.

Read

The Economist gives a good account of the issues that faced the Italian car maker Fiat in the year 2010. The article provides data on the number of employees and cars produced in each plant. On a simple calculation of number of cars per employee, some plants had much higher productivity than others. However, the story is more complicated than this.

"Fiat Plays Double or Quits with Chrysler," from *The Economist*, 25 November 2010. www.economist.com/business/2010/11/25/fiat-plays-double-or-quits-with-chrysler.

Questions

- On what basis can the journalist say that the Italian operations of Fiat are not competitive? How can she say that there is a productivity gap?
- How is productivity measured in this article?
- Is there any problem in the way in which productivity is measured in this article?
- Are we sure that in all plants, employees were all working and that no workers were kept on forced vacation or not working for lack of demand?
- Can we compare cars per worker in plants producing large cars with that in plants producing small cars?
- Can we compare labour productivity in plants of different ages and perhaps using different technologies?

Analysis

The journalist observes that the number of cars per employee (average labour productivity) in Italy is lower than in other countries. Therefore, she argues that Italian

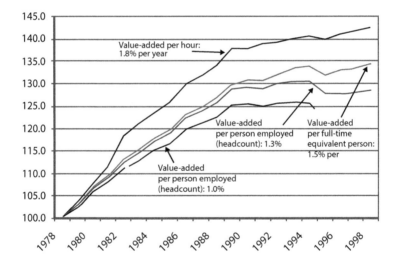

FIGURE 3.1 French market services: Labour productivity based on different measures of employment

We can see that productivity has grown much more when it is measured per hour worked. Output is measured as value added. The figure shows that the growth is maximum per worked hour and lower per employee. Probably the number of employees grew more (or diminished less) than the number of the worked hours. If instead of considering only employees, we consider employed persons,[6] the growth is higher. This seems to suggest that the productivity of employees grew less than that of the other employed persons. These data seem also to refer to an increase in the number of part-time workers: the productivity per full-time equivalent person has grown more than the productivity per person employed (part-time or full-time) or per employee.

Source: OECD (2001:41)

plants are less productive than others (there is a productivity gap in Italy). However, these measurements have some limitations.

1   The article does not say anything about the type of equipment and technology, i.e. the capital, used in each plant. Plants with greater investment of capital in newer technologies should have higher average labour productivity than other plants.
2   The article does not say anything about the degree to which plants are used (capacity utilization). Some plants are perhaps only partially used, for example, for lack of demand. In some plants, employees may be requested to work just a few hours per month. A measurement of output per hour worked would offer clearer results.
3   Some plants may produce very complex and expensive cars and others simpler and cheaper cars. Output would probably be better measured in terms of value added or sales.

A practical case: salaries related to productivity

A company owns two plants: A and B. Both were built in 1990. In 2010 the company renovates plant A with an investment of €5m in new equipment, which is safer and simpler to use. Table 3.1 describes the situation of the two plants before and after the investment. Workers in plant A now say that they have considerably increased their productivity and that they deserve a salary increase that workers in plant B do not deserve. What should the employer do?

Analysis

Plant A is probably more productive because the firm has invested €5m of fresh capital in it. We can observe that labour productivity is a measurement of several things at the same time:

1   The effort of the workers.
2   The skills of the workers.
3   The technology provided to the workers by the company.
4   The capital invested by the company.
5   The environment in which the firm operates (roads, schools, hospitals, policing, among others).
6   The state of demand.

TABLE 3.1 Data on two different plants

	Output 2009	No. of workers 2009	Output 2010	No. of workers 2010
Plant A	500,000	50	800,000	50
Plant B	300,000	25	320,000	25

A better way to measure productivity consists of observing how, on average, the plants in an industry combine capital and labour. We may discover the precise average relationship in the industry between input factors and output. If we know this relationship (the production function), then we can compare the actual results of a firm with the results that an average firm in the industry would achieve with the same use of capital and labour. This comparison is given by the so-called Total Factor Productivity (TFP). While the TFP concept is readily understandable, the calculation of TFP in a particular case requires some skill in statistical analysis. You would be best advised to call in the help of a specialist.

3.3 Marginal productivity

Marginal productivity is "the extra amount of output per unit of extra input".[7] Let's consider it with two examples.

A company has 100 employees, total costs of $500,000 and sales of $1m. Average output or sales per employee (Q/L) is $10,000. Now, this company decides to hire one additional worker. After this change, company sales total $1,015,000. The manager could be interested in knowing the average contribution to sales of the new employee. What should they do? Sales have grown by $15,000. The workforce has been increased by one unit; this is the so called "marginal worker", the last to be hired. We can divide the increase in sales by the increase in the number of workers:

15,000 / 1 = 15,000

The average productivity, in sales terms, of the last, or "marginal", worker is $15,000. It is more precisely called the "**marginal productivity**" of labour in this company.

If for example, he asked for a salary of $16,000 it would probably be better to think twice before accepting such a request. This additional worker would cost more than the additional income that they would generate in the firm. This does not mean that a salary of $14,000 is certainly a good deal. We have just calculated the marginal productivity in terms of sales, not the marginal productivity in terms of value added (see Section 2.2). A salary of $15,000 is just the upper boundary.

If we knew that in hiring this new worker the cost of intermediate consumption (see Section 2.1) would increase by $10,000, we could also calculate the increase in value added:

Increase of Sales $15,000	−	Increase of intermediate consumption $10,000	=	Increase of value added $5,000

We can also calculate the additional value added (marginal productivity in terms of value added) created by hiring this new worker.

We divide the increase of value added by the number of new staff:

$5,000 / 1 = $5,000.

In this case we can notice that only a salary of less than $5,000 would make the hiring of a new worker a profitable operation.

Let us assume that we are going to meet the trade union to agree the salary of the new worker. What are our clear constraints? In this case we can consider the additional value added as the effective additional product created by this new hiring and we can measure the contribution of this worker.

The sum of $5,000 is the measurement of the marginal productivity of labour in value-added terms.

An employer now knows for certain that only by offering a salary lower than $5,000 can the company make some profit from this specific hiring.

This example shows why knowing the marginal productivity of an employee can be very important for those involved in industrial relations and more generally in management.

In reality we can hardly attribute a specific worker's contribution to the success of the firm and we often end up with average measurements. When production becomes very complex, measuring every worker's precise contribution to production is very difficult, if not impossible. In some cases, this leads to the measurement of the productivity of teams, units and divisions.

Labour productivity is only one of the criteria for determining wages; the bargaining power of the sides may play a key part in the definition of the shares of output that each part receives, notwithstanding their productivity. Salary ends up reflecting the marginal productivity of labour and its bargaining power.

When firms produce more, their marginal productivity may change. If it grows, we say that there is increasing marginal productivity, if it diminishes, we say that there is diminishing marginal productivity, and if it remains constant, we can speak of constant marginal productivity. In reality it is frequent that, within a certain range, increases in production lead to increased marginal productivity but that in other ranges production increases lead to decreasing marginal productivity.

Read

How should a 'just reward' be calculated?

Writing in 2011, the economist John Kay raised two related key questions: How can the reward be shared when it is the result of the actions of many different persons? What are the main ways of resolving this problem?

Economic theory developed at the end of the nineteenth century explained that everyone will tend be paid in proportion to their contribution to production. This contribution is called the marginal productivity of labour or of capital. Everybody will be paid proportionally to their marginal productivity. For this reason, the economy is intrinsically fair. There is not much to discuss. The free forces of the market reward everybody according to their merits.

Other authors express a different opinion. According to them, the results of the production process will disproportionately be taken by the group (class) with greater force. Karl Marx, the most high-profile writer in that field, placed the answers within the broader theory of class struggle or class warfare. By the end of the twentieth century, Marx's theories commanded little support within mainstream economics and it seemed that "neo-classical" theory (with measurable marginal productivity as one of its elements) would reign supreme. In subsequent years, however, new developments have reopened the discussion: for example, the fact that the compensation of top CEOs was 30 or 40 times the average wage of their employees in the 1930s, while more recently it has grown to several hundred times the average wage of employees. Remarkably, the insightful investor, Warren Buffett, made the following comment during a recent interview[8]:

BUFFETT: Yeah. The rich people are doing so well in this country. I mean, we never had it so good.
INTERVIEWER: What a radical idea.
BUFFETT: It's class warfare, my class is winning, but they shouldn't be.

Measuring marginal productivity when production techniques involve the work of different people and/or different types of capital is particularly complex and situation-specific.

Kay's enjoyable article seems to reach the sardonic conclusion that in the actual world we live in, the rewards obtained through collective action will usually be divided according to the power relations between the collaborating actors.

To this we might add the observation that Clint Eastwood's bandit makes as he prepares to gun down his target, in the film *Unforgiven*: "'Deserves' got nothin' to do with it".

But perhaps we can draw insights from both approaches?

Why the Rioters should be Reading Rousseau," by John Kay, *Financial Times*, 16 August 2011. www.ft.com/content/4237bcfc-c769-11e0-9cac-00144feabdc0.

Questions

- What is the difference between hunting a deer and hunting a hare?
- Can you mention two theories about the allocation of income?
- How to determine the contribution of a CEO to the success of a company?

Analysis

J.J. Rousseau observed that hunting a hare was an operation that could be carried out by a single hunter, while hunting a deer required the cooperation of several hunters.[9] This implies that attribution of the merit of the result was easy in the case of the hare and difficult in the case of the deer. By the same token, the definition of criteria for distribution of the meat is easy for the hare and more complex for the deer. Hare hunting is an example of simple production, while deer hunting is an example of complex production. The allocation of income between different contributors to a joint production process may be explained by referring to the marginal labour productivity of each player or simply by referring to the bargaining power that each player possesses. The power of each player may depend on the most diverse factors and is not necessarily related to productivity.

3.4 The cornerstone of industrial negotiations: unit labour cost

When a manager considers the cost of labour, wages are just one part of the story. This is true not only because firms should also take account of such costs as social contributions and taxes, but also for another, perhaps more important, reason. The cost of an input factor, for example, labour or capital, cannot be considered in isolation. A firm is sometimes ready to pay extremely high prices for certain inputs, provided that their contribution to the output of the firm is also very high. It is for this reason that many firms choose to invest in countries where the cost of labour is very high, for labour productivity is usually even higher. Alternatively, developing countries with low salaries would be the primary choice of every investor, but in reality, this is not always the case.

In general, the cost of input per unit of production can be calculated as:

$$\text{Cost of input per unit of production} = \frac{\text{Average Cost of a production factor}}{\text{Average Productivity of this production factor}}$$

In the case of labour:

$$\textit{Unit Labour Cost}^{10} = \frac{\textit{Salary}}{\textit{Average Labour Productivity}}$$

This formula clearly shows that the unit labour cost depends on two factors: salary and productivity. Salary is the element which trade unions and employees' representatives in general may influence more through their requests. Labour productivity, as we have seen, is a more ambiguous entity. It certainly depends on the effort of the employees, but it also depends on the organization of the work, on the type and quantity of the equipment that employees use, on the investments the company has made, on the validity of the business strategy of the company (e.g. producing high-value or low-value products) and on many other factors not necessarily within the control of employees. During recessions, productivity often falls because firms are not able to sell, not necessarily because workers are unwilling to work.

Since Average Labour Productivity is given by Output/No of employees,

$$Unit\ Labour\ Cost = \frac{Salary \times Number\ of\ Employees}{Output}$$

Output can be measured in terms of physical output, in terms of sales or in terms of value added.[11] This can be rewritten as follows:

$$Unit\ Labour\ Cost = \frac{Wage\ Bill}{Output}$$

The wage bill is the sum of all salaries which a firm pays. The unit labour cost is the measure of the cost of labour that really matters. In industrial relations this is a key variable.

Finally, it is worth mentioning that there is a symmetrical concept for capital.

The average cost of capital is the total capital cost of producing a given output divided by the output produced. The total cost of capital is the rental per unit of capital (r) multiplied by the stock of capital (K), or, rK. The average cost of capital is rK/Q which, when dividing numerator and denominator by K gives r/(Q/K), or the interest rate divided by the average productivity of capital.

$$Cost\ of\ Capital\ per\ Unit\ of\ Output = \frac{Interest\ Rate}{Average\ Capital\ Productivity}$$

Some technological innovation can change the productivity for capital and increase or diminish the cost of capital per unit of production. The central banks, in particular those of the more powerful economies, influence interest rates. The behaviour of workers may also affect the productivity of capital. Skilled and dedicated workers make the same equipment more productive.

Read

Pay increases "should be linked to productivity"

The quick rise in South Africa's unit labour costs would reverse any competitiveness gains from the rand's weaker exchange rate, the Reserve Bank warned this week. The exchange rate traded between R9.68/$ and R10.17/$ this week, almost 20% weaker than in January. A weaker exchange rate could help make South African exports more competitive, but as long as wage increases outpace productivity increases, competitiveness will not improve overall.

The Reserve Bank said in its Monetary Policy Review this week that unit labour cost growth was a primary driver of the inflation outlook. Unit labour cost is calculated as the ratio of total pay to the gross value added in the formal non-agricultural sector and represents a link between productivity and the cost of labour. The review showed that the growth in unit labour costs was higher than the upper band of the inflation target last year. This was because increases in worker remuneration outpaced the marginal increases in productivity.

Calculations by Mike Holland, director at PriceMetrics, on the recently published GDP data show growth in compensation of employees in manufacturing far outstripped the real growth in manufacturing output for at least the last five years. South Africa does not stack up well in this regard globally and was ranked 134th out of 144 countries in the World Economic Forum's latest Global Competitiveness Index in terms of the extent to which worker pay in the country is linked to worker productivity.

Chris Loewald, deputy head of research at the Reserve Bank, said at this week's Monetary Policy Forum real wage and unit labour cost growth can inhibit job creation, support inflation and reverse the real depreciation gains of a weaker exchange rate. Reserve Bank deputy governor, Francois Groepe, said any wage settlement above the inflation target band may lead to inflation in the absence of productivity improvements. "In the national discourse there is insufficient space allocated to debating the issue of productivity. Ultimately it is about the change in unit labour costs which is very important and which feed into inflation, but also, [it means] we cannot leverage the weakened exchange rate as it erodes the competitive advantage", Mr Groepe said.

Andrew Levy, labour economist at Andrew Levy Employment, said at a conference hosted by the Bureau for Economic Research that in the past decade and half wage increases in South Africa increasingly outstripped increases in output. South Africa's unit labour costs went up, so it costs more to produce less and less. "If wages go up, and there is no link to efficiency, unit labour costs go up, productivity goes down, we become less and less competitive internationally and locally there are inflationary pressures", Mr Levy said. Reserve Bank governor, Gill Marcus, warned that if labour costs keep going up while productivity goes down "it has implications for labour itself in terms of the employment question". Mr Levy said unions often worried that increased productivity of workers meant some workers would lose their jobs, but this was not the case.

Increased productivity leads to a production surplus which could then create more jobs, said Mike Schüssler, economist at www.economists.co.za. It was a narrow view to say productivity just meant South Africa should simply do more with fewer workers, which will cost jobs, he said. "If we do more with less people, those people will be paid more and will have more spending power, demand more services and generate more economic activity". "Creating more value added should make the country generally richer". "Unions call for decent jobs, with medical, pension and decent pay, but you can only have a decent job if you add decent value."

This way for South Africa to raise productivity?

The education system and the many people not completing secondary schooling stand in the way of improving the productivity of South Africa's labour force. Mike Schüssler, economist at Economists. co.za, said that, as industries became more capital-intensive, more skills and training were needed for workers to be productive. "Labour can only be as efficient as workers are trained and managed," he said.

Andrew Levy, labour economist at Andrew Levy Employment, said that, as long as wage talks were handled centrally by bargaining councils, there was no way to link wage increases to productivity. Instead of bargaining for a certain level of increase, unions and sectors had to bargain for an increase range at centralised level, he said. After that, a company could negotiate with a union at plant level to relate the actual increase to productivity and deal with rising unit labour costs. Mr Levy said employers often failed to look for a self-funding wage increase for employees. "There is no attempt to recoup additional wages by increased efficiency", he said. "And to unions: the more productive and efficient the workers are, the more they can earn".

"Pay Increases 'Should be Linked to Productivity'," René Vollgraaff, *Business Day*, 9 June 2013.

Questions

According to this article:

- Why is South African competitiveness not facilitated by a weaker rand?
- Why will overall competitiveness not improve?
- What could be a driver of South African inflation?
- What definition of unit labour cost is used?

Analysis

According to Vollgraaf, even if South Africa has a weaker exchange rate, its competitiveness is not granted because unit labour costs rise quickly, with wage increases outpacing productivity increases. Unit labour cost can also be expressed as the ratio between the wage level and productivity. Its growth may drive the growth of South African inflation. In this article the definition of unit labour cost is "the ratio of total pay to the gross value added". For firms, what really matters is not wage levels but the ratio between wage levels and labour productivity. Therefore, investors do not necessarily choose to invest in countries with low wages; they may choose to invest in countries with higher labour costs, if labour costs are more than compensated for by high productivity. It is not the hourly wage that matters, but the hourly wage compared with the productivity of the hour worked. Finally, it is worth remembering that labour productivity only partially depends on the effort and attitude of workers. It also depends on the chosen organizational model, the adopted technology, the invested capital, the market conditions and the general environment in which the firm operates, for example, availability of transport and training infrastructure. Therefore, the unit labour cost is affected by the choices of trade unions, employers and governments.

Glossary

average productivity The ratio between total output and the quantity of an input factor. Average Labour Productivity is the ratio between total output and the number of workers or the number of hours worked. Average Capital Productivity is the ratio between total output and the total invested capital.

capital intensive A technology, business process or industry that requires large amounts of money and other financial resources, but relatively few workers.

decreasing marginal productivity The situation in which increasing output diminishes marginal productivity.

flexible technology A technique which permits the use of input factors in variable proportions, i.e. it permits substitution between factors.

increasing marginal productivity The situation in which increasing output increases marginal productivity.

labour intensive A technology or business which requires relatively many workers and a smaller quantity of capital.

marginal productivity The extra amount of output per unit of extra input.[12] If it is smaller than the corresponding extra cost, it is more profitable to avoid production of the extra output. On the other hand, if it is greater than the corresponding extra cost, increasing production leads to increased profits. The marginal productivity of labour, when measurable, can be a reference for fixing salaries.

output The amount of something produced by a person or a company.[13]

production function A description of the relationship between inputs and output. "It measures the maximum possible output that you can get from a given amount of input."[14]

rigid technology A technique which uses input factors with specific ratios between them. These ratios cannot be changed. There is complementarity between factors, and one factor cannot be substituted for another.

total factor productivity A measurement of productivity which takes account of the variations in many, potentially all, production factors, i.e. it allows us to tease out the separate contribution that each factor has made to overall productivity. This technique consists of comparing the actual output of a firm with the output of a reference firm. The latter may be obtained using statistical techniques which analyse a) data from the same firm in previous years or b) data from several firms during the same years or c) data from several firms over a number of years.

unit labour cost The ratio between the wage level and average labour productivity. It can also be calculated as the ratio between the wage bill and the output. It is a key variable in business decisions.

wage bill The sum of all wages and salaries paid by a firm.

workforce (of a firm) The persons who work for an organization or business.

Notes

1 See Nicholson (1994:210) or Asimakopolus (1978:165–166).
2 Ibid.
3 Bernheim and Whinston (2008:236).
4 See Battese and Coelli (1988:394) or OECD (2001:12–15, 2001:24).
5 See OECD (2001:40).
6 See OECD (2001:41).

> According to ILO, persons in employment comprise all persons above a specified age who during a specified brief period, either one week or one day, were in the following categories:
>
> • paid employment
> • self- employment

7 Varian (2006:328).
8 Buffet, Warren. 2005. "Interview by By Louu Dobbs", *Lou Dobbs Tonight*, CNN, New York, Sunday, 19 June 2005. http://edition.cnn.com/2005/US/05/10/buffett/index.html.
9 Rousseau, J.-J. (2011). Discourse on the origin and foundations of inequality among men. New York, NY: Bedford/St. Martins.
10 OECD (2007).
11 OECD (2001).
12 Varian (2006:328).
13 Adaptation of the author from www.merriam-webster.com/dictionary/output.
14 Varian (2006:323).

Bibliography

Asimakopolus, A. (1978). *An introduction to economic theory: Microeconomics*. Toronto: Oxford University Press.
Battese, G. E. and Coelli, T. J. (1988). "Prediction of Firm-Level Technical Efficiencies, with a Generalized Frontier Production Function and Panel Data," *Journal of Econometrics*, 38(3): 387–399.

Bernheim, B. and Whinston, M. (2008). *Microeconomics*. New York: McGraw-Hill Higher Education.

The Economist. (2010). "Fiat Plays Double or Quits with Chrysler," *The Economist*, 25 November. www.economist.com/business/2010/11/25/fiat-plays-double-or-quits-with-chrysler.

Kay, J. (2011). "Why Rioters Should Be Reading Rousseau," *The Financial Times*, 16 August. www.ft.com/content/4237bcfc-c769-11e0-9cac-00144feabdc0.

Marsh, P. "Production Processes: A Lightbulb Moment," *The Financial Times*, 28. www.ft.com/content/b59678b4-313b-11e1-a62a-00144feabdc0.

Nicholson, W. (1994). *Intermediate microeconomics and its application*. Fort Worth, TX: Dryden Press.

OECD. (2001). *Measuring productivity, measurement of aggregate and industry-level productivity growth*. Paris: OECD.

OECD. (2007). *OECD system of unit labour cost indicators*. Paris: OECD.

Varian, H. (2006). *Intermediate microeconomics*. New York: W. W. Norton & Company.

Vollgraaff, R. (2013). "Pay Increases 'Should Be Linked to Productivity'," *Business Day*, 9 June. www.businesslive.co.za/bd/national/labour/2013-06-09-pay-increases-should-be-linked-to-productivity/.

4

COSTS

In any firm all stakeholders should be aware that their destiny considerably depends on the costs incurred by the firm. Employers in particular have a duty to inform their counterparts of the constraints attributable to costs. High or low fixed costs, increasing or decreasing marginal costs are indicators of whether or not a business can or must grow. Marginal costs often indicate whether a plant can or cannot continue production operations or employment of staff. In this section we shall also explain the link between productivity and costs, and thereby explain why discussions on containment of costs or increased productivity are two sides of the same coin. Finally, we concentrate our attention on those costs that firms generally face when they operate in a market: transaction costs. We explain that such costs can be a hot topic in relations between firms and public authorities.

4.1 Fixed costs and variable costs

Costs can be variable or fixed. Variable costs depend on how much the firm produces. Fixed costs do not. Over a sufficiently long period all costs are variable because in the long run, getting rid of a cost is always possible, for example if you shut down the firm and stop producing. Fixed costs, in the short term, do not depend on the quantity you produce (Figure 4.1). Symmetrically the short term is the period during which some costs are fixed and the long term is the period during which all costs become variable. This distinction is not always so obvious and neat. To give an example: are maintenance and advertizing fixed or variable costs? You should always carry out some maintenance, but if you produce more, the quantity of maintenance needed may increase. The time framework determines whether costs are fixed or variable.

Fixed costs should not be confused with sunk costs. A cost is sunk if we cannot recover it in the future. Many fixed costs can be recovered at some stage in the future.

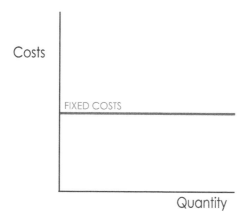

FIGURE 4.1   Fixed costs do not depend on the produced quantity

The following are some typical fixed costs:

- Overheads or administrative costs.
- Taxes on real estate.
- Properties (apartment, house, warehouse, land, etc.) that you cannot easily sell or that you rent through long-term contracts.
- Equipment you own or rent on a long-term basis.
- A mortgage.
- The power required for minimal maintenance.
- Employees that you cannot easily dismiss.
- Long-term supply contracts.

Examples of variable costs, those which change when output changes, are:

- Petrol for your car.
- Paper for your printer.
- Materials and supplies that you only buy when you have to produce additional quantities.
- The power that machines consume when they produce.
- Employees you can easily dismiss.
- Real estate you can rent on a short-term basis.
- Commissions to salesmen.

Total Costs = Fixed Costs + Variable Costs

4.2 Marginal and average costs

How much does an increase in output influence total costs? Knowing this would be a useful tool to decide whether we have to produce more or less. How much additional cost is generated by producing one unit more? What is the average cost of producing ten additional units of output? Many business decisions depend on such information.

$$\boxed{\text{Cost increase}} = \boxed{\begin{array}{l}\text{Total Cost after producing}\\ \text{the additional quantities}\end{array}} - \boxed{\begin{array}{l}\text{Total Cost before producing}\\ \text{the additional quantities.}\end{array}}$$

$$\text{Marginal cost} = \frac{\text{Cost Increase}}{\text{No of additional units}}$$

Are marginal cost and variable cost the same? No, they are not: the marginal cost is the change in variable cost as the level of output changes. In many industries marginal cost over a certain production volume range may decrease,[1] but then, for larger quantities, at least in the short term, it tends to increase. For this reason, we think that in many industries, beyond certain thresholds, firms are ready to offer larger quantities only at higher prices. So, we represent the relationship between quantities that they are ready to sell and prices, that is the supply curve, as an upward-sloping curve.

We often sell every unit of product at the same price. We therefore need to know:

- the average cost of each unit of output;
- whether average cost increases or decreases for different levels of production.

$$\text{Average Cost} = \text{Total Cost}/Q$$

Where Q represents quantity or total output in physical terms.
If total cost is the sum of fixed costs and variable costs then:

$$\frac{\text{Average Cost}}{Q} = \frac{\text{Total Cost}}{Q} = \frac{\text{Fixed Cost} + \text{Variable Cost}}{Q}$$

$$\text{Average Cost} = \text{Unitary Fixed Cost} + \text{Unitary Variable Cost}$$

The average cost of a firm is affected both by the per unit contributions of both fixed costs and variable costs.[2]

The two main production factors are capital and labour. The total cost therefore can be expressed by the sum of the cost of capital and the cost of labour.

$$\text{Total Cost} = \text{Cost of Capital} + \text{Cost of Labour}$$

Therefore, the average cost is:

$$\text{Average Cost} = \frac{\text{Total Cost}}{Q} = \frac{\text{Fixed Cost}}{Q} + \frac{\text{Variable Cost}}{Q}$$

The cost of capital is given by the interest rate multiplied by the invested capital.[3]

The cost of labour is given by the wage (in this case inclusive of social contribution) multiplied by the number of workers.

Therefore, the average cost can be rewritten:

$$\text{Average Cost} = \frac{\text{Capital} \times \text{interest rate}}{Q} + \frac{\text{Wage} \times \text{Number of workers}}{Q}$$

However, the statement above is equivalent to the following:

$$\text{Average Cost} = \frac{\text{interest rate}}{\left(\dfrac{Q}{\text{capital}}\right)} + \frac{\text{wage}}{\text{No. of Worker}}$$

This means that the average cost is given by the sum of the cost of capital and the cost of labour, both per unit of product. The average cost attributable to the output depends not only on the interest rate and the wage that firms pay, but on the productivity of capital (Total Output/Capital or Q/K) and on the productivity of labour (Total Output/[No of Workers] or Q/L). Increasing productivity entails reducing costs and becoming more competitive. Average cost may increase because you increase wages, sometimes depending on the bargaining power of trade unions, or because you reduce productivity, largely depending on the adopted technology, market demand and on the management of the firm. In every debate between employers and trade unions this is a hot topic.

Read

The cost of extracting copper in Zambia

Spectacular growth rates in China, and in its appetite for commodities such as copper, iron ore and oil, have fuelled boom conditions in countries such as Zambia, Angola and Nigeria which are heavily reliant on the extractive industries. For example, China accounts for about 45% of world copper consumption, while for Zambia mining contributes about 75% of foreign exchange earning.

As China's growth slowed in 2014–15, Zambia's Copper Belt was particularly hard hit. The price of copper reached a five-year low of $5,353 a tonne at a time when economists estimated that in the most efficient mines the cost of extracting an additional tonne of copper is about $5,500, i.e. their marginal costs of production, were in the region of $5,500 a tonne. In many, less efficient, mines that cost was higher. Selling the tonne of copper at $5,353 means making losses.

Directors and CEOs in the industry faced the choice: either close down many of the mines, or hang on in the hope that market demand would recover, meanwhile searching ruthlessly for ways of reducing costs.

Read

"Zambia's Copper Belt Reels as Price Falls," Andrew England, *Financial Times*, 26 January 2015. www.ft.com/content/80283f0a-a2df-11e4-ac1c-00144fe ab7de.

Questions

- If in 2015 you were advising the directors of a typical mining company in Zambia, what information would you need to collect?
- Why can copper at $5,353 a tonne be a problem?
- How high is the marginal cost at many Zambian mines which are old, deep and expensive to operate?
- What do high marginal costs imply for many Zambian copper firms?
- What happens to workers when prices dip?

Analysis

In the Zambian town of Kitwe, the legacy of the copper industry can be clearly felt. The article describes a point in time of low copper prices. For many producers, the price of $5,353 a tonne does not even cover the estimated marginal cost of $5,550 a tonne. This means that the price does not even cover the cost of producing an additional tonne of copper, not to mention fixed costs, which of course are not included in marginal costs.

Essentially, at such prices producing an additional tonne of copper is a loss-making operation. In the case of old deep and expensive-to-operate mines, marginal cost is higher and the difficulties greater. For many copper firms there is at least the need to reduce margins. The forecasts are lower growth in Sub-Saharan Africa and job losses.

4.3 Types of costs

Costs can have different structures, which have important implications for the life of firms and for those who earn their living working for them.

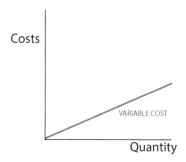

FIGURE 4.2   Linear variable costs

Linear variable costs

Linear variable costs (Figure 4.2) normally indicate constant marginal returns, i.e. constant marginal productivity. This is illustrated every time a new piece of equipment is added or a new worker is engaged and they perform to the precise same levels as the existing. They also indicate that each additional unit of output costs the same.

This is the case of a person who rents a shop (inclusive of utilities) and a photocopying machine. He only pays a *per unit* cost for paper, ink and the labour of a boy who is paid for the number of copies that he makes (piece-work labour). If we consider both fixed costs and linear variable costs, we obtain a picture like Figure 4.3:

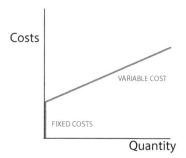

FIGURE 4.3   A company with fixed cost and linear variable costs

Increasing marginal costs: variable costs which grow more and more

The costs (Figure 4.4) of a firm which pays higher and higher overtime salaries to its staff are an example. A business may become less and less profitable as its production level increases, for example, when digging a deeper and deeper mine or building a taller and taller skyscraper. They often indicate decreasing marginal returns. This is the case when, for example, capital is scarce in the short run.

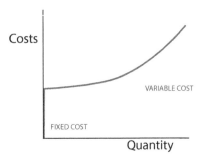

FIGURE 4.4 Total cost in a firm where variable costs grow more and more

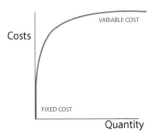

FIGURE 4.5 Total cost in a firm where variable costs grow less and less (decreasing marginal costs)

Diminishing marginal costs: variable costs which grow less and less

These costs can be found, for example, in a business in which experience matters greatly. There is a learning process: as you learn how to perform tasks, the cost of performing them becomes lower and lower (you become more efficient, saving time and money; imagine, for example, when you learn to use Excel!). Usually a curve as per that shown below indicates increasing marginal returns Figure 4.5.

4.4 The supply: is the firm ready to sell a certain quantity? At what price?

The ability of firms to sell a product at a certain price usually changes according to whether they are in a short-term or long-term perspective (see Section 1.2). In the short term they have certain costs which they will have to face in any event, notwithstanding the quantity that they produce (fixed costs); therefore, when they specify the quantity of goods they want to sell at a certain price, in the short run they may ignore fixed costs. They cannot ignore those costs directly attributable to the act of producing; they are variable costs which they could avoid only by not producing anything. In the short term, firms should have revenue at least as high as

FIGURE 4.6 The supply curve

the variable costs, otherwise they would rather not produce anything. This means that the price (per unit revenue) that they demand should be at least as high as the average variable cost or per unit variable cost. But this is usually not enough. Let us assume that, in order to produce more, firms have to pay overtime to their employees, carry out additional maintenance of the plants and in general, carry costs which increase more and more (increasing marginal costs). In such cases, the last unit produced is the most expensive to produce. Usually firms will be willing to produce the last unit of production only if its price will cover the additional costs attributable to its production, that is its marginal cost. So, in the short term, firms are ready to sell a quantity of its product not only at a price at least equal to the average variable cost, but also at least equal to the marginal cost. On this basis they seek higher prices for larger quantities and we can represent this with an upward-sloping curve (Figure 4.6).

In the long term, the firm must not only cover variable costs, it must also cover its fixed costs; if it does not, it is not sustainable and it has the option of stopping production and leaving the industry. Therefore, in the long term, the firm can only sell at a price which is not only greater than marginal cost and unit variable cost, but also greater than average cost (average cost = total cost/quantity).

At industry level, at very low-price levels, only very competitive producers can produce; at higher-price levels, other producers become able to produce and at very high price levels even high-cost producers can join the market with their product. For these reasons, aggregate supply at high-price levels is much greater than at low-price levels.

THE FIRM SUPPLY CURVE: A MORE TECHNICAL PRESENTATION

The firm's supply curve tells us how many units of a product a firm is willing to sell at any given price. A firm will be willing to sell a unit of output as long as the price received for that unit covers the cost of producing that additional unit of output – the marginal cost. Hence the firm will supply a unit of output as long as the price equals the marginal cost. So, at any given price level, we can determine from the marginal cost curve the quantity of output that the firm will be willing to supply. Increasing marginal cost is as depicted in Figure 4.4; the supply curve is as depicted in Figure 4.6.

Keeping in mind that the price must cover average variable cost if the firm is not to shut down in the short run, the supply curve is the firm's marginal cost curve only for prices greater than average variable cost. In the long run, a third condition for production is required, which is that the firm earns a profit. This occurs when the price is greater than the average total cost, that is when the price also covers fixed costs. There are therefore three conditions:

1   In the short run, the firm may supply its product along its marginal cost curve even when price does not cover average total cost, up to the point at which price does cover average variable cost. Below this cost level, the firm shuts down.
2   The supply curve of the firm is one in which price equals marginal cost, provided also that the price exceeds average variable cost.
3   For the firm to be earning profits, the price must be greater than average total cost.

THE GLOBAL OIL SUPPLY

Figure 4.7 shows a line with steps. The first step on the left is at level $25 and has a width of 20. It indicates that about 20% of the world oil production capacity, that extracted in the Middle East (mainly Saudi Arabia, Iran and other countries of the Gulf), can be produced if it is sold at a price equal to, or greater than, $25 a barrel. For oil prices below $25 no producer can produce sustainably and the sustainable supply will be zero. For prices above $40, oil extracted offshore on the shelf also becomes viable. The second large step at level 40 represents that oil. It accounts for a further 20% of total world production capacity. Three percent of the world's extraction capacity is represented by extra heavy oil, which is viable for prices above $48 per barrel. According to this source, onshore Russian production is sustainable at prices above $53 per barrel. At higher prices, other suppliers can produce. For prices above $62, North American shale becomes viable; and for prices above $88, even oil sands can be produced and sold in an economically sustainable way. Every time the price becomes higher, total supply increases with the activation of more expensive production. The quantity which is actually supplied then depends not only on global supply, but on global oil demand. They will cross each other at one point, namely the actual quantity supplied at the world price.

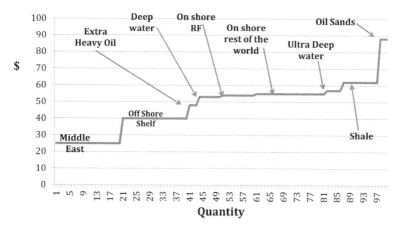

FIGURE 4.7 Supply curve of the world oil industry in 2014

Source of the data: Voxeu.org[4]

Source: Elaboration by the author.

For higher prices, more producers could produce in a sustainable way and greater quantities would be available on the market.

4.5 A special cost: the cost of using the market or transaction cost

Using the market can be expensive. We not only have to pay for those goods and services that we require, we also have to spend money on finding out which goods meet our needs, their price and where we can find them.

Transaction costs are:

> the costs other than the money price that are incurred in trading goods or services. Before a particular mutually beneficial trade can take place, at least one party must figure out that there may be someone with which such a trade is potentially possible, search out one or more such possible trade partners, inform him/them of the opportunity, and negotiate the terms of the exchange. All of these activities involve costs in terms of time, energy and money [telephone calls, internet searches, meetings, business dinners, due diligences-accounting advice, international trips, legal advice among others]. If the terms of the trade are to be more complicated than simple 'cash on

the barrelhead' (for example, if the agreement involves such complications as payment in installments, prepayment for future delivery, warranties or guarantees for quality, provision for future maintenance and service, options for additional future purchases at a guaranteed price, etc.), negotiations for such a detailed contract may itself be prolonged and very costly. After a trade has been agreed upon, there may also be significant costs involved in monitoring or policing the other party to make sure he is honoring the terms of the agreement (and, if he is not, to take appropriate legal or other actions to make him do so). These are the main sorts of transaction costs, then: search and information costs, bargaining and decision costs, policing and enforcement costs.[5]

If these costs are very high, we may decide not to buy a certain input on the market, but instead have a unit within our company producing it. In trade in certain goods, transaction costs may be very high. This is particularly true in the case of know-how (non-patented knowledge concerning production). If you want to sell your know-how, you should be able to explain its focus, after which, your counterpart, having given due consideration, may decide to decline your services. For this reason, firms very often merge with, or acquire companies with a certain know-how in order to obtain it for themselves. In other cases, firms hire personnel who possess the key know-how of a certain company. In the past, it was most common for pharmaceutical companies to include R&D within their own activities to reduce the necessity of buying and selling knowledge. Part of the transaction costs depends on the public authority. It is that authority which decides the rules of civil law, and the limits on solicitors' compensation, litigation duration and cost. In some countries, public authorities or state-owned companies provide infrastructure (telephone lines, the internet, railways and airports) and create data bases, for example telephone directories which can considerably reduce the transaction costs of firms. In the employment field, government-sponsored employment agencies may play a key role in reducing the cost of hiring new staff and the time it involves. For these reasons employers' organizations often ask the government to be active in providing a working legal framework, infrastructure and other services which reduce corporate transaction costs.

Read

The business of exporting: transaction costs facing suppliers in sub-Saharan Africa

"Despite Africa's improved economic performance in recent years, the continent still lags in the area of trade competitiveness. The big question is, Why is

Africa's trade not competitive? Empirical evidence shows that the most binding trade constraint in African countries in general is high transaction costs. Yet most agricultural, horticultural and manufactured exports – the very areas that are most important in South Saharan Africa's trade regime – are transaction intensive. Eifert et al. (2005), for example, show how high indirect costs reduce the productivity and competitiveness of manufacturers across Africa. These costs not only erode the manufacturer's profitability but also the region's trade competitiveness.

Transaction costs in South Saharan Africa are high at every step of establishing and running a business. They range from inadequate and high cost infrastructure to say the least, to costly contract enforcement, high regulatory costs, unsecured land and tenuous property rights. Trade facilitation is a virtually unknown concept in many countries of the region and securing financing for trade transactions is akin to climbing a mountain. Competition is also strangled by the lopsided position of well connected [sic] companies and a concentrated industrial structure, where large firms hold dominant market shares.

Adding to these hurdles, ineffective judiciary systems, policy uncertainty and corruption push the cost of doing business in Africa 20–40% above that of other developing regions (World Bank, 2006). The result of high transaction costs is low profitability for entrepreneurs and thus a hostile investment climate."

"The Business of Exporting: Transaction Costs Facing Suppliers in Sub-Saharan Africa," William M. Lyakurwa, AERC-CREA. www.africaportal. org/publications/the-business-of-exporting-transaction-costs-facing-suppliers-in-sub-saharan-africa/.

Questions

- Why is Africa's trade not competitive?
- Can you give any example of transaction-intensive exports?
- Where in Sub-Saharan Africa are transaction costs high?
- Can you explain what limits competition?
- What are the effects of ineffective judiciary and police systems, and what are the effects of corruption?

On the basis of your experience:

- Why do firms buy certain things in the market and make other things themselves?
- Could they not buy everything on the market?

- How long does it take to find a supplier for an input that your company never purchased before?
- When making a contract for several months or years can you foresee every possible future occurrence?
- Did you ever end up signing a very large contract with many clauses, with the objective of considering every possible situation? Did you ever seek the help of a lawyer in preparing such a contract?
- Do you or your staff spend time verifying that your counterparts (suppliers or clients) comply with the agreed terms of a contract? – e.g. that they deliver the product with the requested features in time or that they pay according to the terms?
- Did you ever complain to anybody for not complying with a contract?
- Did you ever take anybody to court or arbitration for not complying with a contract?

Analysis

An element which reduces the competitiveness of African products is the presence of high transaction costs. Such African exports as agricultural, horticultural and manufactured exports require authorization which make them transaction-cost-intensive, that is to say the administrative costs and those deriving from an environment in which sales and purchases occur are high. Transaction costs in Sub-Saharan Africa are high at every step of establishing and running a business. Infrastructures for reaching the market are often inadequate, having a contract enforced is expensive, regulation is often unclear and expensive, property rights are not well-defined. Competition is also limited by the presence of firms with strong political connections. The ineffectiveness of the judicial system and corruption in general and in the police in particular often hamper the efforts of those who wish to export.

Choice regarding the buying or making of certain components and inputs probably depends also on the transaction costs that the firm would incur when buying them on the market.

Firms often tend to produce inputs, production of which requires confidential information on the firm. Firms are often wary lest that information ends up in the wrong hands. To avoid that risk, produce the input within the firm. Similarly, firms tend to produce inputs in-house when suppliers, for various reasons (their own fault, bad roads, poor security, health problems, etc), may be unreliable. Sometimes in a developing market, finding a reliable and good-quality supplier may be lengthy, time-consuming and expensive. When we draw up a contract, foreseeing every potential issue is difficult, if not impossible and always time-consuming. When you trust your counterpart, things are easier. However, a growing business needs to add new customers and new suppliers. These, at least initially, are unknown entities. We may end up producing very long and complex contracts which are usually difficult to interpret. In many cases we must hire legal specialists or use the services of a lawyer. These are all transaction costs. When the contract is signed, it is often just the beginning. Will our counterpart comply with it? Someone in our firm should check that quantities, quality and times are respected, and if they are not, we should complain, first informally and then, if necessary, formally, via the legal system. All of this costs time and money.

For these reasons, businesses regularly seek to reduce transaction costs. Strong institutions, a properly working government and well-conceived and well-implemented legislation are pillars of the economic development of a country. In many cases, a functioning and fair legal system, clear and easy-to-implement regulations, safe and secure streets, a reliable and trusted police force are worth much more to businesses than tax relief. The implications of increasing or diminishing a firm's transaction costs are very great. When transaction costs are high, the value added of the firm, and what remains for employers and employees, may be very low. Those who represent the interests of employers should be aware of this.

Glossary

average cost   The ratio between total cost and quantity; in the long run, the price of the product must be at least equal to the average cost or the firm will not be sustainable.

diminishing marginal costs   This occurs when the production of additional units entails variable costs which increase less and less.

fixed costs   Costs which do not depend on the quantity produced. Organizations need to pay them even when they are not producing at all, at least in the short term. High fixed costs require that firms produce large volumes of output in order to balance their books.

increasing marginal costs   These occur when the production of additional units entails variable costs which increase more and more.

linear variable costs   Variable costs which are proportional to output, implying constant marginal costs.

marginal cost   This measures the change in cost for a given change of output.

supply   The quantity that firms are ready to produce and sell at a certain price.

transaction costs   Costs other than the money price incurred in trading goods or services.

variable costs   Costs which depend on the quantity that the organization produces.

Notes

1 For example, in the consulting industry, certain additional projects can cost less than earlier ones. Consulting firms use previously accumulated knowledge to solve new problems at very low cost.
2 We further analyse this in unit 5 where we deal with fixed costs divided among a large number of units and the consequent economies of scale.

3 Actually, the cost of capital also includes depreciation and capital gains.
4 www.voxeu.org/article/2014-oil-price-slump-seven-key-questions.
5 Johnson, 2005 www.auburn.edu/~johnspm/gloss/transaction_costs. These costs have been evidenced by Ronald H. Coase in his seminal article "The Nature of the Firm", *Economica*, New Series, 4(16), (Nov 1937), 386–405.

Bibliography

Coase, R. H. (1937). "The Nature of the Firm," *Economica*, New Series, 4(16): 386–405.

Eifert, B., Gelb, A. and Ramachandran, V. (2005). "Business Environment and Comparative Advantage in Africa: Evidence from the Investment Climate Data," Working Paper No. 56. Center for Global Development, Washington, DC.

England, A. (2015). "Zambia's Copper Belt Reels as Price Falls," *Financial Times*, 26 January. www.ft.com/content/80283f0a-a2df-11e4-ac1c-00144feab7de.

Lyakurwa, W. M. (2007). "The Business of Exporting: Transaction Costs Facing Suppliers in Sub-Saharan Africa," AERC-CREA. 23 April. www.africaportal.org/publications/the-business-of-exporting-transaction-costs-facing-suppliers-in-sub-saharan-africa/.

World Bank. (2006). *Doing Business*. [online] Available at: http://www.doingbusiness.org [Accessed 12 January 2007].

5

ECONOMIES OF SCALE

The size of firms matters. Even if in every developed economy the majority of firms is small or very small, and even if most labour is usually employed in small and medium-sized enterprises, an important part of production takes place in large firms and a very large proportion of R&D is also carried out within large firms. Large firms are an essential factor in driving and coordinating the work of many smaller firms which are their suppliers or customers. Moreover, large firms represent a specific environment in terms of relations between employers and employees. We can say that any thriving economy needs both a certain number of large and medium-to-large enterprises and a much greater number of small and medium-to-small enterprises. This section investigates the importance of size in business.

5.1 Reducing the average cost of a firm

Even in a firm using the same equipment and labour force (i.e. substantially a short-run situation – see Section 1.2), producing more may mean producing at lower costs.[1] This may occur because the firm divides up some fixed costs, for example the cost of some piece of equipment, into a larger number of units, or because it is experiencing increasing marginal productivity or decreasing marginal costs. For different reasons producing more may also mean producing better and at lower cost. Here producing more leads to lower average cost. In this case, we are reaching the optimal volume of production in the short run. In Figure 5.1 this can be clearly seen. On the left-hand side we can observe a company with fixed costs and variable costs which grows in a constant manner (constant marginal cost). On the right-hand side we can observe that this same company incurs lower average costs when it produces more units, even if the marginal cost is constant. In other words, the cost of some initial investment (the purchase of a piece of land, machinery or some patent) is divided among a larger number of units.

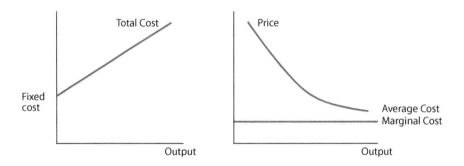

FIGURE 5.1 Total costs (left), average cost and marginal cost (right)

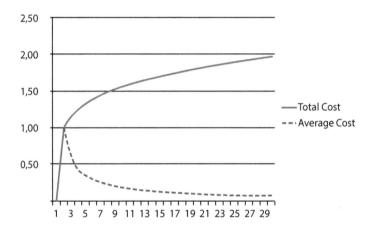

FIGURE 5.2 Total cost and average cost in a firm with only variable costs and diminishing marginal costs

In speaking of production and productivity (see Section 3.2) we have mentioned that when a firm produces more its productivity may increase, decrease or remain constant. We spoke of increasing, diminishing or constant returns to scale. Similarly, when we discussed costs, we spoke of increasing, decreasing or constant marginal costs (see Section 4.2) and showed that cost and productivity are two sides of the same coin.

A reduction in the average costs of the firm sometimes occurs, not because the firm is dividing up fixed costs but because it is experiencing increasing marginal productivity or diminishing marginal cost. For example, when it produces larger volumes both the equipment and the staff work better, the latter because they acquire experience and are more motivated. This case is illustrated graphically in Figure 5.2 and we see that average cost may decrease simply because the firm has total costs which increase less and less.

5.2 The causes of economies of scale

There are economies of scale when larger firms have lower average costs (see Section 4.2) than smaller firms, [2] each unit of production costing them less (i.e. average cost decreases).

This of course creates advantages for some firms and disadvantages for others. When production volumes increase, purchasing specific and more advanced equipment makes sense. Such types of equipment usually permit reduced costs and increased productivity. Moreover, with large volumes, staff can specialize more and handle a narrower range of tasks. Better-prepared staff usually increase productivity and reduce costs. On the other hand, in very small firms, staff may handle a wide range of tasks and therefore cannot specialize in any of them. Similarly, if the firm is very small it usually cannot afford the purchase of very specific and sophisticated equipment and ends up with higher unit costs (higher average costs).

In general, larger firms may balance different risks more satisfactorily. This may, for example, be true when firms have several similar production lines. In this case, the probability of using the warehouse does not grow proportionally with the volume of output, but much less. This is one reason why large firms need to invest in goods in the warehouse and working capital proportionally less than smaller firms.

By the same token, the probability that all customers of a bank with only a thousand customers in one branch in a single village will go to the bank and withdraw a large part of their deposits is much higher than would be the case with a bank with millions of customers in thousands of branches in many towns.

The same is true, albeit in a different way, for firms large enough to be active in different and relatively independent markets (with different products, users or markets); these are known as "diversified firms". The risk of all their clients suddenly ceasing to purchase their goods is much lower than for a firm of limited size active in only one market. Similarly, large firms can more easily increase the number of their suppliers and depend less on each of them.

These are examples of firms that are virtually insured against a total collapse of sales, supplies or, more generally, their business as a whole. This kind of insurance is not provided by insurance companies but by the firms themselves. We can therefore speak of "self-insurance". The larger an organization, the easier it is to develop forms of self-insurance and reduce the cost of handling risks.

A large firm can also retain part of its financial liquidity internally without investing it in the financial market. It can fund different projects, avoid paying commission fees and interest to the banking system and also avoid the constraints and conditions that bankers often impose on borrowers. Finally, by bringing in-house some activities that small firms can only buy on the market, a large firm can reduce the cost of using the market, that is its transaction costs (see Section 4.5).

Whenever firms handle assets (e.g. a machine, plant, building or know-how) which must be acquired in fixed quantities, there are benefits in increasing production to achieve full exploitation of those assets. The cost of those assets is fixed, but the more you produce, the less that cost affects the cost of each unit (diminishing unitary fixed costs, see Section 4.2). In this context we may also consider corporate brands. Once you establish a brand you can keep using it on many units, with no or limited additional costs. Managerial skills follow a similar pattern to a certain degree; a skilled manager can manage more people with little additional effort. Overheads should follow the same rationale even if, as we shall see, they sometimes do not. Medium and large firms can afford R&D costs that small and micro firms cannot. Figure 5.3 shows data for industrialized countries. Generally speaking very small firms tend to carry out relatively less R&D than large firms. This happens not only because of a lack of financial resources but also for other reasons. When you carry out an investment, for example, an investment in innovation, your production volume must be large enough to recoup that investment. Sometimes small firms are not able to produce volumes large enough to recoup significant R&D investment.

In theory, small firms could develop innovations and then sell them to larger firms for a profit. Innovation is basically knowledge. Trade in knowledge may imply very high transaction costs (see Section 4.5). The buyer needs to know what they are going to buy; once that is known, the buyer may not feel the need to pay for something they already possess. Intellectual property lawyers deal with precisely such issues and can potentially find legal solutions, but their services and potential litigation costs may be prohibitive for small firms. For these reasons, only in well-functioning legal systems will small businesses have strong incentives to produce and sell innovations to other companies.

Not only may larger firms have lower average costs through producing more of a single product, they can also benefit from producing several goods. A slaughterhouse

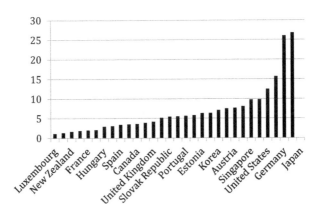

FIGURE 5.3 R&D total expenditure by firms with more than 50 employees compared with that of firms with up to 49 employees

In every OECD country the ratio is greater than 1, i.e. in every OECD country the total R&D expenditure by medium and large firms is a multiple of that by small firms.

In Japan medium large firms spend on R&D 127 times what small firms spend. Data on Japan would require a graph of a different scale.

Source: OECD data about year 2011, elaboration by the author[3]

produces mainly meat, but also leather. A newspaper correspondent may also work for a TV network and give lectures around the world. A factory producing semi-skimmed milk also produces butter. In the Eurotunnel between France and Britain, not only trains pass through but also electricity power cables which connect the French and British power networks. In all these cases, economies arise more from variety than from volume. We call these savings "economies of scope", that is producing a range of goods and so reducing average costs.

Finally, it is worth mentioning that firms can also reduce average costs by being close to other firms in the same industry. There are cities in which fashion shops are mostly situated in certain streets (e.g. Bond Street in London, UK), goldsmiths are concentrated in other streets and banks are confined to one area only (The City of London, UK and Wall Street in New York, US). There are towns which are specialized in light industry (e.g. Dongguan in China, where about 30 per cent of the toys delivered around the globe are made) or one type of product only (cars in Wolfsburg, Germany, car components in Turin, Italy and soccer balls in Sialkot, Pakistan, among others).

Firms may choose to be close to their competitors for several reasons. Customers come to the area because they know that in that area many firms are in that business and a certain product is available. In this way, firms virtually benefit from free advertising. They also benefit from the presence of specialized suppliers. The labour market in the area is rich in people with the skills needed by the industry. Finally, the area may better represent the interests of a certain trade at political levels. Such benefits are called "external economies of scale", that is the benefit that a firm derives from the extensive presence of firms of the same industry in its area. The fact that many firms related to the same industry are in the same area reduces their average costs.

When the average cost of a firm diminishes because there exist many firms in the same industry in its area, we can say that the firm enjoys external economies of scale.

5.3 The limits to economies of scale

We could draw the conclusion that the larger the firm, the better; but the reality is much more complex. Sometimes firms become simply too large and complex and for this reason their average costs increase due to diseconomies of scale. These costs are often caused by the fact that mental capacity is a limited resource. While good managers are able to supervise many people, other managers are not fit for this task. This is particularly true in turbulent times when firms frequently face difficult decisions and sudden changes.

If fixed resources are a major source of economies of scale, they are also a source of diseconomies of scale. A thin market for inputs or outputs may increase a firm's costs; every other fixed factor, the availability of which the firm is unable to increase, will bring about higher costs.

Above, we mentioned that larger firms can save on overheads; but this is not always true. When firms become larger, they must standardize their routines and procedures. Creating rules implies that staff should comply with them. Failure to comply with the rules will not be allowed. In many cases, compliance with rules and risk avoidance become more important than value-creating behaviour. This is so-called "bureaucratic behaviour" and is a serious hazard for firms. Moreover, in some firms, central bureaucracies grow proportionally more than production capacity, particularly during expansion periods. Therefore, for some firms, increasing size means larger bureaucracies and more bureaucratic behaviour, giving rise to lower productivity and higher average costs.

5.4 The minimum efficient size and concentration

How far is the growth of a firm beneficial to society? This is a question that public authorities should answer, at least in those countries which have an antitrust authority. The standard situation occurs when a large firm acquires another firm, creating a very much larger firm. In many countries, acquisitions or mergers of this size are subject to public authorization. Besides political patronage, what objective criteria can public authorities use to decide these cases? Can they simply assume that "the bigger, the better"? No, they cannot. In some cases, firms wish to grow in order to become more efficient and this must be welcomed and encouraged. In other cases, they want to grow merely to eliminate competitors, increase their market share, fix prices and exploit consumers. This should not be welcomed. In the first case, firms, by becoming larger, create new value which market forces and social dialogue can then distribute in society.

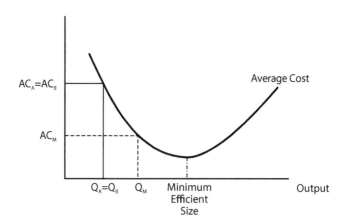

FIGURE 5.4 The minimum efficient size

Consider two firms A and B each producing the same quantity QA = QB and having the same Average Costs, $AC_A = AC_B$. When these two firms merge, they increase the volume produced to Q_M and the average cost declines to AC_M. In this case, the merger improves the efficiency of the economy. If each of the two firms produced a quantity equal to the minimum efficient size already, a merger could create a firm with higher average cost and reduce the efficiency of the economy.

In the second case, an acquisition or merger does not create new value but merely redistributes resources from competitors, clients and suppliers to the coffers of a single firm. To distinguish between the two cases, a tool called "minimum efficient size" (MES Figure 5.4) has been devised. Usually the initial growth of the firm will bring benefits, reducing its average cost (see Section 4.2). As long as the growth of the firm reduces its average cost, such growth must not only be authorized but also encouraged. However, there is a threshold beyond which the growth of the firm is no longer linked with a reduction in its average costs. Beyond such a threshold the growth of the firm is just aimed at increasing its monopoly power. This threshold is the minimum efficient size. A firm which requests authorization for a merger or an acquisition should prove that it has not yet reached its minimum efficient size, otherwise it could expect strong opposition to its initiative. Public authorities may well oppose a firm that exploits its financial resources just to eliminate competitors and increase its market share.

The efficiency implied by economies of scale puts additional resources in the hands of those firms capable of achieving them. These resources may be used to invest in R&D, to achieve technological innovation, to transfer benefits to consumers or simply to increase the market share of a firm. When in an industry the market share of one or a few firms represents a large percentage of the total market, we say that industry is concentrated. Very often a highly concentrated industry ends up being one in which there is not much competition. In such conditions one or a few firms are able to sell their product with considerable margins. This is of course beneficial for the owners and potentially for the employees of the firm, but it can be extremely detrimental to society at large, which sees its wealth transferred to one or few firms. For these reasons, while economies of scale must be welcomed, wariness of excessive concentration is necessary.

THE NATURAL MONOPOLY: WHEN MINIMUM EFFICIENT SIZE IMPLIES THAT THERE IS ROOM FOR ONE PRODUCER ONLY

In some industries (e.g. railways, water supplies, power networks, motorways) average costs continue to decrease over the whole range that the market can absorb. Minimum efficient size can only be achieved when one producer supplies the whole market. This would lead to only one producer and seller in the market: a monopolist. Since this monopoly situation is rooted in the features of these industries and in the structure of their average costs, we call this "natural monopoly".

This single producer could desire the maximum possible profit. To do this, the monopolist may limit the quantity that it sells without fearing competitors because they simply do not exist. This would be an inefficient result and under such conditions, society is worse off. For this reason, in many countries the public authority regulates natural monopolies.

Read

Acquisition or divestment

In a dynamic economy, company managers often seize opportunities to grow the company by acquiring other firms or divisions of other firms. The case for acquisition is usually argued in terms of scale economies. Administrative costs may be reduced, longer production runs may become possible, there may be savings in marketing and distribution.

But for every company that expands by buying a business division from another company, there must also be a seller who sees advantage in offloading that division.

Many companies have greatly benefited by shedding a section or division, which has become marginal to the company's main business. The division's prospects may have seemed good, but it was not well placed to compete with other divisions in the company for management attention or for funds for further investment.

Studies of companies which have slimmed themselves through spinoffs and disposals have found many examples where both parent and spin-off company have achieved significantly higher operating margins in the years subsequent to the demerger.

However, the conclusions of these studies are not always so sure. Some other factors may be at play. The following reading helps to understand why large size may be an asset and why it can be a liability.

Read

"The Logic of Corporate Shrinkage Reasserts Itself," Tony Jackson, *Financial Times*, 4 September 2011. www.ft.com/content/ec51f8d4-d564-11e0-bd7e-00144feab49a.

Questions

- How can we explain that firms in certain periods tend to grow while in other periods there are spin-offs and disposals?
- Do executives have any bias towards small or large size, and why?
- Is there a major difference between states and firms in the tendency towards bureaucracy?

- What happens to corporate bureaucracy when firms become larger?
- Is small necessarily beautiful? Can you give some examples?
- In what way can the financial management of a large firm be different from that of a small firm?
- What is a frequent relationship between large firms and entrepreneurs/business creators?

Analysis

Firms in times of stability tend to become larger partly because this is in the nature of firms, partly because growth can reduce average costs (economies of scale), and partly because managers know that their remuneration is a function of size: the larger the firm, the more they earn; but in times of doubt and depression, the logic of small size may prevail and spin-offs and disposals may become frequent. Firms, like states, may become bureaucratic with a more than proportional growth of central staff and relatively greater attention to procedures and rules than to results. Even so, one cannot say that small is always beautiful. Large firms can better allocate financial resources without passing through the intermediation of the financial system; they can also borrow at lower cost; and they can also be the natural end-product of the efforts of entrepreneurs who have followed the initial phases of an idea.

Glossary

bureaucratization   A process which leads an organization to employ many administrative staff and also causes a large proportion of staff to act more in compliance with set rules and procedures than with creating value.

concentration   The degree to which the output [...] in an industry is accounted for by only a few firms.[4]

constant returns to scale   A condition under which increasing the total output of a firm does not increase its average cost.

diseconomies of scale   A condition under which increasing the total output of a firm increases its average cost.

diversification   Producing for numerous markets, using different suppliers or different technologies.

economies of scale   A condition which occurs when increasing the total output of a firm reduces its average cost.

economies of scope   These economies occur "when a firm producing many products has lower average costs than a firm producing just a few products".[5]

external economies of scale   A condition which occurs when proximity to other firms in the same industry leads to decreasing average cost.

minimum efficient size   The smallest size which permits a firm to achieve the minimum average cost in the industry.

Notes

1   According Bernheim and Whinston (2008:287) "A firm experiences economies of scale when its average cost falls as it produces more". Such definition would consider the phenomenon described in this paragraph as economies of scale. This text follows the definition by Baumol and Blinder (1997:167).
2   "Production is said to involve economies of scale, also referred to as increasing returns to scale, if, when all input quantities are doubled, the quantity of output is more than doubled" (Baumol and Blinder, 1997:167).
3   Ratios calculated in purchasing power dollars. Data retrieved on Oct 26 2015 from http://stats.oecd.org/Index. aspx?DataSetCode=BERD_SIZE# Missing data have been considered as zeros.
4   Sinclair (2000:331).
5   Besanko (2007:81).

Bibliography

Baumol, W. J. and Blinder, A. S. (1997). *Economics, principles, and policy*. New York: Harcourt Brace Jovanovich.

Bernheim, B. and Whinston, M. (2008). *Microeconomics*. New York: McGraw-Hill Higher Education.

Besanko, D. (2007). *Economics of strategy*. Hoboken, NJ: Wiley & Sons.

Jackson, T. (2011). "The Logic of Corporate Shrinkage Reasserts Itself," *Financial Times*, 4 September. www.ft.com/content/ec51f8d4-d564-11e0-bd7e-00144feab49a.

Sinclair, J. (2000). *Collins English dictionary*. London: Harper-Collins.

PART III

Customers and competitors

In this part, we consider the relationship of the firm with its customers and competitors. Firstly, we shall consider the case of a whole industry, which may include many firms or just one in which there is a monopoly. In the case of the monopolist there is one manager with the perception that in some way, he (or she) can influence either price or quantity and must choose what to do. In fact, both quantity and price affect the total revenue of the firm. For every industry and every firm, there is also the major issue of understanding who their competitors are. With the tools to answer these questions we shall be able to consider markets in which firms are numerous and uninfluential, markets in which firms are few and influential, and markets in which firms are numerous but still have some individual influence on their product price. Firms in each of these markets try to make profits but the constraints they face are different, as also are the results.

6

DEMAND FOR THE PRODUCTS OF AN INDUSTRY AND OF A MONOPOLIST

In this section, we concentrate our attention on one industry, which in some cases can be made up of a single firm which we then call a monopolist. We consider how much consumers are ready to buy from the industry, the product price and how this can be affected by many factors, in particular, consumer income. Both price and quantity determine the value of the sales of the firm, its total revenue.

6.1 An industry and the demand for its product

Usually, the higher a good costs, the less consumers demand it.[1] The availability of consumers to buy large quantities of a certain good generally diminishes as the price of that good rises. But price is not the only determinant of a sale. Quality matters; customers are ready to pay a higher price if they perceive a product as of higher quality. Technology also matters; some products such as the Walkman or CD, which attracted widespread consumer interest in the 1980s who were ready to pay for them, now attract buyers less and less. The development of the iPod, of USB memory units and of online downloads has reduced demand for earlier technologies. At 1980 prices, the quantity demanded is now much lower owing to the change in technology. Consumer tastes are also very important: in some periods traditional clothes are the only option, but then fashion swings many consumers towards western trends, which can then be overtaken by various other influences which may make traditional clothes preferred again. Consumers are ready to pay a premium to purchase them. For the same price, a change in tastes causes some goods to be more or less in demand. The availability and price of substitutes also influence the quantity demanded at a given price. For example, the existence of a reliable new railway service makes a toll road less attractive. The more that cheap and good-quality substitutes exist, the lower the price of a good will be.

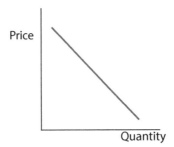

FIGURE 6.1 The demand curve of an industry or of a monopolist

Read

The recommended reading comes from the press agency Reuters and is about the price of a commodity, cocoa, which for different reasons, increases. The text describes how different markets react to this event.

"High Cocoa Prices Set to Curb Demand from Chocolate Makers," David Brough on Reuters, 17 February 2015. www.reuters.com/article/cocoa-demand-outlook/high-cocoa-prices-set-to-curb-demand-from-chocolate-makers-idUSL5N0VQ3B720150217.

Questions

- Why is cocoa demand likely to remain depressed?
- How will chocolate makers behave?
- What is the difference between reactions in North America and Europe on the one hand and in emerging markets on the other?

Analysis

The quantity of cocoa demanded is likely to be low if cocoa bean prices are high. This may lead chocolate producers in industrialized countries to increase chocolate bar prices or to reduce their size. In emerging markets, the option of abandoning cocoa butter in favour of cheaper vegetable oils, for example palm kernel oil, is considered. This is a case of high prices inducing a reduction in demand.

The other major cause of scarce demand is the economic crisis in Europe, a major chocolate consumer.

6.2 Demand and supply

Demand alone (Figure 6.1) does not determine the market price. Demand represents a range of possibilities, indicating for every price level how much customers are ready to buy.

The availability of firms to sell a certain quantity of product at a certain price is called supply (Figure 6.2). We introduced this concept in Section 4.4. We saw that higher oil prices make viable certain sources of crude oil which at lower prices are not viable. In general, higher market prices induce firms to bring to the market greater volumes of output. We can illustrate this with an upward-sloping curve, higher prices corresponding to larger quantities.

A certain quantity can be traded in a sustainable manner only if the price that customers are ready to pay matches the price that firms ask. This is represented by the meeting point of demand and supply (Figure 6.3). If aggregate supply and aggregate demand have a common point, that represents the market's equilibrium point, i.e. there exists a quantity (Q★) with a price (P★) which leads producers to produce and buyers to buy.

For prices higher than P★, suppliers would be ready to produce more, but customers would demand less. This is a situation in which producers' warehouses are full of goods, but there are not enough customers. This situation occurs in many cases when governments fix high prices to support certain category of producers, which then has the effect of reducing the number of buyers interested in purchasing the products. Under such conditions, producers may even look for political support in order to catch the few available customers.

For prices lower than P★, demand is greater than Q★, but at least some suppliers find the price uninteresting and produce no more. More customers are attracted by

FIGURE 6.2 The supply curve

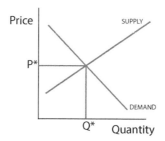

FIGURE 6.3 The equilibrium price is where demand and supply cross each other

this lower price, but under these conditions supply will be lower than demand. We observe queues in shops, waiting lists and customers unable to obtain the product. This applies where public authorities impose artificially low prices without subsidising producers to cover their consequent losses. Usually the result is scarcity, with some people buying the products through recommendations and friendships and others simply unable to buy.

6.3 Total revenue and marginal revenue

Price and quantity determine the revenue of the industry. The total revenue of the industry (Figure 6.4) is the product of price and quantity.

Total revenue = Price × Quantity

The members of an industry may wish to sell at very high prices, but the quantity sold would then diminish or even be nil, with negative consequences for the total revenue of the industry. Selling at very low prices, on the other hand, would also mean low revenue: the sold quantity would be high, but the low price would make total revenue very small.

Prices above a certain price are so high as to deter any customer from making purchases, but then a small price reduction permits the sale of the first unit of output.

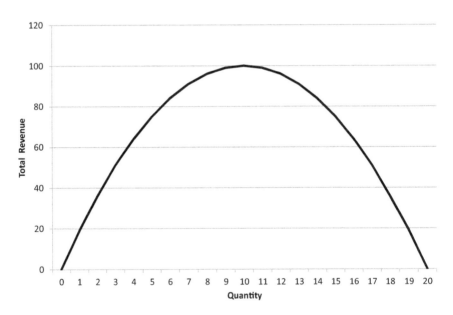

FIGURE 6.4   Total revenue of an industry or of a monopolist

Beyond a certain threshold of output, in this case for quantity greater than 10, the total revenue decreases.

Adding this unit to the previous sales of the firm (nil) generates a considerable increase of revenue. To sell an additional unit the firm probably has to reduce its price. A small reduction in price may permit the firm to almost double its revenue. This may also occur with the third unit: just a small price reduction allows the firm to increase its sales by 50 per cent. In this case we observe that the first unit has brought sales from nil to a certain value, the second has almost doubled sales and the third has caused them to increase by almost 50 per cent. We can expect that further sales will generate further increases in total revenue, but on a declining scale. This is due to the fact that, in order to increase sales, the firm has to accept that customers will only pay a lower price. At a certain point, in order to sell one additional unit, the firm will have to cut its price so much that it will record a reduction in its total revenue and the sale of any further unit will require further price cuts and further reductions in total revenue, up to a point at which in order to sell more, the firm would have to give away its product free of charge.

In Figure 6.5 we can observe the representation of a firm selling a relatively small quantity Q' at a relatively high price P'. Its total revenue is given by P' multiplied by Q' and it is equal to the sum of the area of rectangles 1 and 3. Let us assume that the firm decides to reduce its price to P'', and to increase the quantity sold to Q''. In this

TABLE 6.1 Total revenue: an example with numbers

Price (crowns)	Quantity demanded	Total revenue	Variation of total revenue
32	0	0	
24	16	**384**	384
16	32	**512**	128
8	48	**384**	−128
0	64	0	−384

In the example of Table 6.1, with a high price (32 crowns), customers would not buy anything and total revenue would be nil. A price reduction to 24 would lead to sale of 16 units. Total revenue would increase to 384 crowns. A further price reduction to 16 crowns would lead to the sale of 32 units and total revenue equal to 512 crowns, an increase of 128 crowns. However, an additional price reduction to 8 crowns would lead not only to increased sales (48), but also to lower total revenue: 384 crowns. We would therefore observe a reduction in total revenue by 128 crowns. A final price reduction to 0 would completely destroy total revenue, reducing it by 384 crowns.

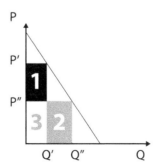

FIGURE 6.5 The monopolist dilemma

second case, the total revenue of the firm will be P" multiplied by Q" and it will be equal to the area of rectangles 3 and 2. The discount makes the firm lose all the revenue represented by rectangle 1, but it gains the revenue on the new units represented in rectangle 2. Rectangle 3 remained unchanged before and after the price change.

Total Revenue A = 1 + 3; Total Revenue B = 2 + 3; The difference in Total Revenue is:

$$\text{Total Revenue B} - \text{TotalRevenueA} = (3+1) - (3+2) = 1 - 2 = \Delta\text{Revenue}$$

It can happen that Δ Revenue is less than zero and that the firm has made a loss-making operation.[2]

We call the difference between the total revenue before and after selling an additional unit "marginal revenue". Marginal revenue is the difference in total revenue caused by the sale of an additional unit of output.

An initial quantity may be 100 units. We sell them at a price of 10 crowns per unit and our total revenue is then 1,000 crowns. We may reduce our price to 9.99 crowns per unit and we can sell an additional unit: we now sell 101 units and our total revenue is 1,008.99 crowns; our total revenue has increased by 8.99 crowns. This is the variation in revenue due to the sale of an additional unit, that is our **marginal revenue**; the unit price of 9.99 crowns diminished revenue from the original 100 units by 1 crown but this was offset by the 9.99 crowns earned from the sale of the additional unit.

Marginal **Revenue** =	Total Revenue **after** increasing the output by one unit	−	Total Revenue **before** increasing the output by one unit

More generally we can say that:

$$\textbf{Marginal Revenue} = \frac{\text{Variation of Revenue}}{\text{Variation of Quantity}}$$

As we have seen, the marginal revenue of a firm can be positive or negative. Firms interested in maximum total revenue increase output for as long as marginal revenue exceeds zero, and then they stop.

Firms with some control over their price often face this dilemma: reducing prices may increase the quantity that they sell, but not necessarily increase their total revenue.

Read

The oil-producers' dilemma

What is the point beyond which it is no longer in producers' interests to push up oil prices?

Open the financial pages at any given date and you will find the same question being debated. For example, in early 2011 the price of Brent crude oil (which is widely used as a reference point) stood at $120 a barrel, after having risen by approximately 50 per cent throughout the previous year. Analysts worried that a further surge, perhaps to $150 a barrel, would place enormous strains on the economies of oil-importing countries, and particularly on emerging economies. Inflation might rise in these countries, central banks might react by raising interest rates, growth might go into reverse and there might be drastic knock-on effects on their future capacity to import oil. Oil demand would be negatively affected. By 2018, with Brent at about $75 a barrel, and we see new arguments that for a major incumbent oil producer, further price rises should be resisted. The price at which oil is traded internationally and the range within which it moves have momentous geopolitical implications, and the process through which this is determined among the major producers can resemble a game of poker between immensely powerful players. But certain features remain relatively constant. For some producers it is urgent to secure maximum foreign exchange in the short term, in order to satisfy the demands and needs of their populations. They argue that it will take time for competitors' fracking and deep drilling to come on stream and that in the meantime there is an opportunity to increase revenues by raising prices.

In contrast, some very large producers, taking a long-term perspective, recognize that high oil prices would destabilize world markets, to the detriment of total oil demand and of their own economies. It is significant that in 2011, officials in Saudi Arabia, a very big producer, suggested that the optimal oil price would be in the range of $70 to $80 a barrel (at a time when it stood at $120 a barrel) and that in 2018 (when it stood at $75 a barrel) Iran, another big producer, took the view that $60–65 a barrel would be the appropriate price.

1   "Oil at $120: EMs Hit Hardest," Stefan Wagstyl, *Financial Times*, 5 April 2011.
2   "Pricey Crude Bad News Even for Oil Producers in Long Term," Faith Birol, IEA, *The Economic Times*, 10 May 2018. https://economictimes. indiatimes.com/markets/expert-view/pricey-crude-bad-news-even-for-oil-producers-in-long-term-faith-birol-iea/articleshow/64110669.cms.

Questions

• Why should high oil prices be bad for oil exporters?
• What effect can high oil prices have on the behaviour of central banks?

- According to these articles, what is the price that Saudi and Iranian officials seek? Why?
- What is the link between economic growth and oil consumption?

Analysis

High oil prices are bad not only for oil importers, but they can also be bad for oil exporters because they can become a threat to global growth and induce a reduction in demand for oil and in the total revenue of oil producers. Moreover, high oil prices can cause inflation. The latter can impel central bankers towards restrictive or non-expansionary monetary policies with further negative effects on economic growth, oil demand and oil revenue. Not by chance do even the officials of Saudi Arabia and Iran, among the biggest world oil producers, aim for a not-too-high price level. They well understand that very high oil prices depress economic growth and therefore reduce oil demand and the oil industry's total revenue. This is one of the many cases where high prices are accompanied by reduced traded volumes and total revenue. The maximum total *revenue* for most *goods* is not generated by the maximum price.

6.4 Price-elasticity

Another way of determining whether increasing quantities generate higher revenue consists of comparing the percentage increase in quantity with the corresponding percentage decrease in price, which is the price reduction that the firm should make in order to sell greater quantities.

$$\textbf{Price} - \textbf{Elasticity} = \frac{\% \text{ Change of Quantity}}{\% \text{ Change of Price}}$$

Usually, to sell larger quantities you have to reduce your price and therefore price-elasticity is negative. What really matters therefore is its size, remembering that its sign is always negative.[3]

Let us assume that a firm was previously selling 100 units at a price of 10. To sell 101 units, i.e. to increase sales by 1 per cent, the firm should reduce its price to 9.99. This is a reduction of 1 per 1,000. Now we see that the ratio between the percentage *increase* in quantity and the percentage reduction in price is −10 (10 if we ignore the sign). This is a number greater than 1 and it indicates that a price reduction will lead to an increase in total revenue. We can also say that demand is elastic. Elastic demand implies that price reductions generate revenue increases.

If elasticity were less than 1, it would indicate that the firm has to reduce prices considerably to achieve a small increase in the quantity sold. That would not be a situation in which you would wish to reduce prices as it would generate a reduction in revenue. Under these conditions, with elasticity less than 1, we say that the firm is facing inelastic or rigid demand.

What can a firm do when confronted with rigid demand? Price decreases do not increase revenue, but price increases do. When a firm or an industry is faced with rigid demand, they can increase revenue by simply increasing prices.

On the other hand, industries and firms faced with very elastic demand can only increase revenue through small price reductions and large increases in the volume of output.

The presence of suitable substitutes and the price sensitivity of users make the demand for a good more elastic. The absence of substitutes decreases the price sensitivity of users and makes their demand more rigid. For such goods as human blood for transfusions, there are few cheap substitutes; when a transfusion is needed, people are ready to pay very high prices. At the same time, if people do not need blood, they do not demand it even when it is cheap. Blood is a good with rigid demand. This is one of the reasons why in several countries blood is provided by the state to protect users from exploitation.

Other factors affecting elasticity are: (1) luxuries *versus* necessities; demand for necessities such as milk is not very dependent on price, (2) those goods accounting for a small fraction of consumer budgets also tend to have less elastic demand, e.g. salt. Major items such as cars are likely to have more elastic demand.

Watch

www.khanacademy.org/economics-finance-domain/microeconomics/elasticity-tutorial/price-elasticity-tutorial/v/perfect-inelasticity-and-perfect-elasticity-of-demand.

Read A

Growth rates in the Russian retail sector slowed in 2013 following a period of rapid expansion. In May of that year however, the Board of Detsky Mir announced that it would pay dividends for the first time in five years. Detski Mir (DM) was Russia's largest retailer of children's goods. There were two possible reasons for expecting that DM's growth rate would continue to rise despite a slowing down of the retail sector as a whole.

First, the nation's rising birth rate promised to support future demand in DM's sector. Second, with rising living standards, many families were in a position to acquire high-quality goods for their children in place of goods designed for the cheap end of the market and mostly imported from China and SE Asia.

DM was well placed to profit from these trends as it held exclusive marketing agreements with US toymakers and with suppliers of educational goods. According to DM spokepersons, demand for children's supplies would be more predictable and less price-elastic than demand in most other retail markets: predictable because growing children need to replace shoes and bicycles, inelastic because parents "would want the best for their children".

The *Financial Times* has an interesting article on this story:

"Russia's Detsky Mir: Buoyant Sales of Children's Goods Prompt IPO Plans," Isabel Gorst, *Financial Times*, 27 May 2013. www.ft.com/content/3c5c1b3e-233d-3292-a0f4-81911b59d63f.

Questions

* What is the difference between goods for general consumption and goods for children?
* What is the outlook for consumer spending?
* What are children's goods defying?
* Where do parents tend to put their children?
* Is demand for children's goods very price-sensitive?
* According to Detsky Mir sources what is the difference between demand for children's goods and that for other consumer products?

Read B

Rigid demand for homes is more of a marketing myth than reality

People often say that property prices on the mainland will just keep on rising but this is not grounded in reality.

Commentators on the mainland property market have often attributed the resilience of home prices and their resistance to pressure to "rigid" buyer demand. I have my doubts. Firstly, the need for accommodation should not be confused with the need to buy and own a home. People's physiological survival, let alone their emotional well-being, is very much diminished if they don't have a roof over their head for prolonged periods – unless perhaps they are marooned in a tropical paradise. Whether a home is rented or bought has little, if any, impact on survival.

But wouldn't hard-earned money be better used to pay off a mortgage instead of rent – to accumulate wealth and not have to worry about finding accommodation in retirement? Of course, and I think buying a home is a good move for most families in the long run, for social and financial reasons. However, the decision still depends on individual circumstances, external and internal, and timing – just ask Hong Kong homeowners who bought at the 1997 peak, or for that matter the Americans who entered their market in 2006.

In short, buying a home is not an optimal or even a good choice all the time in all places and for all people. While the human need for accommodation tends to be rigid, the need to buy a home is not. It is comparatively flexible, or "elastic" to use economics terminology. For instance, when the economy grows, people accumulate money and want to buy things, including homes. Conversely, when the economy contracts, people tend to spend less, and some homeowners may offload their homes, whether forced to do so or not. This is flexibility, not rigidity. Rigidity implies something that one must have, regardless. Some people might behave that way, but most are sensible about what they can afford. Do not confuse a strong urge to buy with rigidity. When a real estate market is in an upcycle and prices are rising, people tend to "feel" more confident (there is comfort in numbers). As a result, there are more buyers, hence higher transacted prices, which in turn entices others to enter the game. This fuels the cycle and prices rise higher. Indeed, in such circumstances, it can easily appear that demand is rigid – i.e., the higher the prices, the higher the demand. But this view is delusional. It is not the case that buyer demand for homes is rigid; rather, it is human nature to pursue investment returns and capital gains out of fear of being left behind in the game.

This phenomenon crosses cultural, national and ethnic boundaries. Whenever economic conditions and market opportunities present themselves, you can bet that this behaviour will happen. If demand to buy homes really is rigid, then – by the same rationale exhibited above – home-buying demand should remain the same, no more and no less, with the same prices, when the market turns down. Naturally, we don't observe such market behaviour.

In some societies, marriage and home-buying are bundled together ("you don't marry my daughter, or son, if you do not buy a home first") which perhaps adds to the demand side. Yet the rigidity lies with the parents, and the peculiar culture, to link the two activities. There is no scientific evidence that home-buying makes a marriage sounder, happier or longer. If anything, the reverse is probably more likely: when there is money to be split from selling a home, divorce may appear, at least, a sounder option.

As such, the idea that there is rigid demand for homes probably has more to do with marketing than reality.

"Rigid Demand for Homes is More of a Marketing Myth than Reality," Stephen Chung, *South China Morning Post*, 20 February 2013. www.scmp. com/property/hong-kong-china/article/1154008/rigid-demand-homes-more-marketing-myth-reality.

Questions

- What is the difference between the human need for accommodation and the need to buy a home?
- Does rigidity imply price sensitivity and attention to affordability?
- Is buyers' demand for homes rigid?
- According to the author, what could be the test for deciding that demand for buying homes is rigid?
- Is the author convinced that demand for homes is rigid?

Analysis

According to Read A, while general consumption is suffering because the economy is not growing, demand for children's goods is forecast to grow strongly. While the outlook for general consumer spending is not altogether encouraging, children's goods defy the general trend because parents tend to put children first, refusing to move towards cheaper goods whenever possible. For this reason, we can say that this type of demand is not very sensitive to price. Demand for children's goods is less elastic than that for consumer products: when their children need new bicycles, parents cannot be too attentive to price levels but must simply make the purchase.

There are also goods that create dependence or even addiction, for example certain narcotics. Demand for such goods may change little, even in the face of substantial price increases, and is therefore rigid or inelastic.

According to Read B, while the human need for accommodation needs to be satisfied at almost any cost, this is not true of the need to buy a home. Price sensitivity and attention to affordability are the opposite of rigidity, which implies constant demand whatever the price. In China most people are sensible about what they can afford. Therefore, according to Chung, we cannot say that demand for homes is rigid, we can only say that at certain times people think that buying properties is a good investment. If demand for buying homes really were rigid, then home-buying demand should remain the same, no more and no less, when there is a downturn in the market. But this has not been observed and therefore, according to Chung, demand for homes is not rigid.

In these two articles, we have two examples. The first concerns children's goods in Russia, where demand scarcely depends on price: parents try to supply their children with the best, regardless of the conditions: that is, demand is rigid. In the second example on homes in mainland China, demand is higher in certain conditions and lower in others, depending on prices: demand is therefore more elastic.

For more advanced readers:

TABLE 6.2 Price-elasticity: an example with numbers

Price (crowns)	Quantity demanded	Total revenue	Variation of total revenue	Price-elasticity
32	0	**0**		Huge
24	16	**384**	384	3
16	32	**512**	128	1
8	48	**384**	−128	1/3
0	64	**0**	−384	0

In the example of Table 6.2, with a high price (32 crowns), a reduction in price would lead to some sales which, if compared with no sales, represents a huge increase in relative terms (Figure 6.6).

At a price level of 24, a small reduction in price would lead to an increase in quantities sold about three times greater. Under such conditions, price reductions lead to higher revenue (elasticity=3).

At a price of 16, a small reduction in price would lead to a similar increase in quantities sold. Under such conditions, price reductions do not lead to higher revenue (elasticity=1).

At a price of 8, a small reduction in price would lead to a much smaller increase in quantities sold. Under such conditions, price reductions lead to revenue reductions (elasticity=1/3).

η = price-elasticity

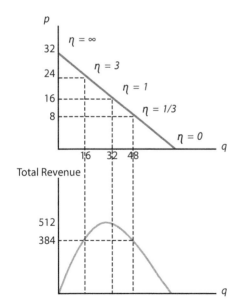

The total revenue is maximum where $\eta = 1$

At values of $\eta > 1$, a **price reduction** will increase total revenue.

At values of $\eta < 1$, a **price increase** will increase total revenue.

η : Elasticity of demand

FIGURE 6.6   The demand for a good, the total revenue and the elasticity

6.5 The effects of income on demand: income-elasticity

In periods of crisis or when people become poorer, they generally spend less; but they do not spend less on every good. We reduce our consumption of most goods but increase our consumption of some. For example, in periods of crisis, people tend to eat less meat and cheese but more bread, rice, potatoes and beans. During crises, many people use their private car less and public transport more, increasing demand for public transport. In rich countries during recent crises, international travel diminished, but visits to local museums increased.

By the same token, in times of boom or when we become richer, we usually increase our expenditure, but not in the same way for every good. For some products the increase is more than proportional, and for others less than proportional, to our income increase. In some countries, when people earn more, alcohol consumption grows even more. In many countries an improving economy brings about much larger expenditures on jewellery.

Paradoxically, but in reality, some businesses can perform fairly well in times of crisis but may have a relatively difficult time during boom periods. This has important implications for decision makers. Certain industrial sectors may benefit from a crisis, others may benefit more than proportionally from booms. Those who handle national policies should be aware that not every sector is affected by changes in the economic environment in the same way. At the same time, we can say that the economy of a country may be more stable if it produces goods for which demand reacts in different ways to periods of recession.

We define income-elasticity as the ratio between the relative variation in the quantity of sales (of a firm or an industry) and the relative variation in income. It is a measure of the change in demand due to a change in consumer income.

$$\textbf{Income} - \textbf{Elasticity} = \frac{\% \text{ Change of Quantity}}{\% \text{ Change of Income}}$$

We call "normal goods" those goods for which consumption decreases when income decreases and, symmetrically, increases when incomes increase. Their income-elasticity is positive. Most goods belong in this category. See, for example, the cases of standard clothes and standard cars.

We call "inferior goods" those goods for which consumption increases when income decreases. Their consumption decreases when income increases and therefore, they have negative income-elasticity. Examples are staple foodstuffs (rice, beans, bread, potatoes, corn, etc.).

We call "luxury goods" those goods for which consumption increases more than proportionally when income increases; their income-elasticity is not only positive but greater than 1. This is, for example, the case with luxury cars, high-fashion brands and jewellery.

How an "inferior good" can also be an excellent good

For many of the items in a typical shopper's basket, it is normal for the volume purchased to rise or fall in line with the shopper's disposable income. The sales of these items are said to have positive income-elasticity.

Sales of some other items move in the opposite direction. When income rises, their sales fall; when it falls, their sales increase. Examples in the economic textbooks often focus on items of diet. Poorer people tend to buy less meat and more potatoes; in today's world, those unable to afford a nutritious menu tend to eat more junk food.

Economists have invented the technical term "inferior goods" for those items in a household's shopping basket whose sales grow during recessions (have negative income-elasticity): as shown by the example, potatoes and junk food.

Market behaviour in the years following the financial crash of 2008 provides a laboratory demonstration of how negative elasticities play out. In the UK, median annual wages fell by 3.2 per cent between 2008 and 2017.[4] The government which came into office in 2010 responded to the post-2008 drop in economic activity with measures opposite to those associated with the names of Franklin D. Roosevelt and John Maynard Keynes. Rather than investing in public works, it imposed draconian cuts on public expenditure.

Prior to 2008, holiday travel to overseas destinations had been a booming market. In the years that followed, an estimated 25 per cent of UK residents changed their holiday habits and booked holidays in the UK. Holidaying in the home country expanded; it had become an "inferior good". In the same period, mid-range department stores such as House of Fraser, Debenhams and John Lewis were adapting their businesses to cover online selling while locked in struggles with low-cost, high-turnover competitors such as Primark and Matalan. In mid-2018, House of Fraser and Debenhams narrowly avoided being taken into administration, while John Lewis reported the first pre-tax loss at its department stores in over a decade. Primark expanded in the same period, benefitting from consumers' negative income-elasticity.

The same patterns played out in the grocery/supermarket sector where mid-range companies such as Sainsburys, Tesco and Morrisons faced fierce competition from price discounters such as Lidl and Aldi. The discounters' goods were far from "inferior" in the normal sense of that word. Lidl and Aldi provided high-quality goods, but with a narrower range and fewer variations. To some customers this may indeed have been an attraction!

6.6 Price cross-elasticity: complements and substitutes

We need to understand the relationships between different goods in order to be able to determine who the competitors of firms and industries are. We also need information to think about the right public policies for supporting and regulating industries. One objective measure of the relationship between different goods is given by the changes occurring in the demand for one good when the price of another good increases.[5] If the demand for one good grows when the price of a second good increases, the two goods are probably substitutes for each other. On the other hand, if the demand for the first good decreases when the price of the second good increases, the two are probably complementary to each other. Price cross-elasticity is a measure of the responsiveness of demand for one product to a variation in the price of another. It is defined as the relative variation in the sales of one good (good 1) divided by the relative variation in the price of a second good (good 2):

$$\textbf{Cross Price - elasticity} = \frac{\% \text{ Change of Quantity of good 1}}{\% \text{ Change of Price of good 2}}$$

If you identify the relationship between two goods, you can understand whether they belong to the same market. If cross-price-elasticity is positive and significantly different from zero, these goods are substitutes and they belong to the same market; for example, gas and oil both belong to the energy market. If price cross-elasticity is negative and significantly different from zero, these goods are complementary, for example, fuel and cars; You cannot use cars without fuel. If it is close to zero, there is no relation between the two goods; chalk and cheese are examples.

Read

What happens when the price of train fares increase? This article shows the decisions of travellers.

Upper class rail passengers not moving to airlines: eco survey

Contrary to popular belief, a rise in *rail fares* has not led upper-class domestic travellers to opt instead for airlines, although domestic airlines offered heavy discounts, said the [insert specific name] Economic Survey [6]2014–15, released on Friday. "We also calculate the cross-elasticity of civil *aviation* traffic to changes in *railways* prices to be 0.5, which indicates that upper class passengers do not easily switch to airlines as a response to hikes in railway prices", the [insert name] Survey says. It adds, "Freight traffic is more price-sensitive than passenger traffic. Within passenger traffic categories, upper class passengers are less price sensitive and may be better placed to internalise prices hikes vis-à-vis other passenger classes".

Soon after the NDA government took charge at the Centre [7]after a landslide victory, passenger rail fares were increased by over 14 per cent and freight rates by 6.5 per cent in June last year. The previous increase was in October 2013. As a result, passenger earnings increased 18 per cent in 2014–15 to Rs 43,002 crore, but passenger volumes declined to almost 1 per cent to 8,350 million. The drop in volumes was largely understood to indicate a small shift to road and air transport.

The [insert name] Survey further highlights a "healthy increase" in international passengers and cargo-handling at Indian airports. "During April – December 2014–15, 101.34 million domestic passengers and 36.74 million international passengers were handled at Indian airports. Domestic passenger traffic throughput increased by 7.1 per cent and international passengers increased by 10.3 per cent during April–December 2014–15", it said. Meanwhile, international cargo throughput at Indian airports increased 8.3 per cent to 1.17 million tonnes, while domestic cargo throughput increased 19.3 per cent to 0.74 million tonnes.

"Upper Class Rail Passengers not Moving to Airlines," *Business Standard*, 28 February 2015. www.business-standard.com/budget/article/upper-class-rail-passengers-not-moving-to-airlines-eco-survey-1150227008021.html.

Questions

- How can the author argue that increases in train prices had a modest effect in pushing richer travellers to use air travel?
- How much were rail passenger fares increased following the NDA victory?
- How much did domestic passenger air traffic increase?
- How great is the cross-elasticity of civil aviation traffic to changes in railway prices?

Analysis

The author of this article observes that an increase in rail fares has not led upper-class domestic travellers to opt instead for air travel. He supports this thesis by showing that while train passenger fares have increased by about 14 per cent, airline passenger numbers have increased by just 7.1 per cent. This means that the cross-price-elasticity between train passenger fares and air passenger numbers is positive, but considerably smaller than 1. This confirms that railways and airlines are competitors. In general, if increasing the price of one good causes an increase in sales of a second good, the two goods are substitutes for each other and competitors.

Glossary

complements   Goods which have negative price cross-elasticity. Consumption of one of these goods facilitates consumption of the other.

demand   The quantity that customers are ready to buy at a certain price.

demand curve   A graphic description of the relation between the price of a good and the quantity demanded of that good.

elastic demand   A condition when a seller who reduces the price of a product can more than proportionally increase the quantity sold, with an increase in total revenue. In this case price-elasticity is greater than 1.

flexible demand   Synonymous with elastic demand.

income-elasticity   This term indicates the ratio between the relative variation in demand for a good and the relative variation in the income of the population.

inelastic demand   A condition which exists when a seller who reduces the price of a product less than proportionally increases the quantity sold, with a decrease in total revenue. In this case, price-elasticity is less than 1. With inelastic demand, price increases increase the seller's total revenue.

inferior goods   Goods which have negative income-elasticity. Their consumption increases during recessions and diminishes during periods of expansion.

luxury goods   Goods which have positive, and greater than unitary, income-elasticity. Their consumption considerably increases during periods of growth. When people become richer, they increase their consumption of luxury goods more than proportionally.

marginal revenue   The addition to total revenue resulting from the addition of one unit to total output.[8]

necessary goods   Goods with price-elasticity less than 1 and close to zero. Their consumption is scarcely affected by their price.

normal goods   Goods which have positive income-elasticity. Their consumption increases during growth periods.

price cross-elasticity   It is a measure of the responsiveness of the quantity demanded of a good to a variation in the price of a different product; when positive and significantly different from zero, the products are substitutes for each other; when negative and significantly different from zero, they are complementary to each other; when close to zero, the goods are unrelated.

price-elasticity   A measure of the responsiveness of demand for a good to its price; a key tool for those responsible for pricing policies.

rigid demand   Synonymous with inelastic demand.

substitute goods   Goods which have positive price cross-elasticity, which are in competition with each other and belong to the same market.

total revenue   The product of price and quantity, PxQ. It is the amount of money that a firm receives from the sale of its output.

unrelated goods   Goods with price cross-elasticity close to zero; they belong to different markets and do not compete with each other.

Notes

1   This is the so-called law of demand (Bernheim and Whinston, 2008:174).
2   Variation of Revenue/Variation of Quantity would be the marginal revenue of this operation.
3   There are a few exceptional cases of goods that sell more when they are more expensive, but for simplicity, we will ignore them.
4   Ahmed (2018).
5   Actually, people look at relative prices: they compare the price of one good with the price of other goods which can satisfy the same need. The price of one good (A) may increase but if it increases relatively less than the price of the alternative good (B), it means that the first good (A) has become relatively cheaper than the alternative (B).

6 The Economic Survey is a major financial document about the Indian economy. It is published every year by the Indian government.
7 The Author of this reading probably refers to the Indian Central government.
8 Baumol and Blinder (1997:G6).

Bibliography

Ahmed, K. (2018). "Workers Are £800 a Year Poorer Post-Crisis," *BBC*. www.bbc.com/news/business-45487695.

Baumol, W. J. and Blinder, A. S. (1997). *Economics, principles, and policy*. New York: Harcourt Brace Jovanovich.

Bernheim, B. and Whinston, M. (2008). *Microeconomics*. New York: McGraw-Hill Higher Education.

Brough, D. (2015). "High Cocoa Prices Set to Curb Demand from Chocolate Makers," *Reuters*, 17 February. www.reuters.com/article/cocoa-demand-outlook/high-cocoa-prices-set-to-curb-demand-from-chocolate-makers-idUSL5N0VQ3B720150217.

Business Standard. (2015). "Upper Class Rail Passengers not Moving to Airlines," *Business Standard*, 28 February. www.business-standard.com/budget/article/upper-class-rail-passengers-not-moving-to-airlines-eco-survey-115022700802_1.html.

Chung, S. (2013). "Rigid Demand for Homes Is More of a Marketing Myth Than Reality," *South China Morning Post*, 20 February. www.scmp.com/property/hong-kong-china/article/1154008/rigid-demand-homes-more-marketing-myth-reality.

Gorst, I. (2013). "Russia's Detsky Mir: Buoyant Sales of Children's Goods Prompt IPO Plans," *Financial Times*, 27 May. www.ft.com/content/3c5c1b3e-233d-3292-a0f4-81911b59d63f.

7

MARKET ENVIRONMENTS

In this section we consider the relation between firms and their competitors. The profits of investors and the salaries of those working for them usually depend on the type and number of competitors. The condition of a monopolist firm is usually very different from that of many thousands of firms operating in perfect competition or even from that of a few major players in an oligopoly. Their behaviour and profit performance are very different, as is their ability to create well-paid jobs. It is essential that social actors have a clear understanding of these differences and take them into account.

7.1 Monopoly

A monopoly exists when a product is sold by only one seller. A single producer represents an entire industry. This singularity is usually obtained through barriers to the entry of competitors. Barriers may take different forms.

BARRIERS TO ENTRY

Barriers may be intrinsic to the nature of the product as in the case of many network-type services (water utilities, gas utilities, power utilities, telephone landlines, railways, roads among others). All these networks require high initial investments (fixed costs Section 4.3) and relatively low running costs (marginal costs, to be precise, Section 4.2). A competitor would have to set up a similar infrastructure with very high initial costs and at the end each company would have just half the number of customers that the original monopolist had and therefore an average cost (Section 4.2) double the previous level. We can say that in these industries the minimum efficient size (Section 5.4) is very large and greater than half the total industry. In these industries the entry of a second firm is not only very difficult, but also often not desirable, for the entrance of the competitor will entail higher prices for customers. These are the cases of so-called "natural monopolies". For them, the most frequently adopted solution is some form of state regulation.

Barriers to entry may derive from assets that firms need to acquire to operate in a certain field, but which can hardly be re-sold at a price comparable to the initial outlay (sunk costs, see Section 1.2). Other barriers to entry may derive from the fact that only one firm possesses the technology, has a patent or has a government licence to run a certain business.

In reality a "perfect monopoly" is not very frequent, because almost every good has some substitute (see Chapter 6). Even so, many situations are close to that of a perfect monopoly. Some business people wish to become monopolists and we often hear this situation decried, but why?

The monopolist firm has no competitors and it perceives that to sell larger quantities it has to reduce prices (see Section 4.2). The firm is also aware that this leads to variations in its turnover (total revenue, Section 6.3). Let us be clear: monopolists are not almighty; if they wish to sell larger quantities, they should reduce prices and if they want to raise prices, they should accept that they will sell less (Section 6.3). If we assume that the firm wants to make a profit, we should also assume that the firm will avoid producing more if by so doing it would increase costs more than revenue.[1] The firm would otherwise end up reducing its profits, something it would prefer not to do. It should be noted that the monopolist firm clearly understands that the price it requests and the additional revenue generated by selling more, are not the same thing. The latter is always lower than the former. We said that the additional costs (marginal costs, see Section 4.2) should be less than the additional revenue (marginal revenue, see Section 6.3). The firm can increase production up to the point at which they are equal, but no further. However, if firms want to produce up to the point at which marginal cost equals marginal revenue, but if marginal revenue is always less than price, it means that monopolists sell at a price greater than marginal cost. Every firm tends to sell more as long as additional revenues (marginal revenue) are greater than additional costs (marginal costs) and it stops when they are equal. However, only the monopolist benefits from a large difference between price and marginal cost. Not only that, the monopolist is the one best positioned to hold back total output in order to increase its profit. The monopolist firm produces less than what it could and, by so doing, earns more. Monopolists are in a position that often permits them to sell at a price greater than marginal cost and average cost. The firm cannot only remunerate capital and labour at their standard rate, it makes extra money, a positive economic profit (see Section 1.4), which a firm with many competitors (see perfect competition, Section 7.2) could not make. With this profit the monopolist firm may remunerate capital and labour at higher rates than those that would normally apply in a competitive market. Capitalists or workers, or indeed both, benefit from rent. The discovery that many monopolist or quasi-monopolist firms remunerate their invested capital or their workers highly should not come as a surprise. For the reasons mentioned above, the employees of a monopolist firm will often make larger demands than employees of firms operating in highly competitive markets.

The buyers pay more and the monopolist earns more. We could be indifferent to this: someone becomes richer and someone else poorer. How can we judge whether this is good or bad? If it were just a matter of income distribution, one could say that, at the end of the day, it is true that the monopolist has an advantage, but also that in a fair market that advantage has been created through its own efforts and maybe it is deserved. It is not only a matter of income distribution, even though we shall see that income distribution may have consequences for economic growth, but also, one of efficiency. In order to keep prices higher, the monopolist firm artificially reduces output. Certain units are simply not produced. Those non-produced units yield neither benefits to buyers nor profits to the monopolist; they do not exist. To achieve its goals, the monopolist not only charges consumers heavily (more than marginal cost), but also reduces the quantity of goods that society can enjoy. In this sense we can say that monopolists are inefficient. They lead economies to produce less than they could.[2]

Read

The effects of state-imposed monopolies

A well-researched article in the *Philippine Daily Inquirer* illustrates how "protecting" an industry can inflict lasting damage not just on the consuming public but also on the industry itself.

Before the rules of the Asean [3]Economic Community came into force at the end of 2015, lively discussion took place in each Asean country on how prospective tariff reductions on intra-Asean trade would affect each economy. In the Philippines, attention focussed on rice, which is the primary food staple there and whose production costs were significantly higher than those of rice-producing neighbours.

Successive Philippine governments had protected the rice industry by placing rice importation under the control of a state monopoly, through the National Food Authority. Over time, this policy had imposed higher prices on the Philippine consumer while reducing the incentive for rice producers to modernize their farming practices. Moreover, corrupt officials had often found ways to benefit from being the agents through whom state control was implemented.

It could not be argued that rice production was an "infant industry" needing monopoly protection to be nursed towards viable independence. Perhaps it was a mature industry in need of time-limited support for a programme of restructuring and cost reduction, in the face of well-entrenched vested interests.

"Rifle vs. Shotgun," Cielito F. Habito, *Philippine Daily Inquirer*, 17 March 2015.

Questions

- According to the author, why did the Philippines fail to become competitive in rice cultivation?
- What were the consequences of a state monopoly on rice?
- What were the effects of the law on cabotage?

Analysis

According to the author, the protection of rice farmers and the activity of the National Food Authority, with the creation of a state monopoly, have acted against the interests of Filipinos, farmers included. In this way, the import of rice was prevented, there was less incentive to reduce production costs and prices were higher. Since rice forms the base of the Filipino diet, more expensive rice implies that all salaries must be higher, thus reducing the price competitiveness of all Filipino goods. A similar situation occurs in the field of cabotage, where foreign ships cannot move goods between Filipino ports. Higher freight costs between national ports have caused the import of foreign goods often to be cheaper than bringing in crops from national plantations.

This article presents some examples of a major defect of monopolies: restricting supply, increasing prices and reducing incentives to innovate. The creation of profits does not push producers to become more efficient and can also create serious distortions.

For the sake of completion, we should add that many industrialized countries (EU, US, Japan, Switzerland, Norway, etc) heavily subsidize their agriculture and therefore:

1 Singling out the Philippines as a special case would not be correct.
2 The fact that protection of agriculture necessarily slows down economic development is controversial, to say the least.

7.2 Perfect competition

There are situations in which the producers of some goods are numerous and none of them can significantly influence the price of the good. If the product is standard – for example coffee, wheat, corn, copper, cocoa, or rice – i.e., if the product is a commodity, this is particularly true. Buyers see no difference between buying from one producer or from another. They just look at price, at the lowest price. The question is whether producers can agree to fix a price, which would not only remunerate capital and labour at their marginal cost, but also leave firms with some additional profit? The answer is that they cannot, they are usually too numerous to be able to build a network and reach an agreement. In a few cases, when all the producers in a country are represented by an industry association or by the national government, then industry representatives or governments may find an agreement and fix a price. In this case, the true players are a few associations or governments, not a very large number of firms. Without any agreement there is strong competition between sellers who end up selling at the cost of the last produced, the marginal cost (see Section 4.2). Of course, this price can be sustainable, that is it can apply over the long term only if it also covers the average cost (see Section 4.2). In essence, the firm should be able to pay all its costs, including a salary for the owner (opportunity cost of labour, see Section 1.1) and some remuneration for the capital invested in the firm (opportunity cost of capital), but nothing more (its economic profit [see Section 1.4] is zero). There are no means of accumulating wealth, only remuneration of what is used at a standard price. There are no large margins to be split between employers and employees. On some occasions it may happen that the market price even falls below average cost. Under such conditions some firms will have trouble and will be compelled to leave the market, reducing the total output available on the market. This reduction may then lead to a readjustment of prices, which will increase. In some cases, prices may even go above the level of average cost for a period. For some time, firms will have some extra money, a profit, besides the simple remuneration of capital and labour. Starting production in these industries is not difficult; there are no barriers to entry (see Section 7.1) and information is freely available to everybody. The news of firms making money will spread very fast and new firms will appear on the market, increasing total supply, bringing prices back to the level of average cost and eliminating profits. Consumers may be happy because there is the largest possible volume of output on the market at the lowest possible price. However, sometimes this is not true; in some cases, as in the case of coffee, millions of producers sell their harvest to a few buyers (oligopsony, see Section 7.3) and those few buyers are able to keep a substantial part of the benefit for themselves, sharing only a limited amount with consumers.

Read

"Economics of coffee". Wikipedia. https://en.wikipedia.org/wiki/Economics_of_coffee.

Questions

- Does coffee cultivation require considerable quantities of capital?
- Do you think that there are large barriers preventing somebody in a coffee-producing country from becoming a coffee farmer?
- How many coffee bean producers are there in the world?
- Where is the price of coffee fixed?
- What made the price of coffee decline in the 1990s?
- What type of market is coffee production?

Analysis

Coffee farming requires considerable quantities of labour and relatively little quantities of capital, since it is labour intensive (see Section 3.4) and automation is rarely used for this crop. For these reasons, we can assume that the barriers to entry (see Section 7.1) in this industry are low for a citizen of a coffee producing country. Not by chance do we observe that coffee farmers throughout the world number about 25m. However, none of them can determine the price of their product. The international price of coffee is decided in international exchanges such as the New York Board of Trade, New York Mercantile Exchange, New York Intercontinental Exchange, and the London International Financial Futures and Options Exchange. In 2008, the first ten coffee roasters were buying about 40 per cent of world coffee production. Their influence on the world price was of course important. Until the 1990s, there was an International Coffee Agreement, a kind of **cartel**, keeping prices at around 100 US cent/lb.; but then the elimination of the agreement, the expansion of Brazilian coffee plantations and the entry into the market of Vietnam, brought prices to considerably lower levels and to conditions close to perfect competition. Very low prices led some farmers to leave the trade because they were no longer able to cover their (average) costs. In general, prices somehow remunerate input factors but do not allow real profits. The average age of African coffee farmers is 60; this leads one to conclude that the low salaries associated with coffee production do not attract the younger generation. Low salaries (salaries close to marginal cost) in industries in perfect competition are the rule.

7.3 Oligopoly

In industrialized countries the key industries are often made up of just a few companies. Think of car manufacturers, aircraft manufacturers, pharmaceutical industries, mobile phone operators and manufacturers, to give just a few examples. Few companies produce the goods, which can be identical or merely similar, there is product differentiation. Car makers, for example, produce cars, but each brand and each model is in some way different. Telephone companies provide services which are similar but usually not identical.

Since the players are few, meeting and agreeing on prices or non-competition are real possibilities. If they fully coordinate their actions, they can make their sector behave as if it were a monopoly,[4] an industry with a single seller (see Section 7.1). If they achieve that, they restrain total output and make large extra profits which are not a simple return to the invested capital at market prices, but a true accumulation of wealth. Cooperation between competitors is called collusion. A group of sellers of a product who have joined together to control its production, sale and price in the hope of obtaining the advantages of a monopoly is called a cartel.[5]

Collusion is an agreement between firms to charge the same price or otherwise not compete. The price agreed on will not always be the monopoly price. Collusion can take the form of an explicit agreement, an official cartel, or can be tacit.

Collusion works well only if every firm respects the terms of the agreement, limiting its output and not selling at prices below that agreed. Of course, especially when prices are high the temptation to cheat and to sell more at lower prices is strong. This can put collusion in jeopardy. Cartels therefore have some intrinsic instability.

If the few firms, the members of an oligopolistic industry, start to compete with each other on price, they may end up in a situation not very different from that of an industry with perfect competition (see Section 7.2). With total competition, profits go down to nil. Capital and labour get paid at their (marginal) cost price, but nothing more, there is no extra profit.

In many countries, collusion is forbidden or at least regulated. The US, the EU and many other countries have antitrust authorities whose task is to prevent and penalise collusion. In some cases, collusion is explicit. Producers coordinate their actions in an organized and structured way with a "cartel". In many countries, cartels are forbidden and therefore collusion can only be implicit. Firms do not formalize their cooperation, but they coordinate their actions to limit production and keep prices high. Where collusion works, firms may also achieve very high margins which in different ways, are then shared between employers and employees.

In some cases, cartels are not between producers but between countries, as in the case of OPEC, the cartel of several oil-producing countries. In other cases, markets, which in their nature would be perfectly competitive, become regulated by cartels. One example of this type was the International Coffee Agreement that regulated the coffee market between 1963 and 1989.

The outcomes of an oligopoly cannot be easily foreseen; much depends on the behaviour of the few major players. Each of them may follow different strategies, taking into account their expectations about the possible reactions of other firms to their own actions. All this makes the analysis of oligopolies extremely complex. We should just remember that collusion often occurs and oligopolies are often able to sell at a margin which goes beyond the simple remuneration of labour and capital at rates achievable in markets with perfect competition. Margins can be used to give higher dividends to shareholders, to pay suppliers better prices, to invest in innovation or to pay higher salaries to employees.

WHEN BUYERS ARE FEW: OLIGOPSONY AND MONOPSONY

As we observe monopolistic and oligopolistic markets, we may also observe markets where there is only one or very few buyers. In these cases, we speak of monopsony (only one buyer) or oligopsony (a few buyers). We may for example observe monopsony of labour in the labour market of a region where there is only one large employer. We observe oligopsony in such markets as the coffee market (see Section 7.2) or the cocoa market. In the latter case, a few large chocolate makers buy a large part of world output. In markets with monopsony or oligopsony, one or few buyers face many competing sellers; the buyer can substantially influence the price of the good or the input factor that it buys. It can fix that price, which maximizes its profit but limits the use and the remuneration of the purchased input, also creating inefficiencies. Under such conditions the constitution of cartels by the suppliers of inputs can bring symmetry into a market that was initially in a non-symmetrical condition. Sometimes in a region or country there are many potential workers and just one or a few employers. This can be considered an example of monopsony or oligopsony of labour. In such conditions, the economic reasons for the existence of labour trade unions and minimum wages are particularly strong, because they aim to bring symmetry and balance to a labour market which was previously asymmetrical and potentially inefficient.

The fact that margins are sometimes used to fund R&D and to foster innovation is the most common argument in favour of oligopolies and monopolies. In practice this sometimes happens but sometimes does not. A different argument in favour of oligopolies is that they tend to stabilize prices. They often have margins. When their costs increase for some external reason, in many cases they are able and willing not to transmit these increases to customers. Often, they do this so as not to lose market share and to keep consumers faithful to their brands.

Read

Few new chocolate bars on the market

In US parlance "candy" includes chocolate and all the other tasty items which used to be sold in the old-fashioned sweet shop. Nowadays the main candy retailers in the US are supermarkets, in any of which a huge number of brands will compete for your attention. The competitive market in operation, you may conclude.

In fact, in the year 2013, two major companies, Hershey and Mars, dominated this market. Between them they controlled some 75 per cent of the national chocolate market and 60 per cent of the candy market overall.

The market looked very different fifty years before. You could buy a Hershey bar or a Mars bar anywhere across the nation but Mars and Hershey competed with a multiplicity of smaller producers many of whom served only their own local region.

How did this market develop into today's oligopoly (few sellers)? First, the major players embarked on a strategy of purchasing their smaller rivals. As the majors grew, their financial muscle and their marketing tactics were more than a match for firms that wished to remain independent. For example, major producers pay substantial fees to a supermarket chain to ensure that their products are displayed in the most prominent slots. Smaller producers struggle to win shelf space. Again, as the supermarket chains have also consolidated and as major producers cut deals with major retailers, smaller operators can be left out in the cold.

One consequence of oligopoly seems to be that innovation has stalled. Few genuinely new products have emerged in these markets in recent years. Commentators ask: where were the US's famed antitrust laws when all of this was taking place? Perhaps the answer is that regulatory laws need to be interpreted through court proceedings; and that major firms can afford the best lawyers.

Read

"Why So Little Candy Variety? Blame the Chocolate Oligopoly," Lina Kahn, *Time*, 1 November 2013. http://ideas.time.com/2013/11/01/why-so-little-candy-variety-blame-the-chocolate-oligopoly/.

Questions

- How many companies produce the 40 brands of candy available in supermarkets?
- Why did diversity not last in the candy market?
- Why is the playing field tilted?
- Is there any barrier to entering the candy industry today?
- Is innovation fostered by the present situation in the candy industry?
- How could we achieve a more diverse market?

Analysis

In the US, most of the 40 brands of candy available in a supermarket belong to just three companies. The US candy market can therefore be defined as an oligopoly. Step by step large firms have taken over other firms; this has led to a reduction in variety. The playing field is tilted because size gives considerable advantages to a few players. These advantages or barriers to entry (see Section 7.1) consist of money to pay for access to supermarkets' shelves, to achieve economies of scale (see Section 5.2), to make a bar of sufficient quality at a reasonable price, and to make life difficult for new producers. This situation has not fostered innovation and since the 1980s no new candy has been introduced. The only possible solution to this situation is stronger and better-enforced antitrust legislation. In conclusion, the US candy industry is an oligopolistic industry with some product differentiation. Not all candy is the same, there are differences in flavour, presentation and price. Few players have sufficient margins to make investments that permit them to dominate the market and to prevent the entry of any significant new competitor.

7.4 Monopolistic competition

In every continent, the majority of firms are small businesses, in some cases officially registered firms, in other cases informal (see Section 19.2) activities. Many shops, craft activities, workshops, restaurants, hotels, consumer services such as hairdressing, and other small and medium-sized businesses, fall in this category. There is no real barrier to entry into these industries and access is certainly possible.

Free access to these industries (low barriers to entry) implies that, every time there is some profit, new individuals may set up firms and bring profits in the sector to zero. These firms are able to provide a living to the owners and to the members of their families or to the employees who work with them. They remunerate the invested capital, but no more than that. Once you take into account the opportunity cost of labour and the opportunity cost of capital (see Section 1.1), they do not make any extra profit.

They bring additional variety to the world. For some of them variety is attributable to their unique position, for example, the shop nearest to our home, for others it consists of a greater or smaller difference in the product that they sell and in the service they provide. Their specific characteristics give them a limited possibility of controlling prices. For this reason, we call this type of competition "monopolistic". For example, up to a certain degree the street corner shop or the plumber can in some way decide their own prices. This level of discretion is however quite limited. The customer knows that by walking just a few metres further, they can find other shops or can call other plumbers.

Their limited size does not allow them to achieve economies of scale (see Section 5.2): they are too small for that. For this reason, they can never achieve production costs (average costs) as low as those of larger producers. In this sense they represent a form of inefficiency. However, firms operating in monopolistic competition constitute the backbone of societies, offering employment opportunities to billions of people and playing an important economic role as suppliers and customers of bigger firms. For many people they are also a great opportunity for going into business; some who have previously worked in firms operating in monopolistic competition then move on to create or manage larger firms.

Finally, we cannot underestimate the role of this market environment in distributing economic power between very many actors; this strengthens the total demand for the goods of a country and for the working of democracy.

MONOPOLISTIC COMPETITION

Monopolistic competition is a market structure in which barriers to entry are low and many firms compete by selling similar, but not identical, products. The goods offered for sale are somewhat differentiated.

In this form of competition, it is important to stress that pricing is not the most important strategic decision confronting firms in this industry. A much more important issue for such firms is how to differentiate their products from those of existing rivals; an example is convenience stores. Although the product list on any given store's shelves is also found in other stores, the product lists of different stores are not identical. Location is also an important differentiating feature of convenience stores.

Glossary

antitrust A policy or an authority with the aim of detecting and sometimes limiting the dominance of one or few market players (monopolist or oligopolist) on the market, preventing them from abusing their position. Antitrust authorities are charged with the task of preventing, detecting and penalising forms of collusion between rival firms and the creation of cartels.

barriers to entry They are those factors that allow incumbent firms to earn positive economic profits (extra profits), while making it unprofitable for newcomers to enter the industry. Structural entry barriers result when the incumbent has natural cost or marketing advantages, or benefits from favourable regulations. Strategic entry barriers result when the incumbent aggressively deters entry.[6]

cartel "A group of sellers of a product who have joined together to control its production, sale and price in the hope of obtaining the advantages of monopoly."[7] Cartels are usually forbidden by antitrust legislation.

commodity A raw material or primary agricultural product that can be bought and sold, such as copper or coffee,[8] without distinction of brand. Their prices are usually determined in international markets.

infant industry   Some economists argue that countries which develop certain industries for the first time, e.g. developing countries, initially may have much higher average costs than competing countries. This can be caused by several reasons and the main one is probably that at the beginning, the produced output will be small and economies of scale will be absent. This could prevent developing countries from ever entering certain industries, remaining permanent producers of raw materials. For these reasons, some economists support the idea that some form of protection (trade barriers) should be granted to these industries in these countries for a limited period of time.

monopolistic competition   A market environment with many small firms and no barriers to entry. Firms are in some way different from each other (e.g. their position, service, product design) and have some limited power over the price of the product that they sell. Firms are unable to attain a large enough size to fully exploit economies of scale; for this reason, they should sell at higher prices and thus they represent a form of inefficiency. At the same time, these firms play a key role in bringing variety (of products, owners, service, or design among others) into the market. This is also a key environment for entrepreneurs to learn their trade and test their skills.

monopoly   A situation in which one sole firm provides a certain good in the absence of competitors. The firm may influence price or quantity. To sell at a higher price the firm may choose to sell smaller quantities. For this reason, monopoly introduces inefficiency into the market, limiting the quantity that users receive. Monopolist firms usually enjoy margins which are shared in different proportions between employers and workers.

monopsony   A condition when a firm is the sole buyer of a certain input, for example labour or a raw material. The monopsonist may decide to buy a lesser quantity of input than competitive buyers would buy; it will also offer a lower price. This will create some form of inefficiency in the market.

natural monopoly   A situation in which monopoly is the most efficient arrangement, as introducing other firms would considerably increase average costs (see Section 4.2). In cases of natural monopoly, some sort of government regulation is often required to avoid exploitation of users and unnecessary inefficiencies.

oligopoly   An environment in which the market share of a few firms is so large as to allow them to collude to keep prices artificially high.

oligopsony   A situation in which buyers are few with consequences similar to those of monopsony.

perfect competition   A situation in which there exist very many substantially identical sellers of a homogeneous product, often a commodity. Sellers do not know each other and cannot fix prices and therefore, they are price takers. It is the market environment which puts on the market the maximum possible quantity of output at the minimum possible price, and in this sense, is very efficient. Firms can remunerate capital and labour at their marginal cost, but cannot make extra profits. Firms operating in perfect competition have usually extremely narrow margins of manoeuvre in deciding wage levels.

Notes

1 Here we assume that the costs caused by any additional unit become higher and higher (increasing marginal costs).
2 There is the so-called deadweight loss (Varian, 2006:431–432; Bernheim and Whinston, 2008:526–527; Nicholson 1994:357).
3 The Association of Southeast Asian Nations, or ASEAN, was established on 8 August 1967 in Bangkok, Thailand, with the signing of the ASEAN Declaration (Bangkok Declaration) by the Founding Fathers of ASEAN, namely Indonesia, Malaysia, Philippines, Singapore and Thailand. Brunei Darussalam then joined on 7 January 1984, Viet Nam on 28 July 1995, Lao PDR and Myanmar on 23 July 1997, and Cambodia on 30 April 1999, making up what is today the ten Member States of ASEAN.
4 "All else being equal, firms would prefer prices to be closer to their monopoly levels than to the levels reached under Bertrand or Cournot competition" (Besanko, 2007:252–253); "A cartel is simply a group of firms that jointly collude to behave like a single monopolist" Varian (2006:496); "A successful cartel may end up charging the monopoly price and obtaining monopoly profits" (Baumol and Blinder, 1997:284).
5 Baumol and Blinder (1997:284).
6 Besanko (2007:289). They quote their own sources.
7 Baumol and Blinder (1997:284).
8 www.oxforddictionaries.com/definition/english/commodity.

Bibliography

Baumol, W. J. and Blinder, A. S. (1997). *Economics, principles, and policy*. New York: Harcourt Brace Jovanovich.

Bernheim, B. and Whinston, M. (2008). *Microeconomics*. New York: McGraw-Hill Higher Education.

Besanko, D. (2007). *Economics of strategy*. Hoboken, NJ: Wiley & Sons.

Habito, C. F. (2015). "Rifle vs. Shotgun," *Philippine Daily Inquirer*, 17 March. www.pressreader.com/philippines/philippine-daily-inquirer/20150317/281698318227791.

Kahn, L. (2013). "Why So Little Candy Variety? Blame the Chocolate Oligopoly," *Time*, 1 November. http://ideas.time.com/2013/11/01/why-so-little-candy-variety-blame-the-chocolate-oligopoly/.

Nicholson, W. (1994). *Intermediate microeconomics and its application*. Fort Worth, TX: Dryden Press.

OECD. (2007). *OECD system of unit labour cost indicators*. Paris: OECD.

Varian, H. (2006). *Intermediate microeconomics*. New York: W. W. Norton & Company.

Macroeconomics

The decisions of policy makers, those of companies and those of trade unions should take into account the economic context in which firms operate: the economy of the region, of the country and of the planet. In this context there is interaction between the private sector, government authorities and foreign entities. All these actors handle both real goods and financial assets. Macroeconomics covers these topics, i.e. the economic environment in which firms and families operate.

PART IV

Introduction to macroeconomics

In this part we introduce the key words that those contributing to the making of the economic policy of a country should know. Firstly, we describe the main types of goods and financial assets.

Goods (food, clothes, raw materials, houses, equipment, health care, semi-finished goods, bridges, school buildings, educational services, among others) have inherent value and are able to provide direct utility to their users.

Financial assets (money, bonds and shares, among others) also have a huge influence on our everyday life. They have no inherent value and are only useful because they represent claims against real assets, i.e. goods. However, they can be used as units of account, means of exchange, stores of value, instruments for taking risks (and potentially receive compensation for this) or for protection against risks.

We present first of all the key words of national accounts, describing the market for goods, then we introduce the most important financial asset: money and its relationship with prices.

8

KEY WORDS OF NATIONAL ACCOUNTS

Some key words appear in any negotiation concerning employment and public policies. Participants in such negotiations cannot afford to ignore them. For this reason, this section introduces the key terms concerning the market of goods in national accounts. The discipline, which defines and measures macroeconomic variables is called "National Accounting". It defines the key concepts and how to measure them. Just as financial accounting (income statement, profit and losses account, and balance sheet) enables us to measure the activity of a firm, national accounting enables us to measure the activity of a country or region.

THE SYSTEM OF NATIONAL ACCOUNTS (SNA)

The System of National Accounts (SNA) is the internationally agreed standard set of recommendations on how to compile measures of economic activity. The SNA describes a coherent, consistent and integrated set of macroeconomic accounts in the context of a set of internationally agreed concepts, definitions, classifications and accounting rules.

In addition, the SNA provides an overview of economic processes, recording how production is distributed between consumers, businesses, government and foreign nations. It shows how income originating in production, modified by taxes and transfers, flows to these groups and how they allocate these flows to consumption, saving and investment. In consequence, the national accounts are one of the building blocks of macroeconomic statistics, forming a basis for economic analysis and policy formulation.[1]

We start by considering the source of the goods that a country uses, and then the possible uses of what is available.

8.1 Supply (sources) of goods: production (GDP) and imports

The goods that we need may be produced domestically or abroad. If they are bought abroad, they are imported. They represent the imports of a country. They come from foreign organizations which are not usually accountable to the authorities of our country. They may or may not wish to trade with our country.

Domestic firms produce either intermediate or final goods. Intermediate goods constitute the "Inter-Industry Use" or intermediate consumption of firms (see Section 2.1). Intermediate goods are purchased by the firm and are used up in the firm's production process. They usually do not remain with the firm for more than one production cycle. Their value is embodied in the products that the firms produce. Metal rolls, transformed into components of cars, or electric power used to light a theatre or a classroom, are examples of intermediate goods.

Final goods are those which are sold to the final user. They are not processed further before reaching their ultimate, final user. The final user may be a firm, which buys durable production goods, i.e. a firm buying investment goods, for example equipment; it may be a family, it may be a public administration or it may be a foreign resident.

We have explained above that any goods not used for intermediate consumption are final goods. The sum of all the values of final goods produced in a country is termed the Gross Domestic Product (GDP).

If we consider the value of the final goods at their current price, we have **Nominal GDP** or **GDP at Current Prices**. If we consider the value of the final goods at the prices of a different year (a reference year), we obtain **GDP at Constant Prices** or **Real GDP**.

Nominal GDP or GDP at current prices must be used for comparisons with all the economic variables for the same year. Did consumption in 2016 represent a large share of the production of our country? To answer this question, we should compare the consumption in 2016 with the nominal GDP (or GDP at current prices) 2016.

Was the production in 2016 bigger than the production in 2015? To answer this, we should compare the real GDP 2016 (or GDP 2016 at constant prices) with the real GDP 2015. The real GDP or GDP at constant prices is what we use to compare the production in different years.

The sum, or "the aggregate" as economists say, of the value added (see Section 2.1) by all private firms and public administrations operating in a country is an alternative way of defining the GDP of a country. Finally, the production or GDP of a country is also equivalent to the remuneration of all those who have supplied capital (land, buildings, equipment and financial capital, among others) or labour (unskilled, skilled and managerial among others) for the production in the country. It is fair to say that, when we reduce the sum of salaries and profits in a country, we reduce the GDP of that country.

8.2 Uses of goods: household consumption, private investment, government spending and export

The final user of final goods can be a resident family, a firm, a public administration or a foreign resident (family, firm or government). We classify final goods according to their destination.

When resident families purchase goods, we speak of "consumption goods" (C). According to national accounts, families only carry out consumption, with just one exception: families buying new houses or new flats. This is considered "residential investment" and it is the only form of investment that families can carry out.[2] During the following periods, new houses permit consumption, offering accommodation to families (housing services), virtually without involving any additional labour. Consumption is usually the main destiny of goods in a country and is also the major component of internal demand (the sum of all uses except export). Usually countries are stronger when they can rely on strong internal demand.

When a resident firm purchases final goods, then we speak of "private productive investment". The general term "Investment" or "Gross Capital Formation" includes not only purchases of buildings, equipment and immaterial assets (licences, brands and patents among others) by firms (fixed productive investments), but also changes in firms' inventories and purchases of new buildings by families (residential investments). The three components of investment have quite different characteristics.

"Private fixed productive investments" represent intentional increases in the real capital of firms. Usually fixed productive investments entail an increase in the productivity of the firm or the employment of more workers. They increase the production capacity of a country. The growth of private fixed productive investments usually indicates that firms are optimistic about the future and it is often a source of the growth of the country's income. Making new useful investments is probably one of the major functions of firms.

"Residential investments" denote intentional increases in housing capacity for families; they increase the possibility of future consumption (including housing services), and they employ labour mainly when under construction, but not afterwards. For this reason, they are not "productive" investments. They are carried out by non-professional buyers (families) and are also highly exposed to speculation and "bubbles", excessive growths of prices. We should be very careful, even suspicious, when most of a country's development depends on these investments.

"Changes in inventories" are often not intentional; firms have to change their inventories when they sell more or less than they had previously planned. If, after a period of normal economic growth, inventories start to increase abnormally, they often indicate that firms are no longer able to sell their output and may face difficulties. Changes in inventories are a bellwether of the economy, and for this reason, are carefully monitored by policymakers. When final goods are purchased by a part of government (federal, national or local), then we speak of **Government Spending (G)**. This is the sum of government consumption (salaries of public employees and intermediate consumption of the public sector) and government investment, the purchases of equipment and buildings by the public sector. In national accounts, government spending does not include pensions, benefits or interest on the public debt; pensions and benefits are also called "transfers". It includes all purchases by the public administration, public procurement, and all payments to public employees for their services (army, police, National Health Service, teachers, firefighters and other civil and public servants). Much of the public policy debate concerns the size, destination and funding of government spending.

Precise statistics also distinguish goods purchased by non-profit institutions serving households. This item is often small and is sometimes ignored or added to other items.[3]

When final goods are purchased by a non-resident entity (firm, family or government), then we speak of **Exports** (X). Exports are an indicator of the competitiveness of domestic production and are essential for facilitating the purchase abroad of those goods that a country cannot produce itself.

Gross Domestic Product =
+ Household Consumption
+ Private Investments
+ Government Spending
+ Exports
− Imports
G D P = C + I + G + X − IM

Wear, obsolescence and accidents affect not only private equipment and buildings, but also bridges, roads and public hospitals. Depreciation (see Section 1.2) of capital affects not only businesses, but also countries. Consumption of fixed capital or **depreciation** denotes the reduction in the value of fixed assets used in production by private and public organizations, as a result of physical deterioration, normal obsolescence or accidental damage during the accounting period.

Net Domestic Product (NDP) is obtained through the formula NDP = GDP − Depreciation. In theory, Net Domestic Product would represent the production of a country more precisely than GDP. In reality, our measurement of depreciation is often imprecise. This is the reason why we use GDP more than NDP.

Read

Residential investment: bubbles and low productivity

The economist, Nouriel Roubini, was one of the few members of his profession not to be taken by surprise when the financial crisis of 2008 came near to overwhelming the major world economies.

Focussing on the world's leading economy, Roubini had argued that since the 1980s the US had been growing fast only during periods characterized by asset bubbles, each followed by periods of disruption, financial losses and foregone growth.

The real estate of the 1980s had been followed by a crisis for the Savings and Loan banks, a credit crunch and the severe recession of 1990–91. The 1990s had seen a market bubble in high tech/internet stocks and when this burst in 2000, a recession followed. Then a great expansion in money and credit in the years after 2000 and a parallel easing in the regulation of mortgages and other loans had created a further housing and credit bubble ending in 2008 with a crisis of historic proportions.

Roubini believes that the US has over-invested in residential housing stock in recent years and that this is an unproductive form of capital, unlike investment in equipment and plants and human capital. These increase the productivity of labour. Moreover, many of those investing in housing were simply speculating on future price increases. Roubini maintains too that the US over-invested in the financial sector. "We've had a model of growth in which over the last 15 or 20 years, too much human capital went into finance rather than more productive activities." He believes that leading economies like the US need to develop a different growth model where the most creative managers will be drawn into the productive sectors rather than as now, attracted by the current high salaries, into financial services.

Read

"Dr. Doom Has Some Good News," James Fallows, *The Atlantic*, July/August 2009.

Questions

- When did the US economy grow fast since 1980s?
- What were the effects of such periods of growth?
- What is the most unproductive form of capital, according to Professor Roubini?
- What is the advantage of non-residential capital?
- What is the corollary of the housing boom?
- What other wrong allocation of resources can occur with the above-mentioned booms?

Analysis

According to Professor Roubini, since 1980s, the US economy only grew rapidly during asset bubbles, which eventually burst with significant economic and financial costs. Residential investment, i.e. investment in residential housing, is according to him the most unproductive form of investment, because while it increases utility, that is to say, it supports a form of consumption, namely the consumption of housing services, it does not increase labour productivity. This does not occur with fixed productive investment.

A corollary of housing booms is that they also bring overinvestment into the financial sector. With this overinvestment also come wrong incentives. Too many young people study finance and too few study science and engineering. This leads to a wrong allocation of the human capital of a country, from innovative and productive to speculative destinations.

In Table 8.1 Government Spending is split between Government Investment (see Chapter 14), which is part of Total Investment and Government Consumption,

TABLE 8.1 Supply (sources) and uses in some major economies

Year 2013	Supply		Uses			
	GDP	Import	Household consumption	Government consumption	Total investment	Export
China	100	23	36	14	48	26
Eurozone	100	40	56	21	20	44
India	100	28	57	12	31	25
Japan	100	19	61	21	21	16
US	100	17	68	15	19	13

Note: The total supply and the total of uses sometimes are not as equal as they should be because of errors created with the treatment of data.

Sources: UNSTAT[4] and ECB[5]

the non-investment part of Government Spending. Total Investment is the sum of Private Investment and Government Investment.

In Table 8.1 we observe the major differences between the structures of the major world economies. The eurozone is the economy most open to the rest of the world: imports and exports represent a large share of its GDP. China and India follow at a distance. The most closed economy is that of the US. This is also the economy which depends most heavily on internal household consumption, which accounts for 68 per cent of its GDP. The opposite is true in China, where internal household consumption is still quite limited (36 per cent of GDP). This table shows that a large share of the world consumption still depends on the consumption of the three richest large economies. Government Consumption is very important in the eurozone and in Japan and much less important in India and China. Investment accounts for a very large share of Chinese GDP (48%) and 31% of Indian GDP. In the three richest economies, it is around 20%. A further example is provided about Mongolia (Table 8.2).

TABLE 8.2 Supply and uses in Mongolia 2014

Supply			Share (%)	Use		Share (%)
Domestic PRODUCTION			73.7	Inter Industry Use		37.7
	Agriculture	7.5			Agriculture	2.2
	Industry	36			Industry	23.5
	Service	30.2			Service	12.1
Import			22.6	Households and Non-profit Institutions		22.5
Taxes less Subsidies on Products			3.7	General Government Consumption		5.2
				Gross Fixed Capital Formation		11.3
				Changes in Inventories and Net Valuables		2.6
				Exports		20.7
Total Supply			**100**	**Total Use**		**100**

Source: National Statistics Office, Mongolia and Asian Development Bank, 2017

This table provides several details.

GDP = Domestic Production (Gross Output) – Inter-industry Use (intermediary goods).

This is actually the definition of GDP at Factor Costs.

GDP at Factor Costs + Taxes less Subsidies on Products = GDP at Market Prices

When we simply say GDP, we usually refer to the GDP at Market Prices.

From this table we learn that industry produces the largest share of Mongol GDP (48.85%). The extraction of minerals plays a major role in the Mongol industry. We can also notice that industry is a major buyer of intermediary goods (Inter-Industry Use).

Glossary

consumption (households final consumption)   All the purchases of resident families excluding purchases of new properties (houses and flats).

depreciation   The annual loss of value of the private and public capital of a country due to wear, obsolescence and accidents.

final goods   Goods sold to their final users, that are not immediately transformed by firms into other goods.

financial assets   Assets without inherent utility; under certain conditions they give their owners the possibility of acquiring goods.

fixed productive investment   Durable goods (mostly equipment and buildings) purchased by firms.

goods   Products with inherent value, able to provide direct utility. Firms produce final goods or intermediate goods.

government consumption   It is approximately the sum of salaries of public employees, plus the intermediate consumption (see Section 2.1) of government plus consumption of public capital (depreciation.).

government spending   Purchases of merchandise and services, including the services of public employees, by all public administrations. It is the sum of Government Consumption and Government Investment.

gross capital formation   See Investment.

gross domestic product (GDP)   a) the sum of the values of all the final goods made in a country; b) the sum of the added value of all the organizations operating in a country; c) the sum of the incomes of all the production factors in a country.

intermediate goods[6]   Goods purchased by domestic firms and transformed into other goods. They represent the sum of the intermediate consumption (see Section 2.1) of all domestic firms and organizations.

inventories   The raw materials, work-in-process goods and completely finished goods that organizations hold to minimize the possibility of running out of stock or to cover planning mistakes.

inventory investment   The difference between production and sales. Firms accumulate inventories if production exceeds sales. It is usually small, but can grow considerably at the beginning of a crisis, when firms start selling less.

investment   The sum of fixed productive investment, changes in inventories and residential investment.

macroeconomics   This is the study of the structure and performance of national economies and of the policies that governments employ to influence economic performance.[7]

national accounts   Measures of economic activity at country or regional level. They describe a coherent, consistent and integrated set of macroeconomic accounts in the context of a set of internationally agreed concepts.

nominal GDP   The sum of the values of the final goods produced in a country, expressed at their current prices. It is used for comparisons with other variables, for example consumption, investment or savings, in the same year.

real GDP   The sum of the values of the final goods produced in a country, expressed at the prices ruling in a reference year. It is used for comparisons of GDP in different years.

residential investment   Spending on the purchase of new houses and apartment buildings by families.[8]

residents   Those who spend most of their time in the home country.

sources   Goods available in a country, subdivided according to their origin. They include domestic goods, the gross domestic product and imported foreign goods.

supply   See sources.

uses   The possible destinations (consumption, investment, government spending or export) of goods available in a country.

Notes

1 http://unstats.un.org/unsd/nationalaccount/sna.asp.
2   According to national accounts, the purchase of financial assets e.g. bonds or shares, is not an investment.
3 Such purchases along with government consumption (see Chapter 14), which is the sum of the salaries of public employees and of the intermediate consumption of the public administration, form an item called "collective consumption".
4 http://unstats.un.org/unsd/snaama/selbasicFast.asp Selected Series: GDP by Expenditure, Percentage Distribution (Shares); retrieved on 29 October 2015.
5 http://sdw.ecb.europa.eu/reports.do?node=1000004819 retrieved on 29 October 2015.
6 Intermediate goods can only be used by the firm once, normally in the current period, and then they are embodied in the new production. Investment goods can be used by the firm more than once, usually in many periods, and their use usually requires labour.
7 Abel et al. (2014:27).
8 Abel et al. (2014:58).

Bibliography

Abel, A. B., Bernanke, B. and Croushore, D. D. (2014). *Macroeconomics*. Boston: Addison-Wesley.
Fallows, J. (2009). "Dr. Doom Has Some Good News," *The Atlantic*, July/August.

9

MONEY AND PRICES

What role does a central bank play in the management of a national economy? How are we to judge if it is doing a good job?

If the economy of a country is like an engine, money is the oil which permits this engine to work well. Without oil the engine stops, with too much oil the engine works very unsatisfactorily or again even stops. The same occurs with money.

This section starts by identifying how money differs from other financial assets. It explains why money is normally defined to include not only cash but also the deposits, which individuals and organizations hold in their accounts with commercial banks. The system through which money is created is then outlined, the different reasons for needing to hold or use money are reviewed and a brief account follows of how both money supply and money demand are influenced by interest rates in the money markets and by the actions of central banks. The section then goes on to consider how money creation can contribute to price increases, i.e. to inflation. Finally, the section asks under what different circumstances inflation might be considered to be either harmful or helpful.

9.1 Money and other financial assets

We have a need not only for goods with inherent value (real goods) but also financial assets, i.e. documents offering us the possibility of obtaining real goods in certain conditions at certain times. Among financial assets, we make a rough distinction between money and all other financial assets.

All our domestic creditors must accept money as payment of our debts without charging us additional costs. If we have a debt of $100 and we pay with a $100 banknote, our debt is extinguished without additional costs. This means that money is the most liquid asset because it gives the right to pay debts at their face value;

and *vice versa* if we wish to pay a $100 debt with goods, for example a pair of shoes which on the market has a value of $100, the creditor may either refuse such a type of payment or say that only a part of the total debt has been paid by delivery of these shoes, for example, $90. In this case, we would still have a debt of $10. Money is "liquid", liberating us from our debt at its face value; other goods, in this case shoes, lack the same degree of liquidity. Not only shoes but even such financial assets as bonds, shares and insurances are not fully liquid. They do not provide the right to pay any debt at its face value at whatever the time.

Money's key advantage of liquidity, makes it an excellent **medium of exchange**, much better and more efficient than bartering, the exchange of goods. Money is also the unit that we use to total the values of very different articles: apples, refrigerators, medical services, accounting services, coal, oil, chalk, cheese. While different amounts of these can be measured in units appropriate to each case (litres, tonnes, hours, etc) only with money do we have a common measure, i.e. monetary value. Money is our **unit of account**. Finally, money has also the great advantage of storing value. Suppose that we wanted to store value in the form of commodities or raw materials. Over time the value would fluctuate as market conditions change. Some commodities, e.g. fresh fish or fruits, are even perishable. Money allows us to maintain a constant value; in other words, money is a **store of value**. A store of value is an asset that serves as a means of holding wealth. Remember however, that by holding money you usually forego the chance to earn interest.[1]

Watch

"Money in the modern economy: an introduction," The Bank of England. www.youtube.com/watch?v=ziTE32hiWdk.

Read

www.bankofengland.co.uk/quarterly-bulletin/2014/q1/money-in-the-modern-economy-an-introduction.

Questions

- What is the advantage of money *versus* barter?
- What is a special form of IOU?
- What is fiat money?
- What makes up most (97%) of the money circulating in the UK?
- What is the main difference between cash and deposits?

Analysis

The major advantage of money *versus* barter is that a buyer does not always need the products of the seller and therefore in many cases some transactions would not take place. That apart, with money, a seller can sell something today and buy something much later, since money stores value. Currency is a special form of IOU issued by the central bank. For example, in the case of the UK pound (£), that IOU consists of the fact that everybody believes that a £20 note is worth £20, that it will keep that value in future and is difficult to counterfeit. Today there are no more promises to give gold to the holders of notes, as there were in the past. In this sense, pounds are "fiat money"; they have a value simply because first the central bank and then everybody else in Britain recognizes that they have a value. Currency is an IOU from the central bank while deposits are IOUs from commercial banks; in the UK monetary system, deposits represent 97 per cent of all money.

Liquid and non-liquid assets

Besides money, there are other financial assets, retention of which permits, under certain conditions, the earning of additional money, for example bonds, shares and insurances. Such assets are not perfectly liquid; they do not guarantee payment of any debt of the same amount as their face value irrespective of time; sometimes they cannot be easily converted into cash. A creditor may accepts them, but may ask for a discount, for example, a bond with value 100 will be accepted as a payment of a debt of 95 or 90. To simplify, in our following presentation, we do not consider all possible financial assets, only bonds, i.e. securities that offer the restitution of the initial sum plus eventual interest on specified dates. Of course, the higher the interest on bonds, the more we are willing to close an eye to their imperfect or scarce liquidity. The higher the interest rate on bonds, the more eager we are to have them.

Deposits are money too

When we pay our bills, we use either cash or bank transfers, debit cards, switch cards, credit cards, cheques, online banking or mobile banking. What is cash is clear: banknotes and coins. All the other means of payment are based on the existence of a deposit in a commercial bank. In deposits we have means of exchange, stores of value and units of account. We can use them to pay our debts. Deposits are money. Money is therefore made up of cash and deposits.

The central bank has the monopoly on the emission of cash and is the bank of the commercial banks. They keep part, usually a small part, of their money in accounts at the central bank. These accounts are called the reserves of the commercial banks.

Commercial banks collect deposits from families and firms and eventually borrow from other banks or issue bonds.[2] They can lend the money of the deposits to firms and families, but not all of it. It is prudent not to lay themselves open to a possible "run on the bank", which would happen if a large number of their customers chose to withdraw their money in their bank accounts at roughly the same time. The banks lend the deposited money to firms and families; each bank keeps aside part of the deposits as reserve, in a bank account at the central bank. Most deposits do not end up in reserves and are available for loan. When the borrower uses the loan to buy items or services from other parties, the money will appear in the deposit accounts held by those parties in their own banks, and the banks may then make further loans based on those extra deposits. This successive growth in deposits based on an initial increase in one bank's reserves is known as the "money multiplier". Some banks, eager to earn more, could play the risky game of expanding their lending to a point where it was higher, relative to their reserves than could be regarded as a prudent or reasonable level. In this way, they would not only create risks for themselves, but also for their depositors and the whole financial system. For this reason, central banks[3] impose a minimum level of reserve that every bank must have. Banks may have more reserves than this statutory requirement. The traditional, and still largely used, way of considering this topic is that the central bank is the first to take the initiative, lending money (actually reserves) to the commercial banks and then permitting them to extend loans to companies and families. In that view, the commercial banks can multiply the money, which they receive from the central bank, through the multiplication process. Today some important sources, e.g. the Bank of England,[4] affirm that things do not work in this way. In most of cases the commercial banks lend money when they think that it can be profitable for them, independently from the deposits that they have. Before running short of reserves, they would ask other banks or the central bank for additional reserves and usually receive them. In this way, they become key players in the process of money creation. Therefore, while the creation of cash and reserves (the monetary base) is strictly under the control of the central bank, the creation of deposits, a very large part of total money, depends on the general public and the banking system. The public may receive credits from banks and use credits to make deposits. In this sense, much money creation depends on commercial banks and the general public.

Brakes to the creation of deposits

While credit creation is largely conducted by commercial banks, several of the actors or parties have the power of imposing limits on the process. Central banks, the public and the same commercial banks can slow down or reverse the money creation process.

The central bank can constrain the process by not providing additional reserves to the commercial banks or by increasing the reserve requirements that it imposes on them. Actions by the public (firms and families) can also have the effect of checking or reversing money creation. Bank customers could lose trust in the banking system, withdraw all their money from the banks and not deposit further money into their bank accounts. This would destroy the ability of the banks to lend by creating new deposits. This occurs in moments of panic (bank rushes), when people decide to keep all their money in cash, perhaps under the mattress. Alternatively, the public (families and firms) may simply refuse to borrow. Commercial banks may be ready to lend huge sums and create many new deposits, but if the public has no desire to borrow, there is little they can do.[5] You can lead a horse to water, but you can't make it drink. They are unable to create money. Finally, the same commercial banks may decide to go easy on money creation. When they perceive that their situation is very unprofitable and risky, for example, because they do not trust the other banks, they can considerably increase the sums that they keep as reserves and restrict further lending.

Lending and the profit of banks

The financial crisis of 2008 demonstrated that the incentive structures for those managing the major banks can lead to an irresponsible expansion of bank lending. In reality commercial banks did not have to wait for permission from the central banks in order to expand lending. Moreover, the compensation of a bank's senior executives and directors are often linked to the profits of banks. When banks make profits, these individuals commonly receive money or shares, the so called "bonuses". When bank executives see some profitable opportunity, they tend to lend, creating new deposits. The central bank could rein them in, by restricting reserves or increasing their reserve requirements, but in the run-up to the year 2008, the central banks in the major industrialized economies adopted a relatively passive role. More generally, when commercial banks see opportunities for profits, usually in years of growth or boom, they lend extensively. When they do not see the prospect of making profits, for example at the beginning of a recession, they lend much less and ask borrowers to pay money back to the bank. These situations are called "credit crunches". This makes their lending and money creation very "pro-cyclical". They grow a lot when the economy goes well and they shrink significantly when there is a crisis. In this way the banking system can often amplify any tendency of an economy towards boom and bust. The prevailing incentive structures in banks are not conducive to correcting these tendencies. In the financial crisis of 2008 some banks went out of business, other banks had to pay big fines, but few of banking's top executives were punished.

Watch

"Money creation in the modern economy," Quarterly Bulletin, The Bank of England.www.youtube.com/watch?v=CvRAqR2pAgw.

Read

www.bankofengland.co.uk/-/media/boe/files/quarterly-bulletin/2014/
money-creation-in-the-modern-economy.pdf?la=en&hash=9A8788FD44A
62D8BB927123544205CE476E01654.

9.2 The demand for and supply of money and the interest rate

People may choose between holding money and bonds or other assets with a return. Money has the advantage that it is absolutely liquid and can therefore pay for any type of debt. It has one major defect: the yield on money is usually nil. Bonds have the great advantage of offering a positive yield, but also have a great defect: they are not legal tender in the way that cash is, and some party to a transaction may refuse them. The person who keeps all their financial wealth in bonds may miss interesting business opportunities through being unable to lay their hands on their money at the right time. The more transactions take place, the more money will be needed: the so-called "transactions motive" for holding money.[6]

On the other hand, the higher the interest rates, the higher the missed interest for those who hold money and therefore, all things being equal, the lower the money demand. In national accounts, we do not have a direct measure of the number of transactions which take place in an economy, but we have a measure of GDP (see Section 8.1) which is assumed to be highly correlated with them. The demand for money is greater when there are many transactions, usually when GDP is greater. However, since holding our financial assets (our financial wealth) in the form of money means not earning interest, the higher the interest rate on bonds, the greater the income opportunity we miss and the greater our opportunity cost (Section 1.1). For this reason, we can say that all things being equal, as interest rates rise, demand for money decreases.[7]

We can, in general, say that the supply of money is under the supervision of the central bank, usually a public authority appointed by the president, government or parliament. It is the central banks which produces the cash, which the public needs, and the reserves that the banks need when they have deposits from the public. The sum of cash and reserves is called "Monetary Base".

See the box below for further details.

THE FOUR CHANNELS OF THE CENTRAL BANK TO CREATE CASH AND RESERVES – THE MONETARY BASE

The Banks

The central bank can lend money (reserves) to commercial banks. Banks may potentially lend money to firms and families. They do this taking into account their own profitability. They can only lend money if some creditworthy person or firm wants to borrow. If no creditworthy entity wants to borrow, perhaps because they have no good investment projects, this channel is blocked. The commercial banks are helpless. In other cases, there are creditworthy firms which borrow from the banks. But these firms do not use money to buy new plants, new equipment or invest in staff. They may borrow to carry out financial operations, for example, to purchase shares in their own company. The prices of goods will not change, but those of financial assets will. In this case, money creation has no real effect except that of increasing the financial wealth of shareholders. Finally, in some cases banks prefer buying financial assets rather than giving credit to firms and families. The interest rate that the central bank demands from banks is called the "discount rate" (US), "official bank rate" (UK), or "base rate" and is one of the key instruments with which the central bank communicates its desire to expand or restrict its credit to the economy.

The open market

The central bank may buy bonds from private entities, not only banks, but also pension funds, investment funds and other corporations. In this way, money goes to banks (as above) or to other financial institutions. These financial institutions may basically behave like banks, encountering the same difficulties and the same alternatives to expanding credit in the economy as we have discussed.

The foreign channel

Foreign residents who wish to buy goods made in our country or financial assets in our currency need our currency to make these purchases. Foreign residents purchase our currency from those who want to hold foreign currencies in order to undertake transactions abroad with those currencies. If the central bank, rather than the private sector, is the counterpart to such transactions then the central bank increases its holdings of the foreign currency by paying with domestic currency and thereby increasing the supply of money in the domestic economy.

The government

The central bank gives money to our government either by buying bonds directly from it or by giving it credit. This channel of monetary creation is described by Friedman (1948), who proposes a system in which budget deficits should be financed by increases in money supply and not interest-bearing securities. Since a dialogue between the central bank and government should usually be easier than one between the central bank and financial institutions, this is the surest way that the central bank has of fostering the demand of goods in an economy. It lends to the government which buys the services of public employees or spends money with public procurement.

Since 1980, this channel, also called "monetary finance", has been used less frequently and forbidden in several jurisdictions.[8] This occurred also because in some countries the use of this channel had coincided with very high inflation.[9] More recently, some unsatisfactory results achieved with the other channels of monetary creation and the presence of deflation have reopened the debate on the topic.[10]

When the central bank action leads to an increase in the quantity of money in circulation, monetary policy is expansionary. When the central bank operates for a reduction in the quantity of money in circulation, monetary policy is restrictive.[11]

Every event, including government spending,[12] which makes the economy grow will increase money demand. If money supply remains constant, increased demand for money will probably bring about a growth in interest rates.

The central bank, with its monetary policy, determines the interest rate that commercial banks pay to it; it may also buy and sell government bonds, influencing their yields.

The interest rate that commercial banks pay to the central bank and the yields on sovereign bonds affect all other interest rates in the economy, in particular those paid by businesses on their loans and those which families pay on their mortgages. This is why policy makers and social negotiators should pay so much attention to the behaviour of the central bank. In the unit on private investment (Chapter 18), we shall again consider the importance of interest rates.

MONEY DEMAND, MONEY SUPPLY AND THE INTEREST RATE

Money demand is the requirement that the public has for cash and deposits. It depends positively on GDP, mainly because when the economy grows, there is greater demand for loans and therefore greater demand for deposits.

Far from it, high interest rates negatively affect money demand. They induce companies and families to reduce their deposits and to purchases bonds. High interest rates also make many investments less profitable (see Section 18.1 for an explanation). For this reason, the total sum of loan requests is usually smaller when interest rates are higher.

The responsibility for money creation, i.e. money supply, rests with the central bank. Today in industrialized countries, this function is largely delegated to commercial banks which facilitate the creation of deposits, i.e. of money, by extending loans to companies and families. This is of course a very controversial topic.

The interest rate operating in an economy at a given point in time depends on the interaction between money demand and money supply.

If the central bank wants to lower the interest rate, it may act towards an expansion of money supply.

It can do this through the commercial banks, if lowers the interest rate that it requests from them. Otherwise the central bank can obtain the same result by reducing the level of mandatory reserves that commercial banks must keep. More generally the central bank can lower interest rates, if it looses the regulation which concerns commercial banks.

The central bank can also use the other three channels of monetary base creation.

If the central bank wants to reduce money supply, it will take the opposite approach.

9.3 Money supply and prices

The central bank can foster or restrict money supply. When it plans its actions, the central bank takes into account that a tightening of credit (i.e. money scarcity) with high levels of interest rates will impede economic growth and employment. However, money abundance can also bring problems. Money may end up either in the market for goods or in the financial markets. If it ends up in the market for goods, the effects will differ according to whether production is growing or not growing. If the economy is growing proportionally to the money flowing into the market of goods, we should not expect inflation. If the new money flowing to the market of goods is more than the growth in the GDP of the country, then that country will experience inflation, i.e. a general increase in the price of goods. When interest rates are very low there is also the risk that useless investments are funded and resources are wasted. If the money flows to the financial markets, we shall not observe inflation in the market of goods, but inflated prices of financial assets, that is inflation in the financial markets. This means that the stock market, the value of bonds and the prices of other financial assets will increase. In some cases, money first flows to the financial market and is transformed by the financial system into mortgages for the purchase of real estate. Some investment in real estate can be a good thing, too much can be a waste of resources (see Section 8.2). In all these cases we can observe the development of "**bubbles**" in the prices of real estate or financial assets, which grow more and more. This growth induces other people to buy these assets and fosters further growth in their prices. These bubbles initially bring euphoria into the economy because the holders of such assets count themselves richer and consume and invest more, but then such bubbles often implode, leaving many people and even banks with more debts than assets. In order to pay their debts back, banks stop lending to families and firms; families and firms stop buying goods, making less demand for goods, and the economy in general, shrinks.

9.4 Banks are special

When things go well, banks make significant profits and when there is a crisis, they could go bankrupt. However, the crisis of a bank is not the same as the crisis of a chocolate firm or of a footwear factory. The collapse of a non-banking business has of course very serious and sometimes dramatic consequences. Production in that firm stops, employees lose their jobs, creditors go unpaid, suppliers lose a client, distributors lose a supplier, shareholders lose their investment, the national treasury misses tax revenue, etc. The same applies to banks but in addition, the many firms and families that have deposited their money at the bank may see their money disappear. This can lead to a chain of bankruptcies. Things are even worse because banks and financial institutions are usually linked by many different relations of credit, debt and risk sharing. The crisis of a single bank, if treated like the bankruptcy of any standard business can have much wider consequences. For these reasons there is general agreement that commercial banks should operate under a form of regulation specific to banking. In some countries the central bank itself performs the regulatory function. In others, a separate entity deals with banking supervision.

BANKING SAFETY NET

Banking Supervision[13] **Checks:**

Capital adequacy. The bank should have enough capital coming from its shareholders. They are those supposed to bear eventual losses, but if the capital of the bank is too small, somebody else (the public authority or the public) will. This is not ideal.

Asset quality. Banks should have lent their money to people who are able to pay them back.

Management. Is the bank well managed?

Earnings. Can the bank make reasonable profits?

Liquidity. Has the bank enough liquid assets or has it assets that can be sold after long procedures and at prices which are much lower than their face value? Is the bank respecting the minimum requirements for reserves?

Sensitivity. How sensitive is the bank to some market event, e.g. how sensitive is it to a crisis in the emerging markets?

The safety of the banking system is not only based on banking supervision, but also on resolution arrangements, deposit insurance and the possibility of borrowing from the central bank.

Resolution arrangements are provisions about what to do in the eventuality of bank failure.

The deposit insurance is a guarantee that is provided to depositors. If their bank goes bankrupt, the insurance will at least give them a proportion of the deposit.

The mission of some central banks

Central banks may have different missions. For example the European Central Bank has the objective of maintaining price stability: safeguarding the value of the euro.[14] This is the case of a central bank mainly focussed on the constant value of the mean of exchange and on the fight against inflation.

The Board of Governors of the US FED has a double mission. "The mission of the Board is to foster the stability, integrity, and efficiency of the nation's monetary, financial, and payment systems so as to promote optimal macroeconomic performance."[15]

The US central bank is not only interested in the stability of prices in the US, as the ECB is in the eurozone; stability, integrity and efficiency are aimed at promoting macroeconomic performance, i.e. economic growth and employment.

The central bank of Nigeria has a mission which is better understood if we consider its vision Be the model central bank delivering price and financial system stability and promoting sustainable economic development.[16]

The vision of the Nigerian central bank shows that its approach is closer to the US approach than to that adopted by the ECB. The Nigerian mission statement is: "To be proactive in providing a stable framework for the economic development of Nigeria, through effective, efficient, and transparent implementation of monetary and exchange rate policy, and management of the financial sector". In this statement too, the exchange rate policy (see Section 10.2) is mentioned; in other countries the exchange rate policy is more in the remit of government than in that of the central bank. Actually, for medium and small economies, where export and import are equivalent to a large share of GDP, the exchange rate plays an even bigger role than for huge markets such as, for example, the US, China or Japan.

The capital or equity of banks and the reserves of banks – the Chicago plan

Most of the money that banks risk does not belong to the owners of the bank, but to somebody else, depositors and creditors in general. This gives rise to a serious systemic problem.[17] When there are losses the public must bear them, not the bankers. Some economists have therefore requested that the capital or equity of the bank, the money from shareholders be at least 20–30 per cent of the amount that they lend. Their advice has been followed in a very limited way.

In the 1930s, a group of economists from the University of Chicago had gone even further saying that even banking supervision and banks with more capital could not avoid that banks, through their big role in money creation, lead the economy to boom and bust; moreover, the fact that most deposits are loaned to the public, today even 99% of them, means that in more unstable times, banks can be short of cash and more generally short of liquidity. Those economists therefore suggested that banks should become real credit intermediaries, losing their present ability to create money from nothing. They recommended giving the monopoly of money creation to the central bank which would supply the commercial banks with the money to lend, while deposits would remain as reserves. Reserves would be equivalent to 100 per cent of deposits. The liquidity of deposits would be guaranteed 100 per cent.

Shadow banking

Hedge funds, with pension funds, money market funds, mutual funds, brokers-dealers and other financial entities belong to the so called "shadow banking system".

"Shadow banking" is a catch-all phrase that encompasses risky investment products, pawnshop and loan-shark operations and so-called peer-to-peer lending between individuals and businesses. Even art dealers like Sotheby's have become shadow banks, making millions of dollars of loans to clients buying masterpieces. The common denominator is that these products and practices flourish outside the regular banking system and often beyond the reach of regulators.[18]

Shadow banking is not regulated as commercial banking is and enjoys a great degree of freedom. This poses two problems.

The first problem is that shadow banks are **de facto competitors** of commercial banks. Since they are less regulated than commercial banks, they can offer customers better conditions. Customers rarely have the possibility to understand that these better conditions are the results of less regulation and higher risk. They accept risks without much deep analysis and underestimate the risks involved. Commercial banks, in order not to lose customers, are therefore under pressure to behave like shadow banks, adopting a similar approach with regard to risk.

The second problem is that commercial banks and shadow banks are **intermingled**. In 2008, Lehman Brothers went bankrupt. Lehman Brothers was not a commercial bank, it was part of shadow banking. Many other institutions that governments had to rescue were not commercial banks, but parts of shadow banking. The US government was called to rescue Fannie Mae, Freddie Mac[19] and also AIG. None of them were commercial banks. However, shadow banks and commercial banks have so many links that any problems in shadow banking would quickly spread to commercial banks. This has led to several requests to regulate shadow banking. This industry has excellent advocates and lobbyist groups as well as huge funds to support its argument. It is no surprise that regulation in shadow banking has only changed in very limited way.

Basel III

The Bank of International Settlements (BIS) is located in Basel, Switzerland. This institution is where the central bankers of 60 countries of the world gather and make common rules, standards and recommendations concerning central banks. After the 2008 financial crisis, the BIS has been charged with the task of making safer rules to avoid the repetition of similar banking crises. There have been some achievements but not in the numbers many scholars and experts had hoped for and worked towards. The main new Basel rules concern increasing the level and quality of capital, enhancing risk capture, constraining bank leverage, improving bank liquidity and limiting pro-cyclicality. They are described below.

- **Increase the level and quality of capital**

Banks are required to maintain more capital of higher quality to cover unexpected losses. Good quality capital should be equivalent to at least 6 per cent of assets (mostly loans to clients and bonds). Very big banks, "Global systemically important banks- G-SIBs" are subject to additional capital requirements.

- **Enhance risk capture**

Banks that engage in ventures with risk should have more capital than other banks. Banks should not only calculate risk with their internal formulas, but should also follow a standardized model. Experts often disagree about what constitutes a risky business.

- **Constrain bank leverage**

Banks can only partially fund their investments by borrowing money from others.

- **Improve bank liquidity**

Banks should have more liquid assets, for example cash or easily tradable bonds.

- **Limit pro-cyclicality**

During periods of growth and expansion, banks should accumulate reserves for "rainy days". In periods of crisis, they can use these reserves to meet their obligations.

The relation between central banks and commercial banks: their balance sheets

TABLE 9.1 The balance sheet of a commercial bank

Assets	*Liabilities*
Bonds and other securities	Deposits in bank accounts
Loans to clients	Bank capital (money from shareholders)
Reserves	Credits from other banks
	Bonds issued by the bank

Assets of commercial banks

The major mission of a commercial bank would be that of collecting savings and extending loans to firms and families. Today, for some banks, this activity may be as important as (or even less important than) purchasing bonds and other securities. Banks may buy bonds from governments (sovereign bonds) or from corporations (corporate bonds). Finally, banks keep part of their resources as reserves under the control of the central bank. Today the mandatory requirement of reserves is quite small. It is between 1 and 2 per cent of the deposit in the eurozone while for example in Georgia, 5 per cent of deposits in local currency should be set aside in reserves. If deposits are in US dollars in Georgia, the mandatory reserve is 25 per cent.

Liabilities of commercial banks

In theory, the major source of funding for a commercial bank should be deposits and shareholder capital. In reality, commercial banks also raise funds by issuing bonds and by borrowing from other banks (Table 9.1), more rarely from the central bank.

TABLE 9.2 The balance sheet of a central bank

Assets	*Liabilities*
Bonds	Currency/circulating cash
Credits to commercial banks	Reserves of banks
Credits to the government	
Reserves of foreign currencies	
Gold	

Assets of central banks

The major assets of central banks (Table 9.2) are the bonds they have bought and their holdings of foreign currencies and gold. They also extend credits to the commercial banks and in some cases to the government.

Liabilities of central banks

The major liability of central banks is the money that they issue which belongs to the public and to the commercial banks.

Can a central bank go bankrupt? No.

Can a central bank run out of foreign currencies and gold? Yes. This could seriously limit the ability of the country to purchase foreign goods and honour foreign debts.

Speculative bubbles A speculative bubble is a social epidemic, the contagion of which is mediated by price movements. News of price increases enriches early investors, creating word-of-mouth stories about their successes, which stir envy and interest. The excitement then lures more and more people into the market, which causes prices to increase further, attracting yet more people and fuelling "new era" stories, and so on in successive feedback loops as the bubble grows. After the bubble bursts, the same contagion fuels a precipitous collapse, as falling prices cause more and more people to exit the market and spread negative stories about the economy.

Robert J. Shiller, Nobel Prize Laureate[20]

Quantitative easing

The policies of "quantitative easing" have reduced the cost of borrowing by the involved governments and to a certain extent interest rates for business. They have been slower or less successful in stimulating demand for goods and increasing inflation. This occurred precisely for the reasons explained above in the description of the channels of creation of cash and reserves. Only a limited part of the new money reaches the market for goods, creating new demand, new products and new jobs; a large part remains in the financial markets. Part of this money has flowed abroad, often reaching developing economies in the form of investment. After 2015 and at least until 2018, the flow was in the opposite direction, leaving some emerging economies in more difficult financial situations.

After the collapse of the US financial firm Lehman Brothers in September 2008, the US Federal Reserve introduced measures aimed at repairing the functioning of financial markets and focussed on liquidity operations to support banks by large-scale asset purchases of mortgage- backed securities and Treasury securities among other such financial instruments. The central idea is that investors who sold these securities to the central bank would take the proceeds and buy other assets, raising their prices. Lower bond yields would then encourage borrowing, and higher equity prices would raise consumption. Both help investment and boost demand. Similar operations have been carried out by the Bank of England, the Bank of Japan, the European Central Bank and other central banks.

9.5 How much inflation is "too much"?

A generalized growth in prices is termed inflation, while a generalized decrease in prices is termed deflation. Are they good or bad? Some limited inflation is usually a good thing; it is a normal element of a healthy economy. Usually the economies of developing countries require higher minimum inflation than advanced industrialized economies. The change occurring in developing countries is quite substantial and may imply inflation. The economies of countries with an advanced process of industrialization and well-developed markets will normally require lower inflation rates. When inflation is higher than a healthy minimum level (2–5 per cent in developed economies, 5–11 per cent in developing economies)[21] it becomes a problem, for several reasons. When inflation is high it also becomes irregular: sometimes it is very high, sometimes less high. Under these conditions, any planning by firms and families can be disrupted. Business needs planning; when you cannot plan, economic activity is impeded.

Inflation redistributes income in the absence of any transparent decision making. It gives an advantage to those groups who are able to compensate for inflation (e.g. shareholders, business owners capable of adjusting their prices and those groups with inflation-adjusted salaries) and penalizes those groups who cannot compensate (bondholders and people with fixed income in general). When you change compensation you also change the incentives of people and their behaviour. They may stop acting in a productive way.

Inflation penalizes creditors and helps debtors because it reduces the real value of payments they have contracted to make. This can lead creditors to stop giving credit, creating a major disruption in the economy.

If inflation distributes income from individuals with low incomes who consume large proportions of their income, to individuals with higher incomes who consume smaller shares of their income, total consumption may decrease. This normally leads to a reduction in total production.

Moreover, very high inflation may convince the public that holding money causes them to make losses and that they should not hold money. This may bring the economy back to barter, an inefficient way of trading. Finally, very high inflation may convince some citizens that they are unfairly treated. This may tear the fabric of society.

In some countries, high inflation has simply led citizens to stop using the national currency and to trade in dollars or other foreign currencies. In order to avoid this lack of trust in the domestic currency, some countries have legally linked their domestic currency to the dollar (dollarization) or to other foreign currencies. In this way, they have renounced a national monetary policy.

For these reasons, we often see monetary authorities set a target for inflation, informing the public of their objective in doing so. This targeting also helps the public formulate its own plans; economists say that "targeting influences expectations".

If people believe that the monetary authority's target is credible, they behave accordingly. For example, they will increase the prices of their products and their salary requests correspondingly. Alternatively, monetary authorities may target interest rates or simply the quantity of money that they issue. Targeting interest rates has the objective of maintaining a foreseeable environment for investors (see Section 18.2), even if investors do not usually look at nominal interest rates but at real interest rates. They look at the combined effects of nominal interest rates and inflation. For central banks, targeting the quantity of money which they issue may be simpler. In this case, the monetary authority renounces direct control over interest rates and inflation.

Deflation is a generalized reduction in prices. If excessive inflation brings problems, does that mean that deflation is a good thing? No, it does not: deflation, besides creating problems similar to those which inflation creates, penalizes debtors and helps creditors. Among debtors there are many businesses which in periods of deflation see their turnover and profits decrease while their liabilities remain constant. This can lead them into bankruptcy. In many countries the major debtor is the state. Deflation reduces the value of GDP at current prices, which is nominal GDP (see Section 8.1), but keeps public debt constant, worsening the debt-to-GDP ratio and any other ratio in which the denominator is GDP. Deflation reduces the financial stability of many governments. It also leads consumers to postpone their purchases on the assumption that goods will later be cheaper. This depresses total consumption, aggregate demand and GDP.

Finally, deflation usually comes as a by-product of recession or stagnation.

THE MEASURES OF INFLATION

The consumer price index (CPI) measures the variation in the price of a basket of goods consumed in the country. It includes both goods produced in the country and abroad. It is very useful for understanding the standard of living of consumers and their purchasing power. When we speak about "real wages" we usually mean wages divided by the consumer price index. The GDP Deflator is given by: Nominal GDP/Real GDP (see Section 8.1). It is an indicator of the variation in the prices of the goods made in the country. It is used to analyse the variations in the competitiveness of a country.

Glossary

base rate   The interest rate which banks pay to the central bank.

bonds   Documents that attest that the holder has a credit towards the company or government which has issued them. They give a fixed income every year and at the maturity date they guarantee the repayment of their face value to the holder. They can be traded.

bubbles   Situations during which the prices of some assets (real estate, financial assets or even tulip bulbs) grow more and more. This growth of prices induces other people to buy these types of assets which fosters further growth in their prices. Bubbles initially bring euphoria into the economy because the holders of such assets think of becoming richer and consuming and investing more, but bubbles often then implode, leaving many people and even banks with more debts than assets.

cash or currency   Banknotes and coins, i.e. the physical output of the central bank.

central bank   A public authority with exclusive responsibility for the production and management of cash and bank reserves in a country. Usually it also supervises the country's banking system. It is the source of money supply through four channels (see below) and with the cooperation of several actors, principally commercial banks.

channels of money creation   Banks, financial institutions, foreign buyers of domestic goods and government are the possible channels that the central bank can use in the process of money creation (see Section 9.3).

commercial bank   Ordinary banks, which issue credit to the public, so facilitating the creation of deposits and therefore of money. In accordance with the law they must hold a small percentage of deposits as a reserve.

Consumer Price Index   An index indicating the variation of the price of a basket of goods representing merchandize and services consumed within a country. It is used to analyse the purchasing power of consumers, viz. their standard of living.

deflation   A general reduction in price levels.

deposits   Credits of firms and individuals, corresponding to what they have lent to commercial banks. They represent the largest part of money supply, since they can be used to pay debts with bank transfers, cheques, debit cards or credit cards.

discount rate   See *base rate*.

expansionary monetary policy   Measures taken by the central bank aimed at increasing the rate of growth of the nation's money supply.[22]

GDP deflator   The ratio between Nominal GDP and Real GDP. It indicates the variation in the prices of the goods made in a country. It is used to analyse the price competitiveness of a country.

inflation   A general increase in price levels.

inflation targeting   A monetary policy aimed at maintaining inflation close to a certain value. It contributes to the creation of expectations that inflation will not be appreciably different from the stated value.

IOU   An informal document acknowledging debt.

legal tender   A debtor cannot successfully be sued for non-payment if he pays in court in legal tender.[23] Cash is legal tender.

liquidity   The feature of cash, cash equivalents and other assets (liquid assets) that can easily be converted into cash (liquidated); the suitability of an asset for paying debts at their face value; the degree to which an asset or security can be bought or sold in the market without affecting the asset's price. Liquidity is characterized by a high level of trading activity. Assets that can easily be bought or sold are known as liquid assets.[24]

maturity date   The date on which the principal amount of a bond or other debt instrument becomes due and is repaid to the investor, and interest payments stop.

monetary base   The output of the central bank, i.e. the sum of reserves of banks and cash of the public.

monetary policy   A set of measures, usually carried out by the central bank, to increase or decrease money supply and interest rates.

money   Those financial assets that can be used directly to buy goods. It is made up of cash and deposits.

money demand   Deposits and cash that the public (families and firms) desires to hold. It increases when the number of transactions increases and diminishes when interest rates increase.

money supply   The currency that the central bank puts into public circulation plus the deposits that individuals hold in banks and other financial intermediaries which can be used to make payments.

quantitative easing   Expansive monetary policy which the central banks of the major industrialized economies carried out following the major 2008–2009 recession, by buying financial assets from banks and paying for them by creating electronic cash that did not previously exist. The purpose is to encourage banks to use the new money to buy assets which support investment expenditure in the economy.

restrictive monetary policy   The action of the central bank aimed at reducing the rate of growth of the nation's money supply.[25]

Notes

1 These are the money functions that monetary theory treats in depth: medium of exchange, unit of account and store of value.

2 These are written promises of the banks to pay certain sums at certain dates.

3 Commercial banks are regulated by their central bank or by some other watchdog of the banking sector.

4 McLeay et al. (2013).

5 Why doesn't the public want to borrow? Probably because it is worried about its ability to repay debts. This occurs for example in a depressed economy.
6 The theory of money demand includes at least two other motives to detain money. The precautionary motive derives from the problem of providing for uncertain contingencies (Tsiang, 1969). The speculative motive derives from the desire of not missing investment opportunities that may arise, "experience indicates that the aggregate demand for money to satisfy the speculative-motive usually shows a continuous response to gradual changes in the rate of interest, i.e. there is a continuous curve relating changes in the demand for money to satisfy the speculative motive and changes in the rate of interest as given by changes in the prices of bonds and debts of various maturities" (Keynes, 1934:198).
7 The interest rate also plays a role in the choice between present consumption and future consumption (saving). The higher the interest is, the more families are pushed to save for the future.
8 For example, Article 123 of the Lisbon Treaty prohibits its use by the European Central Bank.
9 In those years (1980s to the present), a theory of "central bank independence" has been developed.
10 See Turner (2015) for a recent contribution in support of this way of creating money.
11 Actually, the central bank can also influence the interest rates in other ways. It can increase or reduce the interest rate that commercial banks have to pay to borrow from the central bank. Alternatively, the central bank may oblige commercial banks to put a larger share of the deposits which the public has given to them, as reserves with the central bank.
12 When government raises taxes and cuts its spending, probably the demand of money, actually the demand of loans, will diminish.
13 www.stlouisfed.org/in-plain-english/safety-and-soundness.
14 www.ecb.europa.eu/ecb/orga/escb/ecb-mission/html/index.en.html.
15 www.federalreserve.gov/publications/gpra/2011-mission-values-and-goals-of-the-board-of-governors.htm#subsection-142-21B7B547.
16 www.cbn.gov.ng/aboutcbn/mission.asp (capital letters in the original).
17 See Admati and Hellwig (2013) for a discussion of this topic.
18 Jun Luo (2018). www.bloomberg.com/quicktake/shadow-banking.
19 www.fhfa.gov/SupervisionRegulation/FannieMaeandFreddieMac/Pages/About-Fannie-Mae---Freddie-Mac.aspx.
20 Shiller (2012) "Bubbles without Markets", Project Syndicate, July 23 3012. www.project-syndicate.org/commentary/bubbles-without-markets#TFLjX6R9lUcEk0ej.99.
21 Islam, I. (2014) "Macroeconomic Policy After the Global Recession of 2008-2009: A Development Perspective." In The Twin Challenges of Reducing Poverty and Creating Employment. New York, NY: United Nations, 2014. pp. 123–139.
22 See Abel et al. (2014:34).
23 www.royalmint.com/aboutus/policies-and-guidelines/legal-tender-guidelines.
24 See also www.investopedia.com/terms/l/liquidity.asp.
25 See Abel et al. (2014:34).

Bibliography

Abel, A. B., Bernanke, B. and Croushore, D. D. (2014). *Macroeconomics*. Boston: Addison-Wesley.

Admati, A. R. and Hellwig, M. F. (2013). *The bankers new clothes: What's wrong with banking and what to do about it*. Princeton, NJ: Princeton University Press.

Friedman, M. (1948). "A Monetary and Fiscal Framework for Economic Stability," *American Economic Review*, 38(June): 245–264.

Islam, I. (2014). "Macroeconomic Policy After the Global Recession of 2008–2009: A Development Perspective." in *The Twin Challenges of Reducing Poverty and Creating Employment*. New York, NY: United Nations.

Keynes, J. M. (1934). *The general theory of employment interest and money.* Harcourt, 1964.

Luo, J. (2018). "Shadow Banking," *Bloomberg*, 24 September. www.bloomberg.com/quicktake/shadow-banking.

McLeay, M., Radia, A. and Thomas, R. (2013). "Money Creation in the Modern Economy," in *Quarterly Bulletin*, 2014 Q1. London: Bank of England.

Shiller, R. J. (2012). "Bubbles Without Markets," *Project Syndicate*, 23 July. www.project-syndicate.org/commentary/bubbles-without-markets#TFLjX6R9lUcEk0ej.99.

Tsiang, S. C. (1969). "The Precautionary Demand for Money: An Inventory Theoretical Analysis," *Journal of Political Economy*, 77(1) (January–February): 99–117.

Turner, A. (2015). *The Case for Monetary Finance: An Essentially Political Issue*, Paper presented at the 16th Jacques Polak Annual Research Conference Hosted by the International Monetary Fund, Washington, DC, 5–6 November.

PART V
Foreign economic relations

All countries have some degree of openness to the rest of the world. Trade is of course the main form of foreign economic relations, but financial relations are also extremely important. They occur, for example, when countries borrow from or lend to other countries. They represent huge opportunities but also major constraints.

This part describes these relations and presents the major accounts that report on them.

10

THE FOREIGN TRADE OF GOODS

Exports and imports

Imports are important because they are part of the resources (supply or sources, Section 8.1) that a country can use to satisfy its needs, and therefore imports contribute to the standard of living of a country. Exports are important because they are a possible use (uses, Section 8.2) of the goods made in a country and therefore their presence stimulates production and employment in the exporting country. They are also the best means that a country can employ to accumulate resources to pay for its imports, avoiding large liabilities with and dependence on the rest of the world. Imports and exports depend on the quality of the products, on the exchange rate, on local prices and on the economy of the client countries. In the following sections we first analyse the role played by quality, the exchange rate and prices in trade; finally, we separately try to answer two questions: why do imports grow? Why do exports grow?

10.1 The quality of goods

One way for countries to be competitive is by producing high-quality products for which buyers are ready to pay high prices. High-quality products usually embody technological knowledge, rare skills and design. Moreover, quality products are not sold in market environments of perfect competition (Section 7.2), but in those of oligopoly (Section 7.3), monopolistic competition (Section 7.4) or even monopoly (Section 7.1). In conditions close to perfect competition, margins are very low or nil while under conditions of oligopoly or monopoly, margins can be substantial. Quality-based competition leaves firms larger margins which they can then split between employers and employees. In the long term, a strategy based on quality permits producers higher standards of living. On the other hand, strategies based mainly on prices imply strong pressures on wages, suppliers and profits.

Competitiveness based on quality often requires highly skilled workers and sophisticated equipment. A country has skilled workers if it complies with certain conditions. It must have a good health system which keeps them healthy and avoids the spread of diseases. A strong training system will aid the supply of good workers. Countries must also be able to retain their best workers. For this reason, education and health care should not only be considered as consumption, but also as investment. Furthermore, quality products are the result of investments in technology and physical capital. These aspects require a system which fosters innovation and affords the right protection to property rights, as well as to human life and human rights. More skilled workers are often the first to emigrate if human rights are not sufficiently protected in a country.

Why do we trade?

Economists explain trade in different ways. Some practitioners and scholars introduced the **mercantilist approach** several centuries ago.[1] This emphasized that trade is a kind of zero-sum game in which victory for one country means the defeat of the other. In this view, trade is not only an economic activity but is also a way of increasing the power of a country. According to a mercantilist view, countries should accumulate a surplus on their foreign trade. In this way they become richer. This theory has frequently been attacked by many free-market economists, but it has also been frequently applied with success by some countries. Of course, a mercantilist approach can work for a long period only if the economy of the mercantilist country is relatively small when compared with the rest of the world economy. If a very large economy, for example the eurozone, wanted to follow this policy it would face insurmountable obstacles sooner or later. A large trade surplus for the eurozone would imply a large trade deficit for the rest of the world. That would not be sustainable over a long period.

Some explanations of trade make reference to countries which could produce the same goods without large differences in quality or brand. Their explanation of trade focusses on the so-called absolute advantage.[2] In this view, every country should produce those goods that it can produce at a cheaper price and import the other goods. According to this view everybody would be better off under this system. Imagine two countries with the same population: Country A and Country B. Initially they use half of their workforce to produce bicycles and half to produce potatoes. They produce potatoes and bicycles fundamentally of the same quality. In Table 10.1 we can see what they can produce and consume without trade.

TABLE 10.1 Absolute advantage and no trade

	Production		Consumption	
	Bicycle	Potatoes	Bicycle	Potatoes
Country A	10	2	10	2
Country B	3	9	3	9

Now let us consider the case of when they start to trade (Table 10.2). Country A is very good at producing bicycles, while country B has a clear advantage in producing potatoes.

After trade, everybody is producing what it can do best and total production is higher. Every country consumes more than before.

A second explanation of trade refers to the so-called comparative advantage.[3] Even if a country were more productive (or less expensive) than other countries in every field, the less productive (or more expensive) country could specialize in those goods that it can produce at relatively lower before-trade prices. Even if those prices are higher than those requested elsewhere, this country would still benefit from making what it can produce at relatively lower prices and buying what it produces at relatively higher prices. Before trade (Table 10.3), we observe that country A is more productive at producing both bicycles and potatoes. Even so, for country A, each tonne of potatoes has an opportunity cost of 2.5 bicycles, while in country B the opportunity cost (Section 1.1) of potatoes is much higher: 9 bicycles. This because in country A the production of a tonne of potatoes entails not producing 2.5 bicycles, while in country B the production of a tonne of potatoes entails not producing 9 bicycles. In country B everything is expensive, but potatoes have the highest opportunity cost. Therefore, for country B producing bicycles is better. Bicycles have a low opportunity cost: one-ninth of a tonne of potatoes. In country A, bicycles have a higher opportunity cost: four-tenths of a tonne of potatoes.

TABLE 10.2 Absolute advantage with trade

	Production		Consumption	
	Bicycle	Potatoes	Bicycle	Potatoes
Country A	20	0	15	4
Country B	0	18	5	14

TABLE 10.3 Comparative advantage and no trade

	Production		Consumption	
	Bicycle	Potatoes	Bicycle	Potatoes
Country A	10	4	10	4
Country B	9	1	9	1

TABLE 10.4 Comparative advantage with trade

	Production		Consumption	
	Bicycle	Potatoes	Bicycle	Potatoes
Country A	0	8	10	5
Country B	18	0	8	3

After trade (Table 10.4), we observe that country B obtains three tonnes of potatoes, i.e. two tonnes more than before. Country B pays for these three tonnes of potatoes with ten bicycles. Prior to trade, in country B, three tonnes of potatoes had a price of 27 bicycles. Country B has a comparative advantage in producing bicycles. This occurs because for country B, the production of bicycles has a very low opportunity cost. To produce one bicycle, they have to renounce just one-ninth of a tonne of potatoes.

The absolute and the comparative advantage theories may be applied with success if at least two conditions apply. Firstly, countries must be able to switch from one product to another without major costs and in a short period of time. Secondly, these approaches work well in a peaceful world. In such conditions, countries do not use trade as a strategic weapon to force other countries to do what they want. In a non-peaceful world, the country which completely abandons the production of food could be blackmailed. It could potentially face a choice between starving and obeying foreign orders.

The theory of **factor endowment**[4] suggests that a country should export those goods for which production requires large quantities of the production factor (see Section 1.1) which is more abundant in that country. Therefore, according to this theory, developing countries with plenty of workers and little capital should specialize in labour-intensive (see Section 3.4) production. In many cases, this can be a successful trade strategy. However, it is also true that developing countries may wish to produce goods with higher value added (see Section 2.1). Production of such goods often may require higher capital-intensity.

Further pursuing this strand, more recent studies have noted that today, it is very frequent that countries do not produce entire products, but contribute to specific steps in the production of final goods. We speak of international supply chains (see Section 2.1) to indicate that different phases of production are undertaken in different countries (see also see Section 2.1). A final assembly company and its suppliers import intermediate goods and services from plants located in different countries. "Instead of simply creating more trade in goods, global integration is increasingly marked by trade of intermediate goods and services, also known as 'fragmentation', 'offshoring' or 'task trade'".[5]

Of course, those who are able to retain or attract the production phases requiring more quality, higher technical skills and generally higher value, also retain the largest part of the total value added (see Section 2.1). They are able to pay high wages and make high profits.

Other economists stress that goods are often diversified, with quality and specifications making the difference. Countries often import goods similar to those they produce. The difference is in varieties. Italians import some cheese from France and sell different types of cheese to France. The same may occur with fashion or with cars. The type of goods that a country consumes also depends on the income of its citizens. Countries with similar incomes often sell and buy from each other.

When firms produce large quantities, they may achieve lower unit costs (economies of scale, see Section 5.2). This can encourage countries to export. Exporting is a way of increasing production and permits firms to achieve those economies of scale that they could not achieve only in their internal market. Not by chance, small countries are those in which exports account for a large share of GDP (see Section 20.2). Certain firms operating in small countries could not achieve economies of scale by simply selling within their domestic market. Exports help them to achieve those output volumes which the minimum efficient size (Section 5.4) requires.

10.2 The (nominal) exchange rate and the exchange rate regimes

While it is true that, in a medium-to-long term perspective, the best way to export more and import less is by enhancing the quality of the contribution made by a country to the production of goods, this requires some time. In the short term, the competitiveness of a country depends on prices. Every buyer will compare goods from different countries and their respective prices. However, in import and export operations and foreign trade generally, there is an additional complication: the prices of domestic goods are expressed in the domestic currency while the prices of foreign goods are expressed in a foreign currency.[6]

The exchange rate, or to be precise the nominal exchange rate, is (a) the price of our currency in a foreign currency or (b) the price of a foreign currency in our currency. Both definitions are correct, but here for simplicity we always use "a". Therefore, speaking of the exchange rate between the dollar and the euro from a eurozone perspective, we shall say that a euro could be bought for $1.09 in April 2015. When the price in US dollars of one euro moves from 1.09 to 1.12, the euro appreciates. The opposite movement is called depreciation.

The exchange rate can be in three different regimes: flexible, fixed or mixed.

The exchange rate may float freely and will be called "**flexible**" if the authorities of a country are not committed to any specific rate, leaving market forces to determine it. Several aspects need to be considered, and are listed below:

- The authorities of the country should not spend time and financial resources defending the exchange rate.
- A flexible exchange rate allows the country to carry out an effective monetary policy.
- A flexible exchange rate takes into account the flows of money to and from the country, adapting to them. When trade flows are the main source of payments to and from the country, a flexible exchange rate permits avoidance of excessive trade deficits (imports less than exports) and trade surpluses (exports exceeding imports). A country with a trade deficit and no international lenders will experience low international demand for its currency and high internal demand for foreign currencies and this will lead the domestic currency to become cheaper in terms of foreign currency, that is to depreciate, and *vice versa*. This will diminish the relative price of domestic goods, making them

more attractive. It will also diminish the attractiveness of foreign goods by making them more expensive.

- The mechanism described above may not work if the rest of the world is willing to lend more to the country concerned. As long as the rest of the world keeps on lending, for example because it is happy to export to this country even with a flexible exchange rate, the trade deficit will not be adjusted.
- A flexible exchange rate is not a great help if the country is simply not able to produce domestically those goods it currently buys abroad; it can merely reduce the consumption of those foreign goods which are not strictly necessary. By the same token, a flexible exchange rate does not help a country to export more if its production capacity (Section 3.4) is extremely limited.
- A flexible exchange rate creates additional costs for domestic firms active in foreign trade. They have to face a risk connected with variations in the exchange rate.
- A flexible exchange rate could deter excessive lending to a country, but a depreciation of the exchange rate may make the burden of debt in foreign currency much higher.

Alternatively, the national authorities may decide that they desire the exchange rate between their currency and a foreign currency (or a basket of foreign currencies) to remain fixed. To defend the exchange rate at this rate they should be ready to buy or sell any quantity of the domestic currency at the **fixed exchange rate**. This policy has several implications.

- It facilitates trade between the countries adopting this policy. Businesses trade without having to take note of fluctuations in the exchange rate.
- It facilitates investment in a country, eliminating exchange rate risks for investors. This can also facilitate foreign investment and foreign credit. These are sometimes arranged without due consideration of the related risks. This was the case with Argentina, and with peripheral European countries (e.g. Greece, Spain and Portugal) during the first 7–8 years of the euro. They were examples of what occurs according to the so-called Frenkel cycle.[7] They were receiving considerable quantities of capital. The inflowing capital created a boom, mostly in the values of real estate. This fostered inflationary (Section 9.3) processes. These processes increased the prices of domestic goods more than those of imported goods (appreciation of the real exchange rate, see Section 10.3). Imports became cheaper and more attractive than local products. This led these countries into trade and current account deficits (Section 12.1). They therefore accumulated liabilities with the rest of the world. As a consequence, these countries became less and less able to honour their debts and went into financial crisis.
- Some countries also fix their exchange rate *vis-à-vis* the currency of another country to constrain their monetary authorities; countries with fixed exchange rates have reduced discretion over their own monetary policy. This policy

makes sense for those countries which trust foreign monetary authorities more than their own.

• When speculators challenge the fixed exchange rate, the central bank should use its reserves of foreign currency to defend the fixed exchange rate. This may even lead to the total destruction of the national reserves of foreign currency. This of course would be an undesirable outcome.

Between full flexibility and fixity there are intermediate solutions and **mixed regimes**; when the authorities of a country commit themselves to limiting the extent of the fluctuations of their currency, this is the so-called "fluctuation within a band", or do not make any commitment but let it be understood that they could discretionally intervene. Speculators are warned that something could happen to them.

THE FRENKEL CYCLE

This model was originated by the analysis of the economist, Roberto Frenkel, first relating to the process of "dollarization" of the Argentinian economy, as well as other Latin-American countries, but was then applied to the European environment after the introduction of the euro. The Frenkel model considers the evolutionary phases of a weak economic system affected by structural problems, low competitiveness, bad public finances and other imbalances, when reforms are not undertaken and the country has to compete with more stable and performing systems, all bound by a common currency and thus a unique external exchange rate. During the first stage, when the common currency is adopted, capital movements are liberalized and the more problematic country will benefit from large capital inflows as its yields will probably be higher, while the exchange risk is absent or at least limited. However, during the second phase such trends, while benefitting the economy, also fuel excessive public and private debts, as well as bubbles in the equity and property markets. If reforms and adjustments are not adopted, an external or internal factor – whether geopolitical, financial (as the 2008 crisis) or other – may determine a "turning point": foreign investments cease and leave the country, and a spiral of distrust, if not panic, sets in. That takes the situation to the next phase, when GDP stagnates or decreases, along with consumption and investment, so that the government has to cut public expenditure and raise taxes, thus further worsening the recessionary trend. Finally, the country may – or must – leave the common monetary system or the pegging parity – under the market pressure, devaluing its money or reverting to its original currency. Of course, such a choice may be voluntary, preventative and by mutual consent among the parties, but its consequences are significant in any event.[8]

Read

The Dutch Disease

When a nation's exports increase relative to its imports, the media will normally treat this as news to be celebrated. The balance of trade has "improved". But in some cases, not everyone in the nation may want to celebrate. In 1977, *The Economist* used the term 'The Dutch Disease' for a condition that at first seemed paradoxical, and since then the label has been widely used. A huge new gasfield had been found in the northern Netherlands some 18 years earlier, and its exploitation had greatly benefitted the Dutch GDP. But over the same period, Dutch businesses in many other sectors ranging from agriculture to engineering had gone into steep decline.

The same story unfolded in some developing economies where extraction of primary resources such as minerals and hydrocarbons grew rapidly while home-grown local businesses were finding it harder to survive. The linkage is to be found in currency markets, where exchange rates are determined. As exports of the extractive industries grow, the value of the local currency increases. Imports therefore become cheaper relative to locally made products, to a point where local production is undercut.

Why has this not happened in countries such as China and Germany, which consistently show a large surplus of exports over inputs? The answer lies in the composition of those exports. In the case of China, the surplus was achieved by exporting a wide portfolio, ranging from clothing and toys to high-tech intermediate components and high-tech finished goods. The industrial base producing these goods sucked in the labour released from traditional occupations in the countryside.

Export growth in Germany was mainly in the form of relatively high-tech products created across a widely distributed industrial base. To the extent that a "Dutch Disease" resulted from the export successes, the sufferers tended to be in eurozone countries other than Germany. In contrast, the exports from resource-rich African or Latin American countries, e.g. Nigeria, have been dominated by the extractive or primary industries, and the resources have usually been exported in raw form, to be processed in the countries of destination. Instead of building the broad industrial base that sustains mass employment, these countries see the narrow resource sector prosper against a background of poverty and stagnation. The employment, and the value added, accrue elsewhere.

The case of Nigeria, a country whose economy has been heavily transformed by oil, is presented in the reading.

Read

"Nigeria unravelled," Tom Burgis, *Financial Times*, 13 February 2015. www. ft.com/content/b1d519c2-b240-11e4-b380-00144feab7de.

Questions

- Why was the gas field not necessarily a blessing for the Netherlands?
- What enters the economy via the currency?
- What happens to imports?
- What happens to farming and to industry?
- What happens to the processing ability of African-resource states?
- What happened to African manufacturing?
- What about telecommunications and financial services?

Analysis

What happened in 1959 when energy companies found gas in the Netherlands is an experience common to many other countries which export raw materials in response to strong international demand. This situation takes its name from the Dutch case and is called "Dutch Disease". In the Netherlands and elsewhere, it led many people in the non-raw-material, non-energy sector to lose their jobs. This happened because the exports of gas boosted the exchange rate, i.e. the value of the national currency in terms of foreign currency. Foreign countries need the national currency to buy the natural resources possessed by the country. This also leads to increased monetary creation through the foreign channel of money creation (Section 9.3). The availability of money and the lower price of imports leads to inflation and to people buying foreign goods and abandoning production in national manufacturing and national farming. All national goods which may have a foreign substitute feel the pain: consumers find them expensive and stop buying them. Money will go towards foreign goods or towards national goods without foreign substitutes, the non-tradable goods: first and foremost, real estate, financial services, utilities and telecommunications. This will lead to real estate booms, with all the negative consequences they imply in terms of low productivity growth and speculation (see the reference to the interview with Professor Roubini, Section 8.2). When this occurs in countries which have just started to build up their own industry, this may mean the end of their industrialization process. The African ability to process raw materials has been undermined by exports of raw materials. African manufacturing represented 11 per cent of GDP in 2008, compared with 15 per cent in 1990.

    The Dutch Disease may also occur in a sudden inflow of foreign capital, for example portfolio investments (Section 11.1) in a country. This occurred in peripheral EU countries (Ireland, Portugal, Spain and Greece in particular) after the adoption of the euro. It also occurred in many emerging economies between 2008 and 2013, when the central banks of the major reserve currencies (US dollar, euro, UK pound and Yen) started expansive monetary policies, reducing the interest rates paid on assets in those currencies. International capitals were no longer able to earn yields in the markets of the most advanced economies and so they turned hurriedly to emerging economies, causing the currencies of those economies to appreciate.

10.3 The real exchange rate

In international trade, not only the exchange rate, but also prices, matter. Domestic and foreign buyers, when considering whether to buy a domestic or foreign product, take into account the price of our domestic goods and the price of our currency in terms of foreign currencies: the higher they are, the less willing they are to buy our goods. However, they also take into account the prices of foreign goods: the higher they are, the more they are willing to buy our goods. All this can be summarized by saying that, in international trade, the variable to be considered in price terms is the real exchange rate: the price of domestic goods in relation to that of foreign goods.

$$Real\ Exchange\ Rate = \frac{Domestic\ Prices \times Nominal\ Exchange\ Rate}{Foreign\ prices}$$

This implies that there is a real exchange rate even between countries using the same currency; it suffices that they have different prices. When prices in a country grow much more than those in a competing country but the nominal exchange rate remains unchanged, the former country will become less competitive than the latter.

10.4 The determinants of imports

A country can use what it produces or what it imports, i.e. what it buys abroad. Imports are part of the country's supply of goods (see Section 8.1). Imports may contribute to the welfare of the importing country and to the development of its production capacity, but when we regularly import more than we export, we accumulate liabilities; these can be in the form of debts with the rest of the world or in the form of sales to foreigners of our properties or companies. Accumulating excessive liabilities risks putting our country in a condition of weakness, subordination and dependence.

Whether we import more or less depends on several factors:

- The **limitations of our production capacity** or the absence of certain resources in our country; for example, we may not have the sophisticated skills needed to make medicines or we do not have oil reserves to produce petrol. If we do not have certain resources, finding substitutes may be long and complex.

- The **quality** of our own products (see Section 10.1); our citizens and firms will prefer foreign goods when the quality of our own goods is perceived as low.
- **Our real exchange rate** (see Section 10.3); if it is too high – i.e., our prices are comparatively too high or our currency is over-valued – we import more. When the real exchange rate is higher, importing foreign goods is cheaper.
- Our **level of economic activity**, i.e. our GDP (see Section 8.1); when we produce more, we first need more foreign inputs and then, our income is higher and we consume more. A proportion of the goods we consume is made abroad and we must import them. When our GDP is higher, we import more.

Read

When the US trade deficit declined

When Donald Trump campaigned for the US presidency, he declared that one of his priorities would be to greatly reduce the US trade deficit. The balance of exports and imports had been in deficit every year since the US government had started to publish trade statistics, in 1948, and usually it had risen from each year to the next.

The greatest fall in the deficit had happened in 2009, when a global recession followed on the heels of the financial crisis of 2008. In this recession, US imports fell by 26%. The trade deficit in goods fell from $816 billion to $501 billion, i.e. from 5.7 to 3.5% of GDP. Imports of consumer goods fell by 11% and US industry's reaction was even greater: imports of industrial goods dropped by 41%. The US GDP was falling and import was falling too.

The US economy started to pick up after 2009, the trade deficit resumed its upward trajectory and President Trump embarked on his campaign to bring the deficit down again by other means, short of a global recession.

Read

"Recession's Silver Lining: U.S. Trade Deficit is Down the Most on Record," Floyd Norris, *The New York Times*, 12 February 2010. www.nytimes.com/2010/02/13/business/economy/13charts.html.

Questions

- What was the good news about the US economy in 2009?
- What was it that fell?

- What was the cause of such improvement?
- Will the deficit continue to decline?
- Why was the improvement so sharp?
- When, historically, has there been a surge in imports?

Analysis

During the 2009 recession, one of the few items of good economic news was that the US trade deficit was diminishing, owing to a 26 per cent decline in imports. The cause of this was the heavy economic recession. The trade deficit and imports were supposed to continue to decline if the US economy was not recovering or at least recovering more slowly than the economies of the rest of the world. The reduction in the trade deficit and the decrease in US imports were so sharp that this recession, with its fall in US GDP, raised serious concerns among US consumers who accordingly reduced their spending. We should expect imports to recover if the economy recovers. In general, we can conclude that our imports fall when our GDP falls and rise when our GDP grows.

10.5 The determinants of exports

Our exports, the goods that we sell to foreign residents, are part of the demand for nationally produced goods. The more we export, the more we produce and the more we can create jobs. Exports also guarantee that we have the resources to buy the imports we need, without accumulating liabilities with the rest of the world. We can even acquire assets abroad with our exports. In some measure, this can be an insurance policy for our country; the ownership of assets abroad can guarantee the country future flows of returns on those assets; for example, in 2018, Japan had conspicuous assets abroad and this contributed to its financial solidity. However, we should also be careful about building excessive assets abroad, for our assets abroad are foreign countries' liabilities, and there is a risk that our debtors may not pay their debts and may default. Our properties abroad could create resentment and be confiscated. We have limited control over what happens beyond our borders. To consider the determinants of our exports, i.e. the goods we sell to foreign residents, we have to take into account that our exports are foreigners' imports. The determinants of our exports are therefore similar to those of our imports, with just the necessary adaptations.

Our exports depend on several factors:

- The **uniqueness of our resources** or **the scarcity of certain resources abroad**, which may make the rest of the world almost dependent on us, guaranteeing at least part of our exports. Think, for example, of the position of Saudi Arabia in the oil market. Satisfying world oil demand in the absence of Saudi Arabian exports would usually not be possible or at least would be very difficult.

- This situation can of course change over time, because the rest of the world can slowly find alternatives. The situation of Bolivian lithium[9] is similar to that of Saudi oil.
- The quality of our products, since the higher it is, the more we shall export (see Section 10.1). Foreign residents prefer our goods when their quality is perceived as high.
- Our real exchange rate (see Section 10.3), for if it is too high – i.e., our prices are comparatively too high or our currency is over-appreciated – we export less. When our real exchange rate is higher, exporting our goods is more difficult.
- On the level of economic activity, the world's GDP (see Section 8.1), or more precisely the GDP of those countries which are the main destinations of our exports, for when our foreign clients produce more, they need more of the inputs which we produce. Moreover, when their income is higher they consume more of the goods we make. When the economies of our trade partners improve, our exports also improve. For this reason, we can say that we are interdependent: we depend on each other. The success of our partner countries is linked with our own success.

Read

The following example shows that even such a huge country as India may be affected by the economy of other countries.

Euro crisis pulls down India's export growth to 35-mth low

Severe sluggishness in demand in Europe hit India's merchandise exports, which fell for the third consecutive month this financial year. Compared with $26.3 billion in the corresponding period last year, exports fell 14.8 per cent to $22.4 billion in July.

This was the steepest fall in 35 months (exports had declined 23.59 per cent in August 2009).

Imports, too, contracted for the third consecutive month, falling 7.78 per cent to $37.9bn billion, against $41.1 billion in July last year.

Crude oil imports fell 5.52 per cent to $12.22 billion, while non-oil imports declined 8.57 per cent to $25.70 billion, indicating a sluggish industrial scenario in the domestic economy.

"Contraction in this segment (imports) points to a slowdown in industrial activity, as it indicates a fall in consumption expenditure, as well as imports that are export-linked", said D. K. Joshi, chief economist, CRISIL.

As the fall in exports was more than that in imports, the trade deficit widened to $15.5 billion in July, against $11.08 billion in the corresponding month last year, prompting Moody's Analytics senior economist Glenn Levine to term it a "monster trade deficit".

For the April–July period, exports declined 5.05 per cent to $97.6 billion, compared with $102.8 billion in the corresponding period last year, while cumulative imports fell 6.47 per cent to $153.2 billion, compared with $163.8 billion in the year-ago period.

The trade deficit for the April–July period stood at $55.5 billion, against $60.9 in the year-ago period.

Last month, Commerce Secretary S. R. Rao had said the crisis in Europe was affecting India's external trade, and the current global outlook was contributing to woes.

"Euro Crisis Pulls Down India's Export Growth to 35-mth Low," *Business Standard*, New Delhi, 4 September 2012. www.business-standard.com/article/economy-policy/euro-crisis-pulls-down-india-s-export-growth-to-35-mth-low-112090400014_1.html.

Questions

- Why did India's merchandize exports fall?
- What did the Commerce Secretary say?
- If this case could be generalized, what would be the general rule?

Analysis

The problems with the European economy are felt in India. Faltering European demand implies not only that Europeans buy fewer European goods, but also that they have reduced their demand for Indian goods. This means that Indian exports to Europe are diminishing. Lower demand (and lower GDP) in Europe means a lower level of Indian exports to Europe. The Commerce Secretary S. R. Rao declared that both the crisis in Europe and the current global outlook were contributing to an undesirable situation.

The general conclusion we can draw is that, if even the exports of such a large country as India depend on the growth of GDP in other parts of the world, this is probably true for many countries.

Glossary

appreciation of currency   An increase in the exchange rate in a setting of flexible exchange rates.

depreciation of currency   A reduction in the exchange rate in a setting of flexible exchange rates.

devaluation   A reduction in the exchange rate in a setting of fixed exchange rates.

Dutch Disease   There is an increase in the value of the local currency due to a sharp inflow of foreign currency, consequence for example of the discovery of large oil reserves. The appreciation makes the country's other products less competitive in terms of price on the export market. This phenomenon also leads to bigger imports, eventually damaging the domestic manufacturing sector.

exchange rate   The quantity of foreign currency needed to buy one unit of our currency (definition used in this text), or *vice versa* the quantity of domestic currency needed to buy one unit of foreign currency.

exports   The goods that we sell to foreign countries.

fixed exchange rate   An exchange rate which does not change; the authorities of the country are committed to a specific exchange rate between the domestic currency and a basket of foreign currencies.

flexible exchange rate   A free-to-float exchange rate; the authorities of the country are not committed to a specific exchange rate and let it float.

imports   Goods bought abroad by our residents.

real appreciation   An increase in the real exchange rate.

real exchange rate   The price of domestic goods in terms of foreign goods. This is the major measure of the price competitiveness of a country.

revaluation   An increase in the exchange rate in a situation of fixed exchange rates.

Notes

1 See Mun (2013).
2 Smith (1776).
3 Ricardo (1817).
4 Ohlin (1933).
5 Baldwin and Nicoud (2014:51).
6 In common currency areas e.g. CFA, East Caribbean Dollar, euro or countries, using the US dollar, countries may import goods from countries having their same currency.
7 Frenkel and Rapetti (2009); some years later Baldwin et al. (2015) have presented very similar ideas. www.voxeu.org/ sites/default/files/file/Policy%20Insight%2085.pdf.
8 www.vsv-asg.ch/en/publications?katid=lexikon&id=493.
9 www.nytimes.com/2009/02/03/world/americas/03lithium.html?ref=world&_r=0.

Bibliography

Baldwin, R., Beck, T., Bénassy-Quéré, A., Blanchard, O., Corsetti, G., de Grauwe, P., den Haan, W., Giavazzi, F., Gros, D., Kalemli-Ozcan, S., Micossi, S., Papaioannou, E., Pesenti, P., Pissarides, C., Tabellini, G. and Weder di Mauro, B. (2015). "Rebooting the Eurozone: Step 1 – Agreeing a Crisis Narrative," Centre for Economic Policy Research, Policy Insight No. 85, November.

Baldwin, Richard E. and Robert-Nicoud, Frédéric. (2014). "Trade-in-Goods and Trade-in-Tasks: An Integrating Framework," *Journal of International Economics*, 92: 51–62.

Burgis, T. (2015). "Nigeria Unravelled," *Financial Times*, 13 February. www.ft.com/content/b1d519c2-b240-11e4-b380-00144feab7de.

Business Standard. (2012). "Euro Crisis Pulls Down India's Export Growth to 35-mth Low," *Business Standard*. New Delhi, 4 September. www.business-standard.com/article/economy-policy/euro-crisis-pulls-down-india-s-export-growth-to-35-mth-low-112090400014_1.html.

Frenkel, R. and Rapetti, M. (2009). "A Developing Country View of the Current Global Crisis: What Should not Be Forgotten and What Should Be Done," *Cambridge Journal of Economics*, 33: 685–702.

Mun, T. (2013). *The complete works: Economics and trade*. Newton Page.

Norris, F. (2010). "Recession's Silver Lining: U.S. Trade Deficit is Down the Most on Record," *New York Times*, 12 February. www.nytimes.com/2010/02/13/business/economy/13charts.html.

Ohlin, B. (1933). *International and interregional trade*. Cambridge, MA: Harvard Economic Studies.

Ricardo, D. (1817). *Ricardo, David, 1772-1823. The Principles of Political Economy & Taxation*. London: New York: J.M. Dent; E.P. Dutton, 1911.

Smith, A. (1776). *An inquiry into the nature and causes of the wealth of nations*. London, Methuen, 1922.

11

FINANCIAL MOVEMENTS

Finance has a central role in the life of people. Better to understand how it works.

The economic relations of countries with the rest of the world concern not only trade in goods (see Section 10.1), but also the movement of capital and labour. In this section we address the movement of capital. Firstly, we present the major types of financial movement, then we consider the advantages and disadvantages of foreign capital entering the country with or without the objective of controlling some business. Is it good if a country receives credits from foreign lenders? Is it good if foreigners buy local companies? Finally, we present some considerations regarding the free movement of capital.

11.1 Main types of financial movements

The most basic type of financial movement is the **trade credit** attached to an export. A firm in one country, in order to export goods to another country, extends trade credit to foreign buyers, giving them the means to make purchases. Many countries (Table 11.1) have specialized agencies or banks to foster trade credit to foreign buyers. This type of credit has the main advantage of fostering national exports, national production and national employment. Its abuse however, may lead to accumulation of non-performing loans and even defaults. For this reason, both businessmen and national authorities should be wary. Extending credit to firms and countries which already have important debts may not always be wise. It gives the impression of striking a good bargain today, but may pave the way for tomorrow's credit losses.

A similar means of extending credit to foreign countries consists of purchasing their currency. The accumulation of **reserves of foreign currencies** is on the one hand a means of stabilizing our currency and our trade, and on the other, is a form of trade credit. We accumulate reserves of a foreign currency and in this way, we

TABLE 11.1 Official export credit agencies in some countries

Australia – Export Finance and Insurance Corporation (EFIC)
Austria – Oesterreichische Kontrollbank AG (OeKB)
Belgium – Office national du Ducroire/Nationale Delcrederedienst (ONDD)
Brazil – Brazilian Developmnet Bank (BNDES)
Canada – Export Development Canada (EDC)
China – Export-Import Bank of China (Exim), China Export & Credit Insurance
  Corporation
Hong Kong – Hong Kong Export Credit Insurance Corporation
Colombia – Banco de Comercio Exterior de Colombia (Bancóldex)
Czech Republic – Export Guarantee and Insurance Corporation (EGAP), Czech Export
  Bank
Denmark – Eksport Kredit Fonden (EKF)
Estonia – Kredex Krediidikindlustus (EST)
Finland – Finnvera and its subsidiary Finnish Export Credit Ltd (FEC)
France – Compagnie Française d'Assurance pour le Commerce Extérieur (COFACE)
Germany – Euler Hermes Kreditversicherungs-AG, AuslandsGeschäftsAbsicherung
  derBundesrepublik Deutschland
Greece – Export Credit Insurance Organisation (ECIO)
Hungary – Hungarian Export Credit Insurance Ltd (MEHIB), Hungarian Export-Import
  Bank
India – Export-Import Bank of India, Export Credit Guarantee Corporation of India
  (ECG)
Iran – Export Development Bank of Iran (EDBI)
Israel – Israel Foreign Trade Risks Insurance Corporation, (ASHRA)
Italy – SACE S.p.A. Servizi Assicurativi del Commercio Estero
Japan – Japan Bank for International Cooperation, Nippon Export and Investment
  Insurance
Jordan – Jordan Loan Guarantee Cooperation (JLGC), Loan Guarantee & Export Credit
  Guarantee
South Korea – Korea Trade Insurance Corporation (K-SURE), The Export-Import Bank
  of Korea
Luxembourg – Office du Ducroire (ODD)
Mexico – Banco Nacional de Comercio Exterior (Bancomext)
The Netherlands – Atradius
New Zealand – Export Credit Office (ECO)
Norway – The Norwegian Guarantee Institute for Export Credits (GIEK)
Poland – Korporacja Ubezpieczén Kredytów Eksportowych (KUKE)
Portugal – Companhia de Seguro de Créditos
Russia – Export Insurance Agency of Russia
Slovakia – Export-Import Bank of the Slovak Republic (Eximbank SR)
Sri Lanka – Sri Lanka Export Credit Insurance Corporation (SLECIC)
Spain – Compañía Española de Seguros de Crédito a la Exportación CESCE
Sweden – Exportkreditnämnden (EKN)
Switzerland – Swiss Export Risk Insurance (SERV)
Turkey – Export Credit Bank of Turkey (Türk Eximbank)
United Kingdom – Export Credits Guarantee Department (ECGD)
United States – Export-Import Bank of the United States (Ex-Im Bank)
South Africa – Export-Import Credit Insurance Agengcy (EICIA)

usually permit the holders of the foreign currency to obtain our currency and buy our goods. The considerations on foreign trade credit apply. Accumulating foreign reserves supports our exports but exposes us to the risk of losses on foreign currency depreciation.

Sometimes foreign capital enters a country for the purchase of securities, mainly bonds and shares. **Bonds** are documents representing a tradable credit, usually in respect of a corporation or a government. They provide a fixed income every year and full repayment of their face value at their maturity date (Section 9.1), the moment of so-called "redemption". **Shares** are documents representing a tradable participation in the capital of a corporation. They have a value determined by market demand and supply. In some cases, they are traded on the stock exchange market. They do not give a fixed income but they entitle their holders to receive so-called dividends when the corporation decides to distribute part of its profits and reserves.

In the case of the purchase of foreign bonds and of limited purchases of foreign shares (less than 10 per cent of total capital) we speak of "**foreign portfolio investments**". These are investments designed to earn a yield and make a profit without controlling or managing a business, merely supplying some capital to a business or government, and making a return on it.

Foreign direct investment (FDI). When a company or institution acquires some or all of the ownership of a business in another country, and takes control of that business's operations, this will normally be labelled as "Foreign Direct Investment" (FDI). The word "control" is key, as FDI is to be contrasted with portfolio foreign investment, where a company or individual in one country acquires stakes or securities issued by companies or institutions in another country without any claim to control the activities of those organizations. The aim in making an FDI is to acquire or create assets in a foreign country in order to generate income there through the control of the operations. "Control" is not an exact concept, and for practical purposes a working convention has been accepted internationally that whoever holds at least 10 per cent of a company's voting shares can be said to control it. In practice, the ownership of much smaller blocks of voting shares may be enough to control a company when the other shares are held in even smaller blocks, and again factors other than capital, such as technology, management skills and ownership of key inputs may enable effective control to be exerted. However, the 10 per cent rule has provided a useful framework for considering the significance of cross-border investment and in tracking changes in FDI over time.

11.2 Advantages and disadvantages of foreign portfolio investments

Portfolio investments offer the advantage of providing financial resources without entailing cessation of the control of business by domestic businesses authorities, permitting them to pursue their investment projects autonomously. When portfolio foreign investments involve the purchase of the bonds issued by our government, they may provide our national government with the resources to fund such major investments as the construction of dams, roads, bridges, power stations, schools and hospitals. Sometimes they may be very cheap sources of funding for very important projects. Foreign credits are particularly cheap when international financial markets have an abundance of money. This usually occurs because the central banks of the major industrialized economies have increased their money supply (see Section 9.3), bringing interest rates down. Under such conditions international investors may find the financial markets of industrialized economies very unattractive because of the too low yields that they offer, which would not provide them with good profits. Under these conditions they often consider moving their capital to developing countries. Developing countries may therefore face intensive marketing activity by large financial corporations and financial organizations which aim at pushing developing countries to issue bonds or simply take credits. For these organizations loans to developing countries are a major source of earnings. In some cases, such organizations have the status of privileged creditors: repayments to them have priority and therefore the risk they run is very low. The best interests of the recipient country may or may not be served by taking a credit. The conflict of interest of those financial organizations which claim to care for developing countries is quite evident.

In developing countries, the possibility in bad cases of corrupt practice by certain officials in respect of important development projects constitutes the other side of the coin. Under these conditions, the debt of developing countries may increase dangerously.

Countries mainly pay their foreign debts with the inflowing foreign currency they earn with their exports. In the case of many developing countries exports are often made up of commodities (Section 7.2), raw materials, or simple manufactured products which are traded at an international price. Often these goods are traded in almost perfectly competitive markets (see Section 7.2) which developing country producers can influence only in minimal measure. The value of exports depends on the quantities exported, on the prices of the goods and on the values of the currencies. Countries often receive portfolio investments when they export large quantities of commodities at high prices. Under such conditions the interest to be paid on their debts may represent a relatively small part of the value of their exports. Later the quantities they export may fall and so may the prices of their exports. Meanwhile, interest rates may rise. The burden of debt may suddenly become very heavy because it becomes a large share of the revenue in foreign currency that a country generates with its exports. Under these conditions, countries often need to borrow again to refinance their expiring debts which, under these conditions, they are unable to repay. If international interest rates rise, refinancing operations will be more expensive. Additionally, foreign lenders will often push developing countries to make savings so as to leave cash available to pay their debts. These savings will usually affect welfare, health, education and public employment in general. Tax rises will also be requested which will possibly lead to growing unemployment, decreasing salaries, limitations on social protection, recessions and potentially political instability.

Read

The risks in borrowing in a foreign currency

If you want to keep abreast of exchange rate fluctuations, cross-border capital flows and the so-called currency wars, the website of the Bank for International Settlements (BIS) is a reliable source of current information and analysis. Its archive also contains data necessary for interpreting past episodes of boom and bust, speculative bubbles, currency crises. For example, the first decade of this millennium witnessed a boom in commodity prices, and at the same time, loose monetary policy in leading western economies flooded emerging markets with what appeared to be cheap loans. Those emerging countries which depended heavily on commodity exports saw their currencies appreciate to levels which could not have been sustained for very long. BIS Reports in the years following the boom give a picture of what happened. Thus, in late 2014, the index of emerging market currencies fell against the US dollar by some 8 per cent over a period of three months, while for the weakest currencies included in the index the fall was much greater. The Brazilian real fell by 17 per cent. In a BIS article, Avdjiev et al. (2014) noted that some emerging economies had learnt to be wary of financing their sovereign debt, and the debt of their financial institutions, with dollar-denominated loans. But many non-financial companies in emerging countries were less risk-averse, issuing foreign currency bonds at interest rates high enough to attract western asset managers who faced a shortage of good investment prospects in their own domestic markets. For a while this must have looked like a win–win situation. The corporate borrower in an emerging economy secured funds at lower rates than he could have found locally (if indeed any local funds were available); the western fund manager enjoyed returns higher than he could have found at home.

But funding conditions can change very quickly. This is particularly true when we speak about portfolio investments, i.e. those investments which are only aimed at a return, without the managerial control of the asset, e.g. a company. The US dollar started to appreciate as the Federal Reserve Board wound down its programme of quantitative easing (easy money and low interest rates). Consequently, the emerging market borrowers saw the cost of servicing their dollar-denominated debts increase. Moreover, they might also have needed to find extra collateral, i.e. guarantees, for their loans as the dollar value of existing collateral declined.

It is the familiar story of the difficulty of evaluating risk. It is usually possible nowadays to make informed estimates of exchange-rate exposure in the case of sovereign debt or of debts of the financial sector. But researchers, including those of the BIS, can find scant data from which to estimate the foreign debt exposure of non-financial companies in emerging countries. This is a major source of difficulty in judging how great the risks are to these countries' currencies.

When portfolio investments arrive, they increase the total liquidity of a country.[1] Part of such liquidity may reach the market for goods, increasing their prices and thereby creating inflation (see Section 9.3). Additionally, the flow of capital into the country will lead to appreciation of the domestic currency. These two events, inflation and appreciation of the domestic currency, will reduce the competitiveness of the country; more precisely they will increase its real exchange rate (Section 10.3). While tradable goods become less competitive and less profitable, most money is targeted on non-tradable goods (real estate, finance and utilities among others), creating further distortions. The country will find exporting more difficult, while imports will become relatively cheaper. At the very moment when the country needs foreign currency to pay its debts, it exports less and imports more.

Finally, portfolio investments can flow very rapidly into a country, but also leave very rapidly when domestic or international conditions make this desirable for investors. In this sense portfolio investments may considerably increase the instability of the financial assets and the economy of a country. For this reason, some countries have regulated the inflow of portfolio investments, for example by taxing them. In general, those countries which do not need foreign resources to fund large private or public debts are also less exposed to the drawbacks of portfolio investments.

Portfolio investments have the great advantage of bringing in foreign capital to contribute to the development of a country, for example for the purchase of much-needed foreign equipment and know-how. They have the disadvantage of being very volatile masses of money which can suddenly enter a country, fostering inflation and currency appreciation with their associated loss of competitiveness, and then equally suddenly leave the country, leaving it with falling demand, recession, deflation and depreciation of the national currency. Finally, portfolio investments can contribute to processes which lead countries to accumulate excessive debts which they may then find very hard to repay.

"The Emerging Problem of Foreign Currency Debt: The BIS Issues a Timely Warning about Exchange Mismatches," *Financial Times*, 8 December 2014. www.ft.com/content/4facbbb2-7ed1-11e4-a828-00144feabdc0.

Questions

- What are currency wars?
- What flooded the emerging world?
- Which were the consequences of such floods?
- Where is capital now heading?
- Under the new conditions, what is happening to the Brazilian real?
- What message does a strong dollar send to the developing world?
- What problems do non-financial companies present in emerging economies?
- What was the currency of three-quarters of the debt issued by emerging economies?
- Why did they choose that currency?
- What is the currency mismatch?
- What could be the effects on corporations and countries?
- Why may the problem this time be even worse than during previous crises?

Analysis

For several years, emerging economies have been flooded with large quantities of dollars. This made their currencies appreciate. This was part of the currency wars between large developed economies. These were supporting their economies by printing large quantities of their currencies, which consequently were depreciating. Part of these currency wars also consisted of reducing interest rates on assets expressed in dollars, euros, pounds and yen, in order to increase investments in the respective economies. With such low returns on western assets, western investors were looking for higher yields in emerging economies which were therefore flooded with foreign currencies. This led to the appreciation of local currencies, considerably reducing the competitiveness of emerging economies.

During the following phase with a strong dollar, capitals portfolio investments in particular are leaving emerging economies leading to a depreciation of those economies' currencies. This creates serious consequences for those non-financial companies which have issued bonds in dollars. They had chosen to borrow in dollars because interest rates in that currency were lower, but when the dollar has a greater value, they have to pay their debts in dollars using local assets which scarcely see their value increase. This is the so-called "currency mismatch". Currency mismatches occur whenever borrowers find it cheaper to contract debts in foreign currencies. This will lead many companies to spend less on salaries and investments and some firms will even go bankrupt. All this can do serious damage to developing economies.

Such a situation is complicated by the fact that data on corporate borrowing are less available than those on sovereign borrowing, therefore the precise measure of corporate problems is not well known.

Here we observe boom and bust in portfolio investments. While in moments of boom they may be fashionable and foreign investors may fight to lend their money to developing countries, capital may retreat equally rapidly when interest rates on the dollar rise. So, although portfolio investments may contribute to the growth of developing countries, this cycle may have dangerous consequences in both the inbound and outbound phases.

11.3 Advantages and disadvantages of foreign direct investment (FDI)

Foreign direct investment brings foreign capital into a country which perhaps lacks it. Its arrival is usually in a medium-to-long-term rather than short-term perspective. This is a considerable advantage *vis-à-vis* portfolio investments which sometimes arrive with a short-term perspective of the "bite and run" type. In this way, FDI can better contribute to the development of a country. Thanks to FDI, a country may see long-term business projects taking place within it, contributing to job creation.

The other large advantage of FDI appears if foreign investors bring into the country managerial or technical skills that the country lacks and increases the abilities of local workers. This is probably FDI's greatest merit. Through FDI countries can acquire the knowledge they could autonomously develop only over long periods, if ever. In some cases, FDI also creates linkages with the economy of the foreign company.

Among FDI's disadvantages, we should stress that it does not always bring the desired know-how, especially in those cases when it appears for the wrong reason – for example, when a country sells assets to foreigners just to pay its foreign debt and those foreigners do not bring any know-how into the country, either because they do not wish to or simply because they do not have any.

When can we say that an FDI increases the economic sustainability of a country? An important test consists of looking at the medium term (5–10 years) effects of the FDI on the flows of money entering and leaving the country. We can say that an economically good FDI is one that within such a time frame will bring the country more resources than will drain out of it.

Will the FDI increase the exports of the country? Sometimes foreign buyers develop new firms, (greenfield FDIs) or acquire existing firms (takeovers), which export very little. In these cases, if the foreign buyers have strong export capabilities, they can help the acquired firms, and therefore the country, to export more. If the target firms are already well-established exporters and the buyers have no experience of selling their product, the advantages are fewer.

Will the FDI increase the imports of the acquired firm? This depends on the supply chain (Section 2.2) of the firm before and after the foreign acquisition. Foreign buyers in some cases want to supply the firm with an increased quantity of foreign inputs. Sometimes this is necessary to increase the quality of products and to make the product more competitive in terms of quality (Section 10.1); in other cases, the objective is simply to bring business to foreign suppliers that foreign investors control. In other instances, the foreign buyer could even decide to increase purchases in the local market, reducing imports and helping to improve local suppliers' production. These choices of course affect the total imports of a country which may increase or decrease as a result of the decisions of the new owners.

Another important flow concerns profits. Will the foreign investor transmit profits abroad more than currently happens with the present owners? This could of course increase the flow of cash leaving the country. And certainly, other important considerations also have to be taken into account regarding the social and environmental impact of FDIs.

Read

Restrictions on FII investments in Pharma could help industry, consumers

Reports that the government is likely to impose restrictions on portfolio investments by foreign institutional investors (FIIs) in the domestic pharmaceutical sector have been welcomed as a move that will help both the domestic industry and the Indian consumer, experts have said.

The Department of Industrial Policy & Promotion (DIPP) wants any increase in foreign institutional investment in the listed pharmaceutical companies beyond the 24 per cent threshold to first get permission from the Foreign Investment Promotion Board (FIPB).

As things stand, the 24 per cent limit can be raised through a board resolution and special resolution of shareholders of the companies. India had opened its pharmaceutical sector to foreign direct investment (FDI) in 2002 but drew a distinction between greenfield (new) projects, where a 100 per cent automatic route still exists and brownfield[3] acquisitions.

Speaking to this correspondent, D.G. Shah, Secretary General, Indian Pharmaceutical Alliance (IPA), said, "It would certainly make a difference because some companies use FIIs as a vehicle for acquisition of controlling stake".

Karvy Stock Broking Research Head, Rahul Sharma, told *The Hindu* that, were it to happen, the restrictions would be a "proactive measure by the government to protect not only the interests of the domestic industry but also of consumers as India still makes arguably the cheapest medicines in the world". Fears still remain that if they acquire a significant share of the market, MNC pharma could end up dictating prices.

Indian companies still present an attractive case for acquisition. Typically, international players acquire the domestic companies for their established marketing and distribution networks or for brands and restricting brownfield acquisitions could encourage greenfield projects.

More recently, Indians buying domestic assets have increased. Sun acquiring Ranbaxy and Torrent buying Elder Pharma are examples of this. Shah felt these cases "are more straightforward as an MNC acquisition is fraught with complexity and takes much longer".

"Restrictions on FII investments in Pharma could help industry, consumers," Ramnath Subbu, *The Hindu*, 9 June 2014.[2] www.thehindu.com/business/Industry/restrictions-on-fii-investments-in-pharma-could-help-industry-consumers/article6097926.ece.

Questions

- Why have restrictions on portfolio investments by FIIs in the domestic pharmaceutical sector been welcomed?
- In 2002, what distinction did India draw when it opened its pharmaceutical market to foreign direct investment?
- According to Shah, is there any relationship between portfolio investment and FDI?
- Why, according to Sharma, could government restrictions protect Indian consumers?
- What should be the objective of acquisitions, according to Shah?

Analysis

In this article, India faces the choice of imposing new rules on portfolio investments by FIIs. The idea is one of imposing a public authorization of any purchase of shares beyond the 24 per cent limit. According to new rules, any FII wishing to own more than 24 per cent of an Indian pharmaceutical firm, should seek public permission. The 2002 regulation already makes a distinction between greenfield investments in which the foreign investor creates a firm from scratch, and brownfield investments, takeovers in which the foreign buyer acquires an existing Indian firm. The former enjoyed an unobstructed route while the latter did not. According to Shah, portfolio investments can be a way of acquiring control of existing Indian firms, i.e. carrying out takeovers. According to Sharma,, the restrictions could also protect local consumers since Indian firms produce very cheap drugs. Some foreign buyers could merely be interested in purchasing brands and retail networks in order to sell medicaments at higher prices.

According to Shah, acquisitions should be a tool for bringing technology and assets to India, not merely for benefitting some intermediate player.

In general, we can say that FDI plays a positive role if and when it attracts capital and, most of all, the knowledge that a country could otherwise hardly acquire.

11.4 The freedom of movement of capital[4]

Historically, capital has enjoyed greater or more restricted freedom of movement during different periods. The twentieth century started with great capital freedom. That lasted until World War I (1914–1918). Then a period of much lower mobility occurred until 1970.[5] In the early 1980s, capital mobility increased quite considerably and in 2018, capital could move quite easily. The period of lower capital mobility partially coincided, at least for the US, France and the UK, with a period of reduced inequality.

Capital is supposed to flow from advanced to emerging economies; the theory suggests that capital in developing countries, where there is a relative abundance of labour, should be highly productive. In advanced economies, where there is relative abundance of capital, it should be less productive. Thus, if investors are seeking the highest return, developing countries seem to present the best opportunity for their capital.[6] In reality it is often the other way around (e.g. capital flowing to the US). Capital inflows are supposed to increase the GDP growth of the specific country which receives them. However, most empirical examinations reveal no clear relationship between capital inflows and economic growth. A surge of capital inflow might even lead to economic shocks. Capital is always supposed to flow to the most efficient investment location, but a "home bias" leads to less investment in foreign countries. And even technological spillovers, that is foreign investors spreading technological innovations into destination countries are not as certain about their effects. In some cases, foreign investors tend to locate in foreign low-income countries activities with lower value added and less technological content. Capital mobility has provided advantages for some countries, for example China, which since the mid 1990s, has experienced a period of outstanding growth. However, China, the major winner in this game at least until 2018, has not authorized full capital mobility. Capital has been welcomed in China only under precise rules, and certainly not in a *laissez-faire* regime.

There are fiscal implications of capital mobility. Giving more mobility to one factor than to another has clear implications for the distribution of the tax burden. Taxes tend to be imposed on those production factors which cannot avoid them. Factors with high mobility have the option of moving away, if they do not like the tax regime they face; the minimum possible taxation is provided by tax havens, in which taxation is nil. Factors with scarce mobility do not have this option. In a context in which capital is highly mobile and labour much less so, taxes are paid by the least mobile input factor. Small businesses, with their relatively scarce mobility, share much of the features of labour in this regard. In countries such as the US – an example for many other countries – the share of total revenue paid by corporations has dramatically fallen between the 1950s and today, from about 30 per cent to 11 per cent of total revenue. Governments are faced with the choice between cutting public spending and public services or taxing more those who cannot easily move elsewhere. To avoid these problems, the French economist, Thomas Piketty, has suggested a global wealth tax, but there is absolutely no consensus on its introduction. Under these conditions the room for tax avoidance is large.

Capital mobility implies that capital can move between different jurisdictions with different regulations. In some jurisdictions certain financial operations are allowed but other operations are not. Holders of financial capital can selectively move it according to the type of operation that they want to undertake. This is the so-called "regulatory arbitrage"; it makes certain capital *de facto* unregulated and seriously increases risks in the financial markets. Even if such international authorities as the International Monetary Fund (IMF) and the BIS try to promote regulatory harmonization, the regulatory differences between the different financial markets remain large. In this context the risk of new financial crises can be considerable.

Globalization

One of the hottest topics in national and international debates concerns globalization. However, the definition of the word is not always made clear and the word is not given the same meaning by everyone. Moreover, the views on this topic range from extremely favourable to extremely negative. Globalization is "the movement of money, goods, people, ideas, technologies, and cultures across frontiers".[7]

> Economic 'globalization' is a historical process, the result of human innovation and technological progress. It refers to the increasing integration of economies around the world, particularly through trade and financial flows. The term sometimes also refers to the movement of people (labor) and knowledge (technology) across international borders. There are also broader cultural, political and environmental dimensions of globalization that are not covered here.[8]

According to some authors, it is a relatively recent phenomenon taking place in the last fifty years. "The term globalization – in its modern meaning – was coined in the 1970s to describe the internationalization of markets, especially financial ones, after the oil price increases of the decade, but it reflects a much older reality. The recent period of globalization that seemed ascendant, at least until the global financial crisis, is but one of many such periods – and reversals – that dot human history" (James, 2016). However, this phenomenon could be considered as old as ancient Rome or even older. Probably old phenomena have hugely increased their intensity in recent times. When the quantity of a phenomenon changes so much, even its quality seems affected. The present movements of goods, people, technologies and cultures look more extended and pervasive than those of the past.

Theories in favour, argue that a free movement of goods, capitals, people, technologies and ideas should lead to a more efficient use of resources, cheaper and better goods for consumers and faster growth of developing countries in particular. Resources and goods go where they are more appreciated and where they can create greater value. The achievement of economies of scale in a larger market becomes easier. Globalization

> augurs the advent of multinational enterprises (MNEs) who bring modern up-to-date technology in less developed countries. Not only MNCs[9] bring with them modern technology but also it brings investment funds, organisational structure, managerial culture, distribution network, etc. All these create income and employment in the country.[10]

However, globalization creates an asymmetry between a single global market and multiple national institutions. There is a market with global players and local jurisdictions which are not able to fix the rules of the game. The players fix their own rules. This may lead to results which are short of efficiency and equity.

According to Potrafke (2015), "globalisation has spurred economic growth, promoted gender equality and improved human rights. Moreover, globalisation did not erode welfare state activities, did not have any significant effect on labour market interaction and hardly influenced market deregulation".

"Globalisation has a significant influence on institutional quality, and (...) institutional reforms in turn facilitate and support financial development, in particular the development of the banking sector in East Asia."[11]

According to Dani Rodrik,[12] in the industrialized democracies there was a social bargain based on a generous welfare state alongside economic openness. He claims that deal has come to an end. Citizens do not trust their governments and these are less able to manage their economies. The repetition in other countries of Asia's economic miracles – most notably China's – looks difficult. People argue and quarrel about trade, immigration and capital movements. According to Rodrik:

> If progressive tax policies to reduce inequality are impeded by the mobility of corporations around the world, it should be the latter that gives way, not the former. If countercyclical fiscal and monetary policies are precluded by short-term capital flows, it is finance that should be regulated. . . . We should not fret too much about a reversal in globalisation.

Rodrik states that there is an opportunity to fix the asymmetry between global markets and national powers. This fix may hamper hyper-globalization, but if it is done with the aim of creating more inclusive societies, liberal democracies and economic growth, its achievement should not be incompatible with developing and maintaining an open world economy.

Glossary

capital mobility   The ability of private funds to move across national boundaries in pursuit of higher returns. This mobility depends on the absence of currency restrictions on the inflows and outflows of capital.[13]

export credit agency An organization that provides trade financing to national companies for their activities abroad.

financial regulation The laws and guidelines that govern what financial institutions such as banks, brokers and investment companies are allowed to do.

foreign direct investment Investment by one country in another (usually by companies rather than governments) that implies establishing operations or purchasing tangible assets, including stakes in other businesses. FDI is the purchase or establishment of revenue-generating assets abroad that involves control of the operation or business.

foreign portfolio investments It usually concerns bonds or shares. Foreign portfolio investment (FPI) does not provide the investor with direct control of a business, and thus no direct management of a company. This type of investment is relatively liquid, depending on the volatility of the market in which the investment is made. It is investors who do not want to manage a firm abroad who most commonly use it.

foreign reserves Reserves of foreign currencies, usually held by the central bank of a country to stabilize the national currency and foster exports and inbound investments.

non-tradable goods and services Goods and services which usually cannot be sold to foreign residents, including real estate, public services and personal services such as housekeeping, carers and barbers.

regulatory arbitrage A practice whereby firms take advantage from differences in the regulatory systems of different countries, typically by finding loopholes in these systems. The firms then adapt their intra-company transfers so that, for example, tax payments will be made in the country with the lightest taxation regime.

tax avoidance The behaviour consisting in using legal means to pay the least possible amount of tax. There is a semantic difference between "evasion" and "avoidance". Tax evasion is the practice of using illegal methods to escape paying tax.

tradable goods and services Goods and services which can be sold to foreign residents, for example the products of manufacturing, agriculture, fisheries, mining and the hotel industry.

trade credit Credit extended to clients to permit them to buy the goods provided by the creditor.

Notes

1 They activate the foreign channel (see p. 96) of money creation, see Section 9.3.
2 Copyright of this article belongs to THG PUBLISHING PRIVATE LIMITED/*The Hindu* and according to their Terms of Use THG PUBLISHING PRIVATE LIMITED grants you a limited licence to access and make personal use of this site but not for commercial purposes. We permit the use of materials on this website subject to due credit is given to THG PUBLISHING PRIVATE LIMITED. The use shall also be subject to

non-commercial use and limited to personal or academic dissemination. (including on social media and use on all kinds of media). www.thehindu.com/termsofuse/.

3 The purchase of an existing company. The alternative is the greenfield investment, where the investor starts the business from scratch.

4 Here we refer to a presentation made by some students of the Paris School of Economics: The Pros and Cons of Capital Controls, (2012) Haberer, Leang, Seap, Lux, Nowak.

5 Taylor, Alan M., 1996, International capital mobility in history: the saving investment relationship, Working Paper 5743, NBER, Cambridge, MA, September 1996.

6 Robert Lucas (1990), the Nobel Laureate estimated that the marginal return on capital was 58 times higher in India than in the US in a paper titled "Why doesn't capital flow from rich to poor countries?".

7 James (2016).

8 IMF (2000).

9 MNCs means Multi National Companies.

10 Deepali Pal, www.economicsdiscussion.net/globalization/globalisation-meaning-arguments-for-and-against/14211 retrieved on 1 August 2018.

11 Law et al. (2015).

12 Rodrik (2016).

13 www.businessdictionary.com/definition/mobility-of-capital.html#ixzz3ZMZAhav4.

Bibliography

Avdjiev, S., Chui, M. and Shin, H.S. (2014). "Non-Financial Corporations from Emerging Market Economies and Capital Flows," *BIS Quarterly Review*, 7 December.

Financial Times. (2014). "The Emerging Problem of Foreign Currency Debt: The BIS Issues a Timely Warning About Exchange Mismatches," *Financial Times*, 8 December. www.ft.com/content/4facbbb2-7ed1-11e4-a828-00144feabdc0.

Haberer, Leang Seap and Lux, Nowak. (2012). "The Pros and Cons of Capital Controls," Paris School of Economics presentation. www.parisschoolofeconomics.com/benassy-quere-agnes/Enseignement/Poleco2013-presentation7.pdf.

IMF. (2000). "Globalization: Threat or Opportunity?" www.imf.org/external/np/exr/ib/2000/041200to.htm.

James, H. (2016). "New Concept, Old Reality," *Finance & Development*, 53(4) (December).

Law, S. H., Tan, H. B. and Azman Saini, W. N. (2015). "Globalisation, Institutional Reforms and Financial Development in East Asian Economies," *World Economics*, 38: 379–398. doi:10.1111/twec.12168.

Lucas, R. E. Jr. (1990). "Why Doesn't Capital Flow from Rich to Poor Countries?" *American Economic Review*, 80(2) (May): 92–96.

Pal, Deepali. "Globalisation: Meaning, Arguments for and Against," www.economicsdiscussion.net/globalization/globalisation-meaning-arguments-for-and-against/14211, retrieved on 1 August 2018.

Potrafke, N. (2015). "The Evidence on Globalisation," *World Economics*, 38: 509–552. doi:10.1111/twec.12174.

Rodrik, D. (2016). "There Is No Need to Fret About Deglobalisation," *Financial Times*, 4 October. www.ft.com/content/d9a28a08-895c-11e6-8cb7-e7ada1d123b1.

Subbu, R. (2014). "Restrictions on FII Investments in Pharma Could Help Industry, Consumers," *The Hindu*, 9 June. www.thehindu.com/business/Industry/restrictions-on-fii-investments-in-pharma-could-help-industry-consumers/article6097926.ece.

Taylor, A. M. (1996). "International Capital Mobility in History: The Saving-Investment Relationship," NBER Working Paper No. 5743.

12

INTERNATIONAL ACCOUNTS

How are our economic relations with the rest of the world? Can we afford our present standard of life? Are we accumulating debts? Should we sell our country to foreigners?

Two major statements inform us about the economic and financial relations of a country with the rest of the world. They also describe the major foreign economic constraints that a country faces. Any social negotiation should take such constraints into account. For this reason, the ability to read such accounts is really important. They are the International Investment Position (IIP) and the Balance of Payments. "The balance of payments is a statement that summarizes the economic transactions between residents and non-residents during a specific time period."[1] In terms of national accounts somebody is resident in a country, if they spend more than six months per year in that country. Residence does not depend on passports or work permits, but simply on actual presence in a country.

The Balance of Payments is divided into three accounts:

1 The Current Account (very important).
2 The Capital Account (usually of smaller size and lesser importance).
3 The Financial Account (very important).

Firstly, we analyse each account and then we consider the International Investment Position of a country.

12.1 The current account of the balance of payments

The current account of the Balance of Payments presents the values of all the current operations between a country and the rest of the world. It includes purchases and sales of goods and services, remuneration to capital and labour (input factors, see Section 3.1) received from and given to other countries and the donations received from and given to other countries. Below we consider its major components, with their sign in the current account in brackets.

Exports of goods (+)

The value of exported goods, see Section 10.5.

Imports of goods (−).

The value of imported of goods, see Section 10.4.

Exports of services (+)

The value of services (e.g. transport, tourism, construction, insurance, financial services, ICT services, etc, see Section 10.5), which domestic firms have provided to foreign residents.

Imports of services (−).

The value of services (e.g. transport, tourism, construction, insurance, financial services, ICT services, etc, see Section 10.5), which foreign firms have provided to domestic residents.

Labour incomes from abroad (+)

The value of what our residents have earned abroad through their work (with a positive sign). This applies to people staying predominantly in the country, but working for less than six months per year abroad, for example, seasonal workers.

Labour incomes going abroad (−)

The value of what foreign residents have earned in this country with their work (with a negative sign). This applies to people predominantly resident outside this country, and working here for less than six months.

Capital (or investment) income from abroad (+)

The value of what domestic residents have earned abroad with their capital. Domestic residents may have different assets abroad, e.g. bank deposits, bonds, shares, investments in companies and properties. These assets may generate income, e.g. interests, dividends, profits and rents.

Capital (or investment) income going abroad (−)

The value of what foreign residents have earned in this country with their capital. Foreign residents may have various assets in the home country, e.g. bank deposits, bonds, shares, investments in companies and properties. These assets may generate incomes, e.g. interest, dividends, profits and rents. These incomes are generated in the home country but belong to foreign residents.

Labour and capital income are also known as **primary income**.

Private transfers from abroad (+)

The value of transfers that foreign residents make to residents in the home country. This item includes remittances that a country receives from its citizens permanently living abroad. In countries with many migrants (e.g. Moldova, Peru or the Philippines) this is a precious source of finance.

Private transfers abroad (-)

This is the value of the transfers that home country residents make to foreign residents. This item includes money that migrant workers permanently living in the home country transfer to their country of origin, the so-called remittances (Figure 12.1 and Figure 12.2).

Public transfers from abroad (+)

The value of donations or contributions that the home country receives from other countries or from international organizations, for example, the UN. This item is important for countries which receive significant sums as foreign public assistance from donors.

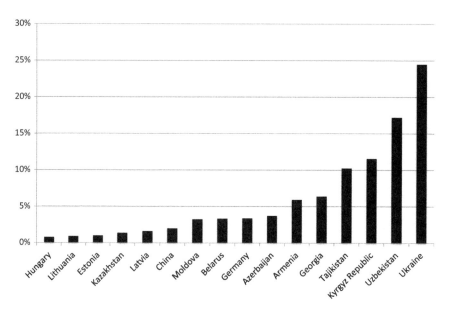

FIGURE 12.1 Main destinations of remittances (private transfers abroad) from Russia in 2017

Elaboration of the author of the World Bank and IMF data[2]

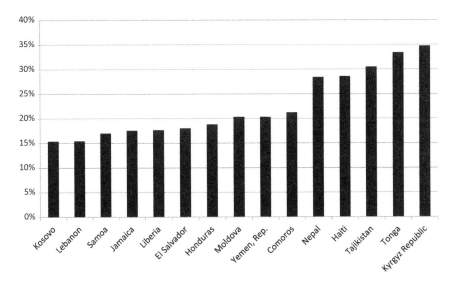

FIGURE 12.2 Remittances as a share of GDP in some countries

Source: Data elaboration by the author on IMF and WB data.[3]

Public transfers abroad (−)

The value of donations or contributions from the home country to other countries or to international organizations such as the UN, for example, the ILO.

Private and public transfers are also known as **secondary incomes**.

The current account balance

The sum of all the foregoing items gives the current account balance (Table 12.1).

When this balance is positive, there is a surplus; it shows that the international economic transactions of a country are making it richer, increasing its assets abroad or reducing the assets that non-residents have in the country. A country with a positive current account balance is accumulating foreign currencies, gold, credits with foreigners or it is diminishing its debt with them; it is acquiring foreign bonds, shares, firms, or properties; or else foreigners are reducing their holdings of such assets in this country. It is becoming richer.

If a country has a current account surplus, it is producing more than its private and public sectors consume and invest.

The current account balance may be referred in absolute terms or as a percentage of GDP.

Every policy should take into account its effects on the current account balance. If a policy generates benefits (GDP and employment growth) for a country,

TABLE 12.1 The current account

+ Exports of goods	
− Imports of goods	**Goods and services**
+ Exports of services	
− Imports of services	
+ Labour incomes from abroad	
− Labour incomes going abroad	**Primary incomes**
+ Capital (or investment) income from abroad	
− Capital (or investment) income going abroad	
+ Private transfers from abroad	
− Private transfers abroad	**Secondary incomes**
+ Public transfers from abroad	
− Public transfers abroad	
= The current account balance	

but entails consistent current account deficits, it should be considered with special care. The current benefits of that policy risk creating serious liabilities for the country.

A small economy can continue to accumulate surpluses over a long period, provided its significance in the world economy is modest. A large economy cannot do so, and needs to avoid being in permanent current account surplus, since its surpluses will always be matched by deficits in other countries (we do not trade with other planets!). If other countries keep accumulating liabilities, this will inevitably generate problems in the international economy, large imbalances being destabilizing.

Read

How were the external economic relations of Georgia in 2014?

Growth and foreign accounts in Georgia according to the Asian Development Outlook 2015

According to the Asian Development Outlook 2015 "GDP expanded by an estimated 4.7% in 2014, up from 3.3% in 2013". The same report explains that "On the demand side, growth came from a 5.5% expansion in consumption and, in particular, a 21.2% rise in investment, mainly in the private sector. However, a major slowdown began in the fourth quarter and continued into 2015 as the drop in oil prices and the impact of economic sanctions on the Russian Federation triggered recession there and much slower growth in other key trading partners. As a consequence, their imports from and remittances to Georgia plunged."

The same document describes the foreign accounts of Georgia. "The current account deficit widened to an estimated 9.5% of GDP from 5.7% in 2013. Higher growth fuelled a 7.1% rise in imports, while exports declined by 1.6%, reflecting a 3.5% drop in the fourth quarter that erased increases in the two previous quarters. Steep currency depreciation in its main trading partners eroded Georgia's competitiveness despite lari depreciation against the US dollar. In addition, Azerbaijan's adoption of Euro 4 automobile standards in April 2014 cut Georgia's exports of second hand vehicles. The fourth quarter drop in exports – followed by the 30.0% decline year on year recorded in January 2015 – also reflected weakening in the economy of the Russian Federation, which by 2014 had become Georgia's third-largest export destination, taking nearly 10.0% of all exports. Tourism receipts declined, and remittances fell by 2.5%, with a notable drop of 16.3% in the fourth quarter and an even heftier decline of 22.5% in January and February 2015 compared with the same period a year earlier. Higher remittance in flows from southern Europe did not offset the drop from the Russian Federation, where remittances to Georgia plunged by 30.1% in the fourth quarter. Despite a slow recovery in Europe, foreign direct investment performed well, exceeding $1.2 billion by official estimates. Gross international reserves amounted at the end of 2014 to $2.7 billion, down only slightly from $2.8 billion in 2013 and equivalent to 3 months of imports. External debt totalled an estimated 64.0% of GDP, excluding intercompany loans equivalent to about 20% of GDP. In July 2014, Georgia entered into a 3-year standby arrangement with the International Monetary Fund that provides a $155 million cushion against external shocks and sets a framework to discipline macro-fiscal policies."

Asian Development Outlook, 2015; Asian Development Bank (2015)

Questions

- Are you surprised that when the Georgian economy's growth increases its current account deficit worsens?
- What is a probable explanation for the decrease in Georgian exports in 2014?
- Which figures depict an unfavourable picture?
- Why should Georgia have an agreement with the IMF on possible borrowing from the fund?
- How can a country improve its current account position?

Analysis

The simple fact that Georgia's growth is increasing may explain why its current account deficit is growing. When a country's growth increases, its imports also usually grow (see Section 10.4). Imports enter in the current account with a negative sign. The greater they are, the more negative is the account. However, we also read that Georgia's major trading partners have depressed economies. This can explain why Georgian exports have fallen. The same happened with remittances to Georgia, with a fall of 23.3 per cent in January 2015 alone. Georgian migrants working abroad probably earn less and send less money to their families in Georgia. Remittances are private transfers from abroad, a positive item in the current account. When they decrease, the current account balance becomes less positive or more negative. These are the reasons why a fall in exports and remittances depicts an unfavourable picture.

If the country does not make debts or sell assets to foreigners, with a current account deficit its currency will depreciate. Not surprisingly, in July 2014 Georgia agreed with the IMF that it could potentially borrow up to $155m from the fund to defend its currency from excessive depreciation. A country with a current account deficit either sells part of its assets to foreigners or builds up debt. In this case the debt would be with the IMF.

12.2 The capital account of the balance of payments

The capital account shows credit and debit entries for non-produced, non-financial assets (for example, land) and capital transfers between residents and non-residents. Why non-produced assets? Because transactions in produced assets are recorded in the current account. Why non- financial assets? Because transactions in financial assets are recorded in the financial account.

The capital account is usually of smaller size than the current account. It includes transactions in respect of:

- Natural resources.
- Contracts, leases and licences.
- Marketing assets.
- Capital transfers.

Natural resources include land, mineral rights, forestry rights, water, fishing rights, air space and the electromagnetic spectrum. International transactions in land and other natural resources usually do not arise since local companies are generally identified as the owners of these immovable assets. If a multinational company seeks to acquire mineral rights in a country, accounting standards lay down that it creates a company in that country. The local company would buy the mining rights and the multinational company would own the local company but not the mining rights.

Capital transfers are transfers which entail the ownership of an asset (other than cash or inventories) transferring from one party to another; they can also oblige one or both parties to acquire or dispose of an asset (other than cash or inventories); or they can entail a creditor forgiving a liability. For some heavily indebted countries, debt forgiveness becomes a major issue at certain times. It is in this account that we find records of debt forgiveness, whenever it occurs.

Capital transfers include the case of a migrant who is a foreign resident and owner of a property in the country of origin. If the migrant retires and decides to go back to live in their native country, they become a local resident again. The capital account will record that the property of a foreign resident is transferred to a local resident. In reality the owner does not change, only their residence changes.

12.3 The financial account of the balance of payments

The financial account records transactions that involve financial assets (e.g. cash, credits, bonds, shares, firms and properties) and liabilities; these transactions take place between residents and non-residents. Its value should be equal to the value of the sum of the current and capital accounts. Therefore, if one ignores the usually modest value of the capital account, one can say that every time a country has a current account deficit, the financial account records the growth of the liabilities of the country or the transfer of national assets to foreigners. The financial account gives us precise information on the nature of those assets. Alternatively, a transaction may involve two financial account entries: a new asset offset by a new liability. Sometimes, the financial account transaction involves the exchange of one asset for another; for example, a bond may be exchanged for currency and deposits. A specific example would be a country which formerly had many foreign bonds and now, after selling them, has greater reserves of foreign currency. In other cases, the transaction may involve the creation of a new financial asset and a corresponding liability. A country sells a bond and increases its currency reserves.

The major items of this account are:

- Direct investment.
- Portfolio investment.
- Financial derivatives and employee stock options.
- Other investments.
- Reserve assets.

In Chapter 11 we described most of these assets.

Financial derivatives are financial assets which derive their value from the performance of different assets such as credits, stocks, bonds, commodities, currencies and interest rates. The 2007–2008 financial crisis was at least partially originated in housing-related securities. Their value depended on the payment of mortgages by some groups of house buyers. When many debtors were no longer able to pay their debts, the securities related to those mortgages lost most of their value.

AN EXAMPLE OF BALANCE OF PAYMENTS

In 2013, the trade balance (goods) of Japan (Table 12.2) was negative (−87,734), the country importing more than it was exporting. Also, the balance of services was negative (−34,786).

We can observe that Japanese residents, as owners of substantial capital abroad, receive considerable sums as primary income (+171,729 in interest and dividends). Japanese private individuals and authorities donated to the rest of the world more than the rest of the world donated to Japan. This is indicated by the figure of "secondary income" (−9,892).

TABLE 12.2 The balance of payments of Japan in 2013 (100m yen)

Current account balance	**39,317**
Goods and services	−122,521
Goods	−87,734
Exports	678,290
Imports	766,024
Services	−34,786
Primary income	171,729
Secondary income	−9,892
Capital account balance	**−7,436**
Financial account	**−9,336**
Direct investment	137,210
Portfolio investment	−265,652
Financial derivatives (other than reserves)	55,516
Other investment	25,085
Reserve assets	38,504
Net errors and omissions	**−41,217**

Source: Bank of Japan

The sum of goods and services (−122,521), primary income (+171,729) and secondary income (+9,892) gives a positive current account balance (+39,317). This implies an improvement in the Net International Investment Position of the country.

Japan attracted direct investment (+137,310); foreign residents purchased financial derivatives worth 55,516, received other investment to a total of 25,085 and received money for people acquiring Japanese money as foreign assets (38,504); all this was more than compensated for by the portfolio investments of Japanese residents. They mostly purchased foreign bonds abroad (265,652). Errors and omissions are of considerable magnitude (−41,217).

Employee stock options are rights which some companies give their employees. These rights concern the possibility of acquiring their company's shares at a stated price, if the employees so desire. Often the receivers are managers. Some corporations pay their managers with both a salary and stock options. This is done with the aim of encouraging managers to have a concern for the value of the firm's shares. In reality stock options are open to abuse, for example when managers increase the value of the shares of the company without adding new value or making new profit. If they buy the shares of their company, they can increase the value of the shares of their company.

Reserve assets are made up of gold and foreign currencies.

The financial account basically matches the value of the current account (totalled with the smaller capital account). When we hear that a country attracts many foreign investments, something recorded in the financial account, we should not celebrate uncritically. We should also note that this country probably runs a current account deficit. If the current account deficit is caused by the purchase of equipment and technology which will improve the country's productivity, it could be a good thing. If the deficit is merely due to the inability of the country to produce what it consumes, the situation can be much more critical. The country is selling national assets to pay for its current consumption.

> When all actual balance of payments entries are totalled, the resulting balance will almost inevitably show a net credit or a net debit. That balance is the result of errors and omissions in compilation of statements. . . . In balance of payments, the standard practice is to show separately an item for net errors and omissions. Labelled by some compilers as a balancing item or statistical discrepancy, that item is intended as an offset to the overstatement or under-statement of the recorded components.[4]

12.4 The international investment position (IIP)

Does the value of a country's assets abroad exceed the value of the assets that foreigners own within the country? In considering its relations with the rest of the world, has the country more assets or more liabilities? Will a country receive financial and property earnings from the rest of the world or will the opposite apply? When considering a country and its financial soundness, will foreigners be happy to lend to it? All these questions find an answer in the IIP of a country.

The IIP is

> a statistical statement that shows at a point in time the value of financial assets of residents of an economy that are claims on non residents or are gold bullion held as reserve assets; and the liabilities of residents of an economy to non residents. The difference between the assets and liabilities is the net position in the IIP [N.IIP] and represents either a net claim on or a net liability to the rest of the world.[5]

If the financial account of the balance of payments describes the assets and the liabilities that a country has accumulated during one year, the IIP describes the total stock of foreign assets and foreign liabilities of a country. When local residents own assets abroad, it is a plus; when foreigners own something in the country, it is a minus.

When a country pays off its foreign debt by selling properties to foreigners, there is no improvement. If properties are generating higher returns than the interest the country is paying to foreigners, the financial situation of the country will worsen, in the sense that the country will send abroad larger quantities of money, becoming poorer than before.

The IIP (Figure 12.3) is not the only variable which explains the willingness of foreign investors to lend to a country, but it is probably the one that explains it most. The reason is as follows: a very positive IIP implies that a country in the years to come will receive positive net capital income from abroad (see Section 12.1), that is to say it will receive rents on properties, profits of firms, dividends, interest on credits and bonds, and other capital income. A country with such positive flows will probably have the financial means to pay its debts. Not only that, all these assets abroad represent a kind of collateral; foreign investors understand that if anything goes wrong with their credit, they will be probably be able to ask a foreign court to block such assets and make them available for payment of the debt.

The other variables which affect the perceived ability of a country to pay its debts are its present and future current account balance (see Section 12.1), its debt/ GDP ratio, its history of recent compliance with obligations, its military importance and the fact that its currency is widely used as a reserve currency. Thus, for example, the US, even if it has a negative IIP and current account balance, may borrow at low

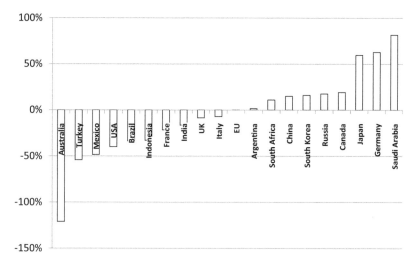

FIGURE 12.3   The net international investment position as a share of GDP of the members of G20 in 2017

Elaboration of the author on IMF data.[6]

interest rates, thanks to the safety that they can guarantee for any money deposited in their banks and to the fact that their currency, the dollar, is widely accepted as international currency.[7]

An international currency is one used outside its home country.[8] Some firms or some authorities of one country may negotiate their transactions with the currency of a different country, using it as means of exchange; they may undertake their accounting with a currency of a foreign country as the unit of account of certain operations; governments and businesses may hold a foreign currency in reserve for "rainy days", storing value for the future. They do this to be able to pay for purchases from foreign partners or to stabilize the value of their own currency, as needed. To emphasize this last use of international currencies, we call them "reserve currencies". The major reserve currency is the US dollar, but the European euro, the British pound, the Japanese yen, the Swiss franc, the Canadian dollar, the Australian dollar and, more recently,[9] the Chinese yuan are also international and reserve currencies.[10]

If India buys goods from China, it may pay China in US dollars rather than in Indian rupees. A currency is useful for settling international transactions when it is issued by a large trading nation (it is a convenient medium of exchange) and when it holds its value *vis-à-vis* other commodities over time (i.e. it is a store of value).

Read

Turkey net international investment position

An analysis of the statement of the Central Bank of the Republic of Turkey of June 2018

According to Central Bank of the Republic of Turkey, Turkey's external assets were $224.7 billion as of June 2018. They have decreased by 3.5 per cent from the end of 2017.

The liabilities of Turkey against non-residents fell to $628.1 billion, diminishing by 9.2 per cent in the same period, according to the Turkish central bank.

The gap between Turkey's assets abroad and liabilities, the net international investment position (N.IIP) of Turkey was minus $403.4 billion in June 2018. It was minus $459.3 billion at the end of last year. The Turkish N.IIP has improved.

The N.IIP shows a snapshot in time and can be either positive or negative. It is the value of the foreign assets owned by a nation, minus the value of local assets owned by foreigners. The N.IIP includes foreign assets and liabilities held by a nation's government, the private sector, and its citizens.

Assets include reserve assets, these were $98.4 billion at the end of June 2018, 8.7 per cent less than at the end of 2017. Other investments, another component of assets, were $75.2 billion, having diminished by 1.6 per cent in the same period.

"Portfolio investment decreased by 12.4 percent and recorded USD 155.6 billion compared to the end of 2017. (. . .). Non-residents' holdings of GDDS (Government Domestic Debt Securities) recorded USD 22.4 billion with a decrease of 27.6 percent. Outstanding eurobond holdings of nonresidents posted USD 46.4 billion with an increase of 4.6 percent." The website of the Turkish Central Bank reports.

Also, currency and bank deposits, one of the sub-items of other investments, a component of assets, diminished by 5.5 per cent to $33 billion when compared with the end of 2017. Turkish entities had in June less foreign currency than before.

On the side of liabilities, direct investment – ownership of business in Turkey by foreigners – at the end of June 2018 was $144.8 billion. They have diminished by 23.5 percent from the end of 2017. According to the Central Bank of the Republic of Turkey, this result was also affected by the low values of Turkish shares and by the depreciation of the Turkish lira. Both factors have contributed to diminish the value in dollars of the holdings of foreigners and therefore of Turkish liabilities.

The bank has added that "Total external loan stock of the banks recorded $93.8 billion, decreasing by 1 per cent compared to the end of 2017" indicating that in the period Turkish banks have borrowed less.

"The total external loan stock of the other sectors recorded $110.2 billion, increasing by 1.9 percent", according to the Central Bank of the Republic of Turkey.

The N.IIP was minus $403.4 billion in June 2018. It was minus $439.5 in the June 2017. In June 2018, the N.IIP of Turkey was approximately equivalent to 47% of Turkish GDP.

> Statement of the Central Bank of the Republic of Turkey
> www.tcmb.gov.tr/wps/wcm/connect/en/tcmb+en/
> main+menu/statistics/balance+of+payments+and+
> related+statistics/international+investment+position

Questions

- Why are Turkey's liabilities down in June 2018?
- What happened to the direct investments of foreigners in Turkey?
- What about the portfolio investments of foreigners in Turkey?

- Which document shows this?
- What is the NIIP according to this text?
- Are you surprised that portfolio investments and non-residents' equity holdings went down? Is this consistent with the story that the Turkish NIIP has improved?
- What about banks' external loans decrease?

Analysis

In June 2018, the decrease in Turkish net liabilities is the effect of several factors, as can be seen in the Turkish Net International Investment Position (N.IIP). The N.IIP is the gap between Turkey's assets abroad and liabilities or the value of overseas assets owned by a nation, minus the value of domestic assets owned by foreigners, including overseas assets and liabilities held by a nation's government, the private sector and its citizens. The fact that portfolio investments and non-residents' equity holdings went down is perfectly consistent with the general story: In the first part of 2018, Turkey suffered a financial crisis, the shares in its stock market lost value and also the Turkish lira depreciated. This made assets denominated in Turkish liras less attractive. Foreigners therefore have reduced their holdings of Turkish bonds and Turkish residents have purchased bonds denominated in euro.

Foreigners became less interested in holding Turkish assets and their shares in Turkish companies lost value. In this way, Turkey had fewer net liabilities.

Glossary

balance of payments   A statement that summarizes the economic transactions between residents and non-residents during a specific time period. It is the sum of the current account, the capital account and the financial account.

capital account   This shows credit and debit entries for non-produced (e.g. land) non-financial assets and capital transfers between residents and non-residents. Usually it is a smaller account.

capital income from abroad   Interest, rents, dividends and other capital incomes that individuals and firms resident in this country have earned abroad.

capital income going abroad, interest, rents   Dividends and other capital incomes that foreign residents have earned in the country.

current account   This presents the values of all the current operations between a country and the rest of the world. It includes the purchases and sales of merchandize and services, remunerations for input factors (capital and labour, Section 3.1) received from and made to other countries, and donations received from and made to other countries.

financial account   This shows net acquisition and disposal of financial assets and liabilities.

IIP   see *international investment position.*

international currency   A currency used outside its home country. Two countries can buy from and sell to each other using the currency of a third country which is not involved in that transaction. A country can do its bookkeeping in a foreign currency or it can keep reserves in a currency which is not its currency. Those currencies, which are widely used for this last purpose, are also called "reserve currencies".

international investment position (IIP)   The value of overseas assets owned by a nation, and the value of domestic assets owned by foreigners, including overseas assets and liabilities held by a nation's government, the private sector and its citizens.

labour income from abroad   Salaries that individuals resident in a country have earned abroad.

labour income going abroad   Salaries that foreign residents have earned in the country.

net capital incomes   The difference between capital incomes from abroad and capital incomes going abroad.

net errors and omissions   When all actual balance of payments entries are totalled, the resulting balance will almost inevitably show a net credit or a net debit. That balance is the result of errors and omissions in the compilation of statements. In the balance of payments, the standard practice is to show separately an item for net errors and omissions. Labelled by some compilers as a balancing item or statistical discrepancy, that item is intended as an offset of the overstatement or understatement of the recorded components.[11]

net international investment position (N.IIP)   The algebraic sum of the assets and the liabilities of the IIP.

net labour incomes   The difference between labour incomes from abroad and labour incomes going abroad.

N.IIP   See *net international investment position*.

primary incomes   Capital and labour incomes.

reserve assets   Gold and foreign currencies that a country holds to meet currency needs and guarantee its ability to pay its obligations. Reserve assets are particularly needed when imports exceed exports and the country cannot borrow to pay its imports.

reserve currency   See international currency.

resident individual   An individual spending more than six months per year in a country.

secondary incomes   Public and private transfers overseas and from overseas.

transfers from abroad   Public or private donations to the government or residents of the country.

transfers going abroad   Public and private donations from this country to other countries.

Notes

1 International Monetary Fund (2009:7).
2 www.knomad.org/sites/default/files/201804/bilateralremittancematrix2017_Apr2018.xlsx.

3 www.knomad.org/sites/default/files/2018-04/Remittancedatainflows%28Apr.
   2018%29.xls.
4 https://stats.oecd.org/glossary/detail.asp?ID=166.
5 International Monetary Fund (2009:7).
6 http://data.imf.org/regular.aspx?key=61468210.
7 Chinn and Frankel (2007:287).
8 Ibid.
9 www.imf.org/external/np/sec/pr/2016/pr1690.htm.
10 http://data.imf.org/?sk=E6A5F467-C14B-4AA8-9F6D-5A09EC4E62A4.
11 https://stats.oecd.org/glossary/detail.asp?ID=166.

Bibliography

Asian Development Outlook. (2015). *Financing Asia's future growth*. Metro Manila: Asian
   Development Bank.
Chinn, M. and Frankel, J. A. (2007). "Will the Euro Eventually Surpass the Dollar as Lead-
   ing International Reserve Currency?" in *G7 current account imbalances: Sustainability and
   adjustment*, edited by H. R. Clarida. Volume ISBN: 0-226-10726-4. University of Chicago
   Press.
International Monetary Fund. (2009). *Balance of payments and international investment position
   manual*. Washington, DC: International Monetary Fund.

PART VI

Fiscal policy

Governments and parliaments play important roles in the economy. Not only do they make laws and regulations and issue directives, but they also raise and spend money. In this way they produce goods and services that the private sector would not produce in sufficient quantity, for example, justice or defence; reduce inequality between citizens and between regions or states of a federation; or stabilize the economy, reducing boom and bust. In Section 14, we analyse government spending in general and in Section 15 government spending on education, R&D.

Governments raise money in different ways. Let us start with those that are generally less important. Governments may be owners of such assets as property, companies or financial assets. Governments may receive returns on publicly owned assets. In other cases, governments acquire cash by disposing of their assets, the so-called privatizations. Through privatizations governments generate immediate revenue, but they also give up future returns on the assets which they sell. Returns on public assets and privatizations are usually secondary sources of government funding.

We have seen that governments may also receive money from the central bank through the "treasury channel" of money creation (see Section 9.3), when this is permitted under domestic legislation. Technically these transfers of money are debts, but the central bank, in some cases, decides not to request these monies back and the transfer is then permanent, i.e., it is a gift.

The last two sources of government financing are the most important. In some cases, governments run public deficits and fund those deficits by borrowing money from the financial markets. In Section 16 we analyse the budget deficit and the public debt.

Finally, governments usually raise most of their revenue through taxes and social contributions. While private businesses are paid if customers decide to buy their services, governments have the power to impose payment of taxes and social contributions. Taxes have considerable consequences for the behaviour of private actors, that is families and firms. By the same token, governments may transfer money to citizens through negative taxes,[1] pensions and benefits, all known as money transfers. Section 13 covers monetary transfers from the private sector (citizens and firms) to the state and from the state to the private sector.

13

MONETARY TRANSFERS

Taxes, benefits, subsidies and social contributions

When money moves from Governments to the private sector (citizens and firms) or *vice versa*, the effects on the economy of a country are usually considerable. This occurs because governments can increase or decrease the amount of money in the pockets of citizens and firms, thereby limiting or increasing their ability to spend on consumption or investment. Governments may also reduce the variability or volatility of an economy if they tax higher incomes at a higher rate and tax lower incomes at a lower rate, thereby practising so-called **progressive taxation**.[2]

This type of taxation takes place in many countries, the US and many EU countries among them. When the economy grows, individuals and companies earn more. In boom years with higher incomes, higher tax rates become applicable. This diminishes the strength of booms. When the economy goes into recession, incomes fall. Low incomes incur low tax rates, and taxation falls even more than income.[3] There are similar effects, albeit smaller, with a single tax rate for every level of income (proportional taxation). Boom and bust effects are mitigated in this way. By the same token, governments may reduce the vicissitudes in their economies if they subsidize people who have completely or partially lost their employment and income through unemployment benefits. Progressive taxes and social protection for those affected by recessions are called **automatic stabilizers**.[4] They are legal provisions that result in automatic increases in government expenditure or decreases in taxes when real output declines (and *vice versa*).

The standard way in which governments raise money is through taxes and social contributions, the so-called government revenue. They can also pay "negative taxes" or benefits to citizens. Taxes are a key feature of government activity. A government which could not impose taxes but would sell its services to buyers that freely decide to buy them would not be a government; it would be a private business.

This section covers transfers of money from citizens (and firms) to government and *vice versa*. It first considers general taxation, non-earmarked transfers, i.e.

transfers that simply occur because the private entities (families and firms) do or do not have income or wealth or because they consume. This section then considers other types of transfer with specific destinations: payroll taxes from the private sector to the state, and benefits and subsidies from the state to the private sector.

Government pays money to the private sector for a further reason: it pays interest to the holders of government debt. These payments will be considered in Section 17 which covers government deficits and debt.

In the final part of this unit, we consider the effects of taxes, social contributions, pensions and benefits on the whole economy.

13.1 General taxation[5]: taxes not earmarked to fund specific expenses

People pay taxes because they have to, not because they like doing it or because they receive something in exchange; they can decide to buy or not buy coffee at the cafeteria or a book in a bookstore, but cannot make a similar decision on taxes. However, in the long run a government which is not useful to its citizens will see its credibility eroded. People will probably try not to pay taxes. As a rule, we can say that taxes are mandatory payments to the state, with no *quid pro quo* as in market transactions.

Taxes can be direct or indirect. A direct tax "is paid directly by an individual or organization to the imposing entity (usually the state). Direct taxes include real estate (property) tax, personal property tax, income tax or taxes on assets. Whereas indirect taxes are levied on someone, such as a seller, and paid by another, for example, a consumer; this is the case of a sales tax paid by the buyer in a retail setting. A direct tax cannot be shifted to another individual or entity. The individual or organization upon which the tax is levied is responsible for the fulfilment of the tax payment. Indirect taxes, on the other hand, are shifted from one taxpayer to another."[6] Moreover direct taxes are applied to the income or wealth of persons, whereas indirect taxes do not take income or wealth into account.

The more frequent direct taxes are personal income tax, the payroll tax, that is the social contribution to fund the pension system and potentially some benefits (see Section 14.2), and corporation tax on the pre-tax accounting profit (see Section 1.3) of corporations. In some cases, corporations may be asked to pay taxes on their total revenue (see Section 6.3). Another important direct tax is inheritance tax which people may be required to pay when they inherit something. Finally, there are also direct taxes on property.

The principal indirect taxes are custom duties on goods entering or leaving the country, excise taxes on goods such as petrol, tobacco, alcohol, air travel and luxuries; sales taxes (a percentage on the value of sales); and value added tax (VAT, see Section 2.1).

Taxes may also be "negative" when government, instead of taking money from citizens and firms, transfer money to them if their income falls below a certain level. This applies when governments provide benefits or subsidies to residents when their incomes are low.[7]

Taxes may affect rich people and poor people in different ways. When **poll taxes** exist, every individual, independently of his or her income, pays the same amounts to the state; rich and poor people pay the same. This may represent a very large share of the income of a poor person and a very small share of the income of a rich person. Poll taxes have the advantage of being simple to administer and, when very low, may not create disincentives to income generation and capital accumulation. They are evidently very regressive, poor people paying a much larger share of their income on them than rich people. They may contribute to inequality which may depress consumption and hinder income growth. They may also deprive poor people of the resources to start their own businesses.

Flat(–rate) or proportional taxes are applied at a fixed rate on everybody, everybody paying the same percentage of their income. For an individual earning $2 per day (less than $800 per year) and being on the threshold of survival, giving up 10 per cent of their income, that is around $80, is much more painful than for somebody earning $200,000 who pays $20,000. The wealthy person will merely renounce some non-essential pleasure, not his or her daily meals. For the same reason, in some cases, flat (rate) taxes are combined with tax exemption on the first layer of income. So, for example the first $10,000 of annual income may be tax free, then every dollar above that threshold may be taxed at a standard rate, for example 33 per cent. If you earn $15,000, you pay 33 per cent of $5,000, that is $1,667, which represents 11 per cent of your total income. If you earn $50,000, you pay 33 per cent of $40,000, that is $13,333, which would represent 26.67 per cent of your total income. Those who earn more pay a greater share of their total income. This follows the principle of **progressive taxation**.

Many countries have or aim for a system of progressive taxation. In a system of progressive taxation richer people should pay a larger percentage of their income (or wealth) than poorer people. Some tax systems may become regressive anyway. A regressive tax system demands from poorer people a percentage of their income higher than that demanded from richer people. Some tax systems aim at progressiveness, but then allow certain deductions (mortgage payments, charitable donations, complementary pensions contribution, investments, etc) or special treatment of certain types of revenue, for example, capital gains, that usually only rich people can afford. In some cases, a progressive system may become regressive after the application of deductions, rich people paying smaller shares of their income than people with lower incomes. This argument is mostly about income tax, taxes such as local taxes, sales taxes and payroll taxes often being less progressive or even regressive.[8]

Read

Why Warren Buffett wants to pay more tax

Warren Buffett, the so-called "Sage of Omaha" and one of the US's richest citizens, attracted headlines in 2013 when he pointed out that he had been paying tax at a lower rate than that paid by his secretary. Not that she was paying more tax than he was, but that her marginal tax rate (the tax due on each extra dollar she earned) was higher than his.

He was commenting on the new tax rates introduced that year by Obama's administration, which included the provision that for those earning more than $400,000 (or $450,000 for couples), capital gains tax would rise from 15 per cent to 20 per cent. Buffett's earnings came in the form of investment gains rather than wages, and a tax rate of 20 per cent would still fall short of the marginal rate his secretary paid on her income.

Buffett has consistently argued that the tax floor should be raised for top earners like himself, so as not to privilege earnings from investment over wage income. Obama's administration supported his proposals, but they were fiercely opposed by a Republican Congress. Buffett concluded that the modest tax changes of 2013 were better than nothing; but far from enough.

"Buffett Says He's Still Paying Lower Tax Rate than his Secretary", Chris Isidore on CNN Money, 4 March 2013, *CNN Money*, http://money.cnn.com/2013/03/04/news/economy/buffett-secretary-taxes/index.html.

"Warren Buffett calls for a minimum tax on the wealthy", *Reuters*, 26 November 2012. www.reuters.com/article/us-buffett-tax/warren-buffett-calls-for-a-minimum-tax-on-the-wealthy-idUSBRE8AP0LY20121126.

Questions

* How much were capital gains taxed in the US in 2013?
* Why was the rise of taxes on capital gains and rich people not the whole story?
* What does it mean that Buffett is "the lowest-paying taxpayer in the office"?
* Why is Buffett advocating a change in the US tax system?

Analysis

In the US, capital gains are an important source of income for rich people, but not for poor people. However, prior to 2013 capital gains were taxed at a rate of 15 per cent, and later 20 per cent, a relatively low rate in the general US tax system. This rise of taxes on capital gains has been matched by an increase of payments (payroll taxes or social contributions) which mostly affect people on lower incomes. The modest increase in the taxation of capital gains and the increase in payroll taxes produces the result that Buffett, one of the richest men on earth, pays the lowest tax rate in his office where, for example, his secretary pays a higher tax rate than he does. This makes the US tax system partially regressive. Buffett advocates a non-regressive tax system, i.e. a tax system in which the actual tax rate of richer people should not be lower than the actual tax rate paid by poorer people.

13.2 Earmarked monetary transfers between private subjects and government: social contributions, pensions and benefits

Payroll taxes (social contributions), social security and benefits are monetary transfers between citizens, firms and government. Employees and employers pay payroll taxes or social contributions in different measure. Social contributions or payroll taxes constitute their contribution to the funding of the pension system and more generally to social security. They are also related to the level of income that workers receive, even if they are not strictly proportional to it. Social security, according to ILO, "involves access to health care and income security, particularly in cases of old age,[9] unemployment, sickness, invalidity, work injury, maternity or loss of a main income earner".[10] Here, we concentrate our attention on monetary transfers, while we analyse government-provided services in Section 15, which is about government's provision of goods and services. Social security includes elements of insurance, mostly for old age and sickness, and elements of assistance or redistribution to the needy. There are various models of social security across countries, involving different payments for different needs. Social protection can be funded both from general taxation and from payroll taxes in different degrees.

Retirement and sick leave are usually at least partially funded from payroll taxes. In this sense payroll taxes are different from other taxes: their revenue is earmarked, i.e. it has a precise destination.

Sometimes trade unions demand a greater involvement of employers in bearing the cost of pensions. Sometimes unions demand that employers pay a larger share of social insurance and payroll taxes. However, for those employers who operate in perfectly competitive markets (see Section 7.2), there can only be a single labour cost, inclusive of wages, taxes and social contributions. In competitive markets, in the short term an increase in payroll taxes is an additional burden for firms and in some cases can also put them at risk. However, if in the medium term the firm operates in perfect competition, an increase in social contributions usually implies a reduction in or lower growth of net salaries, that is what employees take home.[11] Unions should be aware of this before asking employers for increased contributions to social security. This argument is less strong for firms operating as monopolies (Section 7.1) or oligopolies (Section 7.3).

Some countries provide housing benefits to pay for rents, children's benefits (financial support for families with children), food stamps to help with purchases of food, and other benefits for specific needs, for example heating during the cold season. In some cases, families are entitled to certain benefits only if they comply with such conditions as regularly sending children to school or making them available for public vaccination. These are called conditional cash transfers. Such transfers are gradually being implemented in some countries and are a powerful contribution to welfare policies in developing countries.

Finally, we should mention that governments might make transfers to companies, providing them with subsidies. This may occur because those firms produce certain products or carry out certain missions which politicians consider important. Tax exemptions are a special type of subsidy to companies, providing the possibility of paying lower taxes than other firms.

Read

"*Bolsa Família*: Brazil's Quiet Revolution", Deborah Wetzel, Valor Econômico on World Bank website, 4 November 2013. www.worldbank.org/en/news/opinion/2013/11/04/bolsa-familia-Brazil-quiet-revolution.

Bolsa Família: **Brazil's quiet revolution**

Inequality and poverty have walked hand-in-hand in Brazil for decades and even centuries, the result of non-inclusive growth models and regressive social policies. In the second half of the 20th century, Brazil has been one of the most unequal countries in the world, with economists coining expressions such as "Belindia – a society consisting of a tiny Belgium of prosperity in a sea of Indian poverty". For years, the poorest 60% of the population had only 4 % of the wealth, while the richest 20% held 58% of the pie.

Ten years ago this month, President Lula launched the innovative *Bolsa Família* Program (BF), scaling up and coordinating scattered existing initiatives under a powerfully simple concept: trusting poor families with small cash transfers in return for keeping their children in school and attending preventive health-care visits.

BF was met with considerable scepticism. After all, Brazil had traditionally been a big spender in the social sectors, with 22% of GDP spent on education, health, social protection and social security. One of the images used by academics was that throwing money out of a helicopter would be just as efficient to reach the poor, given Brazil's frustration with the lack of results. How could BF, with about half a per cent of GDP, change this bleak scenario?

Ten years after BF has been key to help Brazil more than halve its extreme poverty – from 9.7 to 4.3% of the population. Most impressively, and in contrast to other countries, income inequality also fell markedly, to a Gini coefficient of 0.527, an impressive 15% decrease. BF now reaches nearly 14 million households – 50 million people or around ¼ of the population, and is widely seen as a global success story, a reference point for social policy around the world.

Equally important, qualitative studies have highlighted how the regular cash transfers from the program have helped promote the dignity and autonomy of the poor. This is particularly true for women, who account for over 90% of the beneficiaries.

Besides this immediate poverty impact, a second key goal of BF was to break the transmission of poverty from parents to children by increasing the opportunities for the new generation through better education and health outcomes. Assessing progress on this goal requires longer-term monitoring, but the results up to now have been very promising. BF has increased school attendance and grade progression. For instance, the chances of a 15-year old girl being in school increased by 21%. Children and families are better prepared to study and seize opportunities with more pre-natal care visits, immunization coverage and reduced child mortality. Poverty invariably casts a long shadow on the next generation, but these results leave no doubt that BF has improved the prospects for generations of children. At the same time, fears about unintended consequences such as possible reduced work incentives have not materialized. Indeed, increased labor income has been another critical player in the reduction of poverty and inequality in Brazil during this period.

The Cadastro Único is the essential tool that allowed BF to achieve these landmark successes. It provides the basis for targeting BF benefits, but also links to numerous other social programs and services. It is hence not only the backbone that ensures effective administration of the BF, but also a tool for coordinating social policy and facilitating rapid scale-up of additional efforts such as the recent Brasil Carinhoso program. Efficient administration and good targeting have enabled BF to achieve its success at a very low cost (around 0.6% of GDP), and build the base for ambitious programs such as Brasil sem Miséria and the Busca Ativa effort, to include those not yet reached.

Brazil's experience is showing the way for the rest of the world. Despite its relatively short life, BF has helped stimulate an expansion of conditional cash transfer programs in Latin America and around the world – such programmes are now in more than 40 countries. Last year alone, more than 120 delegations visited Brazil to learn about BF. The World Bank has been a partner to BF from the very beginning; we are learning from it and helping to disseminate it. Our new global goals of eradicating extreme poverty by 2030 and boosting shared prosperity draw from Brazil's experience. Another concrete step is the development of the Brazil Learning Initiative for a World without Poverty (WWP), recently launched in Brasília in partnership with the Ministry of Social Development, Ipea and UNDP's International Policy

Center. The Initiative will help support continued innovation and learning from Brazil's social policy experience.

The ultimate goal of any welfare program is for its success to render it redundant. Brazil is well placed to sustain the achievements over the last decade and is close to reaching the amazing feat of eradicating poverty and hunger for all Brazilians, a true reason to celebrate.

This article was published by Deborah Wetzel, currently World Bank Senior Director for Governance, in November 2013, when she was Country Director for Brazil.

Questions

- What is the biggest and best-known conditional cash transfer scheme in the developing world?
- How many families have been involved in it?
- Has inequality changed in recent years in Brazil? Why?
- Are other countries interested in conditional cash transfers?
- What are the conditions attached to cash transfers?
- What is happening to infant and maternal mortality in Brazil?
- How much does Brazil spend on conditional cash transfers?
- Is *Bolsa Família* money really reaching the poor?

Analysis

Brazil boasts the most extensive and best-known conditional cash transfer scheme: *Bolsa Família*. According to this scheme, poor families are entitled to receive some money from the state only if they regularly send their children to school and make them take advantage of the vaccinations provided by the public health system. This scheme has affected 12m families, considerably reducing inequality, poverty, infant and maternal mortality and improving the educational achievements of many children. This has been achieved at relatively low cost: 1 per cent of GDP. This has of course attracted the attention of other countries in different continents. All this is possible because most of this money, in 80 per cent of cases, really reaches the poor. The Brazilian economy has grown since the introduction of this scheme. Critics would say that it has grown "notwithstanding this scheme", but most of the paid money has been spent on food, education and clothing, supporting domestic demand for goods. This probably is the short-term economic effect of the programme. In the medium term, higher levels of health and education should supply the country with a stronger and better-educated labour force, a key prerequisite for further economic growth.

The ageing of population and the sustainability of pension systems[12] An ageing society is characterized by a growing proportion of the retired to the active working population. Societies age either when fertility rates decline so that fewer children are born, or when longevity increases, or both. Ageing affects virtually all societies today, but more so the industrial countries, which have generally experienced it over a longer period and for which further pronounced ageing is projected over the next four decades, at the end of which a peak in the proportion of the elderly is likely to be attained.

Concerns about the challenges posed by ageing populations have moved to the forefront of the public policy debate in many countries. The fiscal sustainability of public pension schemes is a major issue in many countries. In the industrial countries, public schemes for providing for the retired are predominantly of a pay-as-you-go (PAYG) type, typically with comprehensive coverage, but which are frequently supplemented by funded schemes, mostly operated by the private sector. A standard PAYG system levies payroll taxes on the working population, while paying benefits to the retired, but usually without the close person-based relationship between individual contributions and benefits that characterizes fully funded schemes.

In the early stages of a PAYG system, low contribution rates are sufficient to cover benefits for a relatively small number of beneficiaries, but as the scheme matures, benefits paid out tend to exceed contributions, requiring increases in payroll taxes or budget transfers. However, considerable additional fiscal stress is likely to emerge under a PAYG system as the proportion of the retired elderly rises. And if, as is typically the case, the PAYG scheme also involves various redistributive elements, there is further potential for fiscal stress, especially as the population ages.

A failure to address the resulting fiscal stresses, coming on top of an already burdensome fiscal situation, could inflict serious macroeconomic and structural damage, both on the domestic economy and, in the case of large industrial countries through international linkages, on the world economy.

13.3 The macroeconomic effects of taxes (and social contributions)

In macroeconomics we generally refer to taxes as net taxes, that is the sum of positive taxes minus negative taxes and other cash transfers in general (Table 13.1).

(A + C) = General Government Revenue

Positive taxes and social contributions comprise the General Government Revenue (see the US case in Figure 13.1). They are not only a means of providing resources for government expenditure but also tools for creating incentives and disincentives and

TABLE 13.1 Net public transfers

+ Positive taxes (non-earmarked transfers from families and firms to government)	A
− Negative taxes (transfers from government to families and firms)	B
+ Social contributions or payroll taxes	C
− Pensions and Benefits	D
− Subsidies to companies	E
= Net public transfers or net taxes	

tools for setting up the economic policy of a country. The use of taxes and benefits as incentives affects the behaviour of families and firms. Taxes may foster or hinder work *versus* leisure, consumption *versus* saving, national goods *versus* foreign goods; they may push people to consume more vegetables, education and health care and less alcohol, tobacco and unhealthy and polluting substances. In this sense taxes are messages from the authorities to citizens and companies: do this, don't do that. Every time authorities raise or decrease a tax or a social contribution, they should expect some reaction from citizens and companies. The problem is that sometimes people do not react as the authorities expect. All this is studied in microeconomics. However, the aggregate effects of the behaviour of families and firms impact on the whole economy, and for this reason taxes are also tools of macroeconomic policy.

The income that remains with families after paying taxes and receiving transfers is known as **disposable income**. The decisions of families depend on their disposable income, not what they generate with their employment or with their business. Taxes reduce the income that families save or consume. Corporate taxes may reduce what companies have as investments or as dividends for families. For this reason, when a government considers that its country is producing as much as it can, reaching high capacity utilization (see Section 3.3) and that any further demand may just generate inflation (Section 9.4), a possible tool in its hands consists of raising taxes. Higher personal income taxes may lead to lower consumption and higher corporate taxes may lead to lower investment. Lower consumption may also be achieved with other taxes paid by families, for example property taxes, VAT, taxes on alcohol, tobacco, petrol, gas or other specific substances, or social contributions (payroll taxes). A decrease in income taxes and social insurance taxes paid by workers increases the income available for families,[13] that is their disposable income. A similar effect can be achieved if one increases benefits and subsidies paid to the private sector (families and firms). Usually families use a large share of their disposable income for consumption and therefore, when taxes diminish or benefits increase, consumption increases.

A reduction of $100 in taxes does not necessarily lead to an immediate increase in consumption of $100. People may save. On average, rich people save a larger share of their disposable income than do poor people. Rich people can already satisfy most of their needs and can care for other needs such as providing for their future, i.e. saving. For this reason, reducing taxes on rich people produces different results from such reductions on poor people. If you aim to foster consumption, reducing taxes on poor people is usually the most effective way. If a country does not save and invest enough, a tax reduction on the wealthy may be a solution. However, the transformation of savings into investments is a complex story. With capital mobility (Section 11.4), savings can eventually go abroad. If they remain in the country, but firms do not wish to invest, for example because they do not see business opportunities, savings do not foster investment. Tax reductions for the rich are not a sufficient condition for fostering private investment.

When politicians cut government services and procurement by 100 and reduce taxes by 100, they should usually expect an immediate fall in aggregate demand. Probably the fall of 100 in government spending will only be partially compensated for by the increased consumption of families. In the short term, families will save part of the money they no longer pay in taxes. Only under certain conditions will savings be reflected in investment and aggregate demand revert to its initial level.

Finally, the effects of tax cuts on the choices of families depend on what they expect in the future. If they expect more taxes and hard times, tax cuts bring very modest benefits, because consumers save money for rainy days. On the contrary, if consumers consider those tax cuts as making them permanently richer, they will use the increased disposable income for consumption.[14] In general, tax increases reduce the disposable income of families and therefore consumption and aggregate demand; if demand was already greater than domestic production capacity, tax increases will only curb inflation and imports. If the economy was not fully using its capacity, tax increases may induce a contraction of the economy; this occurs if there is not enough additional government spending. For these reasons, tax policy, pensions, benefits and subsidies may be used to foster or slow down the growth of a country.

Taxes and other monetary transfers can **stabilize** the business cycle and act as automatic stabilizers. This is particularly true if the tax system is progressive[15] and if government pays unemployment benefits to those who lose their jobs. The progressive tax system implies that, when the income of families grows during periods of economic growth, the average tax they pay increases too; however, when in a crisis the income of families decreases, the amount of taxes they pay diminishes more than proportionally. This works well as long as tax brackets – the income levels that attract certain tax rates – are updated when there is inflation (Section 9.4), as for example in the US. If this does not happen, inflation moves people with relatively lower incomes to higher tax brackets, making them pay more tax even if they have not become richer. This phenomenon is called bracket creep or fiscal drag.

In addition, unemployment benefits increase the income of people when they lose their jobs, mostly during recessions; they cease to exist when people find employment. Unemployment benefits make recessions less deep than they would otherwise be, because they restore part of the purchasing power of those who have lost their jobs. Of course, unemployment benefits should not be so high as to create incentives against work and, most of all, should be conditional on the availability of the recipients and their willingness to work. For these reasons they require well-developed offices to administer them.

For the reasons considered above, taxes and benefits can be considered automatic stabilizers and may play an important role in stabilizing the economy and making it less prone to booms and busts.

Read

Aquino urged lower individual income taxes as 'best goodbye gift'

A promise to lower the individual income taxes would be President Benigno Aquino III's "best goodbye gift" to the people when he delivers his final state of the nation address (Sona) this July 27, Senator Sonny Angara said on Wednesday.

"Of the thousands of words in his Sona, one of the most awaited and the one which will be most applauded is the President saying that he will back bills that will lower individual income taxes," Angara, chairman of the Senate committee on ways and means, said in a statement.

As chairman of the committee, the senator is leading the charge in the upper chamber to slash income taxes. He is also the author of a bill compressing the net taxable income brackets, and lowering tax rates especially for low- and middle-income earners. Angara said Aquino's mention of tax reforms in his Sona could mobilize support from the House of Representatives, which would end "the embargo in serious discussion for lower tax rates".

The Senate already approved late last year a bill that would raise the tax cap for the 13th-month pay and other benefits from P30,000 to P82,000. Aquino signed it into law in February 2015. "The Department of Finance has already expressed its openness to review and amend the tax rates and brackets, and we welcome this progress. We should let the executive guys run the numbers and tell us hanggang saan tingin nila pwede ibaba ang rates (up to how much they think the rates can be lowered)," Angara said.

In making one final push for lower income taxes, Angara again calmed concerns by revenue officers that altering tax rates will punch a big hole in the coffers. "Any revenue loss is recoverable. If withholding tax is converted into disposable income, then it can be recouped through the VAT on goods. If part of the salary intended to be remitted to the BIR (Bureau of Internal Revenue) will now be spent for goods, then it can still be recaptured through the tax on the goods bought," the senator explained. "It will also be good for the economy. It is always better to plow money back in circulation, where it can stimulate the production and consumption of goods. Sometimes, instead of government doing the spending for the people, let the people do the spending themselves," he added.

Angara said the bill, once enacted into law, would retain more money in paychecks of ordinary salaried workers and would lead to greater voluntary compliance. "It will also attract human capital and prevent the migration of our own to countries (which) do not reward industry and productivity with high tax rates," he further said.

Angara pointed out that the Philippines has the second highest individual income tax rate in the region at 32 percent next to Thailand and Vietnam's 35 percent, and the highest value added tax (VAT) at 12 percent. He also noted that the country's current individual income tax bracket has remained unchanged since 1997 until today even when the consumer price index has already almost doubled. "We need to think ahead and be competitive in the region but more importantly, we must give the Filipino people a break," said the senator. Currently, a policeman and a teacher whose net taxable income is P150,000 are taxed at the third highest rate. "Currently, a policeman and a teacher whose net taxable income is P150,000 are taxed at the third highest rate. If we will allow this and we will not act immediately to amend our taxation system, maybe next year the tax rate of our teachers, nurses and policemen would be as high as the tax rate of the millionaires and billionaires in the country" the senator said.

This injustice, Angara said, is called "bracket creep" where taxpayers who are not considered high earning are already pushed into high brackets. At some point, economists say, this bracket creep would lead to "fiscal drag" where people will not have any purchasing power left to contribute to the economy due to excessive taxation.

> "Aquino Urged Lower Individual Income Taxes as
> 'Best Goodbye Gift',"Maila Ager, *Inquirer.net*. 15 July 2015

Questions

- According to Senator Angara, with a tax reduction taxes will be converted into what?
- What should be the effect of putting money back into circulation?
- What happened to the tax rates of teachers and policemen?
- What is the injustice, according to the Senator?

Analysis

Senator Angara makes a forecast, which many economists would generally accept: a tax reduction will increase the disposable income of families, that is the income

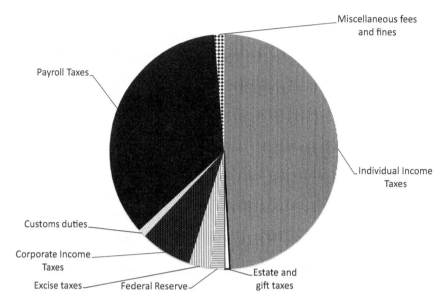

Miscellaneous fees
and fines

Payroll Taxes

Individual Income
Taxes

Customs duties

Corporate Income
Taxes

Excise taxes   Federal Reserve

Estate and
gift taxes

FIGURE 13.1   Revenues projection of the US in 2018

Source: Elaboration of the Author Congressional Budget Office data[16]

which remains after paying taxes. This is particularly true if, as suggested by Senator Angara, the tax reduction is targeted on low- and middle-income earners. Reducing taxes to low-income earners usually implies that much of their newly acquired disposable income is spent on consumer goods and not saved. This would occur in a lesser degree if tax cuts were targeted on higher-income earners. Money back in circulation, in families' pockets, can stimulate the production and consumption of goods. Senator Angara mentions that the income of such relatively low-income workers as nurses and policemen attracts the third highest tax rate. This seems to be something recent. A phenomenon of bracket creep or fiscal drag has probably occurred: receivers of lower incomes have moved into higher tax brackets. This could have occurred either because they have become richer or, more probably, because inflation has increased the nominal value of their salaries. Senator Angara seems to suggest that the cause of this bracket creep is inflation. Lower-income earners would have moved to higher tax brackets without becoming richer.

While it is true that the concept of fiscal drag implies that the movement of certain incomes into higher tax brackets puts pressure on and reduces private demand, it is not generally accepted that fiscal drag is a situation in which "people will not have any purchasing power left to contribute to the economy due to excessive taxation", as stated in the article. This would be a rather extreme case.

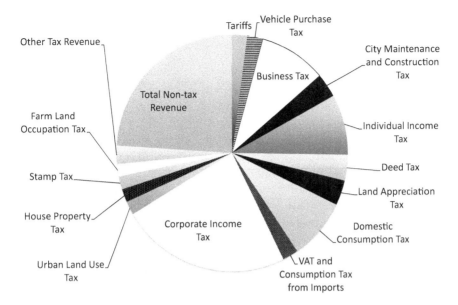

FIGURE 13.2 Revenues of the Chinese central and local government in 2016

Source: Data from www.stats.gov.cn/tjsj/ndsj/2017/indexeh.htm – Elaboration by the author

Glossary

automatic stabilizers Policies that work to reduce fluctuations in the size of a national economy due to business cycle effects, without explicit government action. For example, a progressive income tax structure will lead to an increase in the tax rate as incomes rise, thus reducing economic growth during an economic expansion. The progressive tax structure leads automatically to a reduced tax rate when incomes fall, thus stimulating the economy during a recession. Government welfare and unemployment insurance programmes work in a similar automatic and countercyclical manner, increasing government expenditure during recessions and reducing government expenditure during expansions.[17]

benefit Money provided by the government to people who need financial help because they are unemployed, ill, etc.[18]

bracket creep A situation in which inflation pushes incomes into higher tax brackets. The result is an increase in income taxes but no increase in real purchasing power. This is a problem during periods of high inflation as income tax codes typically take a longer time to change.[19]

burden of a tax The true economic weight of a tax. It is the difference between the individual's real income before and after the tax has been imposed, taking full account of how wages and prices may have adjusted.[20] It may be borne by people who are not those on whom the tax is imposed or levied.

child benefit   Money provided by a government to parents of children who have not yet reached a certain age.

conditional cash transfer   A programme which provides cash payments to poor households that meet certain behavioural requirements, generally related to children's health care and education.

corporate tax   A tax on corporations, usually on their profits.

custom duties   Taxes that people pay to bring a good into or out of a country.

direct taxes   Taxes of which the burden falls on those obliged to pay them. Corporate taxes are direct taxes even if economists agree that others (shareholders, consumers or workers) bear their burden. Income tax and property tax are examples of direct taxes.

disposable income   The income that remains after consumers have received transfers from the government and paid their taxes.[21]

earmarked tax revenue   Money derived from a tax and designated for a specific purpose.

excise   Tax on specific commodities such as gasoline, cigarettes, tobacco and alcohol.

fiscal drag   The increase in the tax taken that usually occurs when an economy is growing. This tends to dampen consumer spending and corporate investment, and therefore to constrain growth from running out of control. It can be a significant side-effect of general inflation, since as money incomes rise, the thresholds at which tax rates become higher (in progressive tax systems) usually stay the same, so that a greater proportion of incomes appear in the higher-paying brackets.

flat(-rate) tax   A tax applied at the same rate on every level of income.

housing benefit   Money which governments provide, usually to low-income individuals to help them to pay their rent or their mortgage.

income stabilizer   A progressive tax system, government benefit or some corporate policy of dividend distribution which diminishes variations in the income of families.

income tax   A tax levied on the income that individuals earn.

indirect taxes   Taxes of which the burden does not fall on those obliged to pay them. VAT, sales tax and custom duties are examples of indirect taxes.

job-seeker allowance   A form of unemployment benefit which exists in the UK.

maternity benefit   Financial support to families during the final phase of the pregnancy period and the first months of life of babies, when mothers find it more difficult to handle their usual job.

negative tax   A payment from the government to those taxpayers who do not reach a certain level of income. It is a form of benefit and belongs to the wider family of subsidies.

payroll tax   A share of wages usually designated to fund pensions and insure workers against sickness, invalidity and unemployment. They are paid by both employers and employees.

pension   A regular payment made by the state to individuals after they have reached a state-defined retirement age; and to others forced into early retirement due to illness or disability.

poll tax   A tax which adults must pay independently from their income or resources.

progressive taxation   Taxation system in which higher incomes incur higher tax rates.

proportional taxation   Taxation system in which all incomes incur the same tax rate.

regressive taxation   Taxation system in which lower incomes incur higher tax rates.

sales tax   A tax imposed by the government at the point of sale on retail goods and services. It is collected by the retailer, passed on to the state and paid by consumers.

social contribution   See *payroll tax*.

subsidy   A sum of money, either one-off or repeated, granted by the state to some organization or industry whose survival or development is considered important by government on grounds which could be any of: national security, social stability, wage enhancement, import substitution, political advantage. Subsidies are of particular concern to those conducting international trade agreements as they may be seen to confer unfair advantage to the recipient.

taxes   Mandatory payments to the state with no quid pro quo, as in market transactions.

unemployment benefit   Payment that governments make to those who are unemployed, on certain conditions.

VAT   Value Added Tax, a tax paid by consumers via the sellers of those goods and services that they buy.

Notes

1 When citizens pay money to government, there is a positive tax and when government pays money to citizens, there is a negative tax.
2 Auerbach and Feenberg (2000) http://users.nber.org/~jroth/w7662.auto.pdf; Mattesini and Rossi (2010) http://economia.unipv.it/alma/mattesini_rossi2011_ok.pdf; McKay and Reis (2012) http://economics.yale.edu/sites/default/files/mckay-130402.pdf.
3 Tax rates do not change, but incomes are automatically taxed at lower tax rate, because they are smaller.
4 See Abel et al. (2014:615–61).
5 This paragraph follows Stiglitz (2000:453).
6 www.investopedia.com/terms/d/directtax.asp.
7 The term "negative income tax" has been used first in politics by Lady Juliet Rhys Williams (1898–1964) and then in economics by Friedman (1967).
8 See also Stiglitz (2000:511).
9 Pensions are in many cases a form of saving or insurance, but this does not always occur. This partially justifies the use of including them in the wide category of monetary transfers.
10 www.ilo.org/global/topics/social-security/lang--en/index.htm.
11 Actually "there is a general consensus among economists that workers, not employers, bear the full burden of the employer share of the social security tax." Stiglitz (2000:511)

In the case of firms operating in oligopolies (p. 78), oligopsonies (p. 79) or monopolies (p. 74) results are more uncertain.
12 Adaptation of the introduction of Chand and Jaeger (2000).
13 See Arnold (2010:147) and www.ons.gov.uk/peoplepopulationandcommunity/per sonalandhouseholdfinances/ expenditure/articles/measuringrealhouseholddisposableinc ome/2015–03–06#gross-disposable-income-gdi.
14 This type of idea started with Ricardo (1888) and the so-called Ricardian equivalence, stating that any increase in public deficit would be offset by additional private savings. Actually, David Ricardo did not believe this as a realist hypothesis.
15 See note 2.
16 www.cbo.gov/about/products/budget-economic-data#7.
17 www.chegg.com/homework-help/definitions/automatic-stabilizers-12.
18 www.oxfordlearnersdictionaries.com/definition/english/benefit_1.
19 http://web.worldbank.org/WBSITE/EXTERNAL/TOPICS/EXTSOCIALPRO TECTION/EXTSAFETYNETSANDTRANSFERS/0,,conten tMDK:20615138~m enuPK:282766~pagePK:148956~piPK:216618~theSitePK:282761,00.html.
20 Stiglitz (2000:483).
21 Blanchard (2009:68).

Bibliography

Abel, A. B., Bernanke, B. and Croushore, D. D. (2014). *Macroeconomics*. Boston: Addison-Wesley.
Ager, M. (2015). "Aquino Urged Lower Individual Income Taxes as 'Best Goodbye Gift'," *Inquirer.net*, 15 July. https://newsinfo.inquirer.net/705305/aquino-urged-to-lower-indivi dual-income-taxes-as-best-goodbye-gift.
Arnold, R. A. (2010). *Macroeconomics*, 9th ed. Mason, OH: South Western, Cengage Learning.
Auerbach, A. J. and Feenberg, D. (2000). "The Significance of Federal Taxes as Automatic Stabilizers," NBER Working Paper No. 7662, April.
Blanchard, O. (2009). *Macroeconomics*. Upper Saddle River, NJ: Pearson Prentice Hall.
Chand, S. K. and Jaeger, A. (2000). "Aging Populations and Public Pension Schemes," Occasional Paper 147, Washington, DC.
Friedman, M. (1967). "The Case for the Negative Income Tax," *National Review*, 7 March, pp. 239–241.
Isidore, C. (2013). "Buffett Says He's Still Paying Lower Tax Rate than his Secretary," *CNN Money*, 4 March. http://money.cnn.com/2013/03/04/news/economy/buffett-secretary-taxes/index.html.
Mattesini, F. and Rossi, L. (2010). "Monetary Policy and Automatic Stabilizers: The Role of Progressive Taxation," Dipartimento di economia politica e metodi quantitative, Università degli Studi di Pavia, # 134 (11–10).
McKay, A. and Reis, R. (2012). "The Role of Automatic Stabilizers in the U.S. Business Cycle," http:// economics.yale.edu/sites/default/files/mckay-130402.pdf.
Reuters. (2012). "Warren Buffett Calls for a Minimum Tax on the Wealthy," 26 November. www.reuters.com/article/us-buffett-tax/warren-buffett-calls-for-a-minimum-tax-on-the-wealthy-idUSBRE8AP0LY20121126.
Ricardo, D. (1888) "Essay on the Funding System" in The Works of David Ricardo. With a Notice of the Life and Writings of the Author, by J.R. McCulloch, London: John Murray, 1888
Stiglitz, J. (2000). *Economics of the public sector*, 3rd ed. New York: W. W. Norton & Company.
Wetzel, D. (2013). "Bolsa Família: Brazil's Quiet Revolution," Valor Econômico on World Bank website, 4 November. www.worldbank.org/en/news/opinion/2013/11/04/bolsa-familia-Brazil-quiet-revolution.

14

GOVERNMENT SPENDING ON GOODS AND SERVICES

Governments are key players in determining the demand of a country and increasing its productivity. Not only do governments affect the quantity of money that families and firms can spend – that is their disposable income – using taxes and other monetary transfers, but governments themselves also demand goods and services, supply the economy with goods that market forces would not produce in the same quantity, and redistribute income. In particular, governments buy the services of their employees and carry out procurement, that is purchases of goods and services from national and foreign firms.

Governments provide different services: defence, police, justice,[1] education, health care, assistance, transport, R&D, urban planning, protection of the cultural heritage, and much more. Governments can produce these services thanks to the services (the work) provided by their employees (Section 14.1) and thanks to the goods and the services they buy from external companies (Section 14.2).

In macroeconomic terms the value of government spending on goods and services includes any expenditure by the government on a currently produced good or service, whether foreign or domestic.[2] In Figure 14.1 the outlays of the US government.

This means the sum of government consumption and government investment.

Government consumption is approximately the sum of salaries of public employees, as governments buy the services of their employees, plus intermediate consumption (Section 2.1) of government[3] plus consumption of capital (depreciation).[4]

Governments not only buy goods and services for public consumption, they also buy them for public investment, the so-called "gross capital formation" (roads, schools, bridges, hospitals, etc) made by or on behalf of government.[5]

14.1 Public employment

Governments contribute to countries' total production through the work of their employees, but seldom sell their services at market prices. For this reason, the value

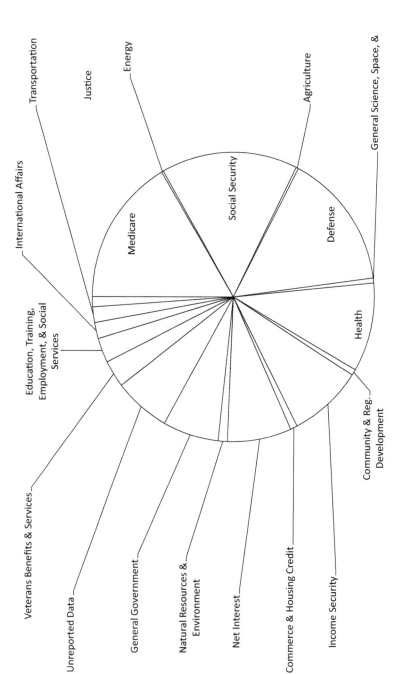

FIGURE 14.1 US Government spending (outlays) by function in 2017

Source: Elaboration of the author of data from www.usaspending.gov/#/explorer/budget_function

added (Section 2.1) by the public sector cannot be measured in the same way as the value added by the private sector, that is in terms of the difference between total revenue (Section 6.3) and intermediate consumption (Section 2.1). Most of the revenue of the public sector is tax revenue and is not directly linked with the quantity and quality of services that the public sector provides. Citizens pay taxes because they have to, not as a payment for specific services that they receive. Government is the only actor with the legal power to impose taxes. Therefore, the value added by the public sector is **calculated as the sum of the salaries of public employees**.[6] Public employment is **a source of stabilization** of the economy because it does not depend immediately on the fluctuations of markets. When the economy goes into recession, GDP decreases and employment diminishes, but public employment does not usually diminish as much as private employment.

The fact that the GDP produced by the public sector is measured as the sum of public salaries implies that, **when we cut public salaries, we automatically diminish the GDP** of a country. This is also true of private salaries. Only if cuts to public salaries can be offset by an equivalent or greater growth in the private sector can they enhance growth, otherwise they give rise to recession (Section 1.2).

The intermediate consumption (Section 2.1) of government is the public procurement of non-durable goods.[7]

Finally, we should notice that when a government increases taxes and public spending by 100 (a balanced budget operation) **the effect on GDP is often positive**. The increase in taxes diminishes the disposable income of the private sector by 100. However, only a part of that disposable income would have been used for consumption and aggregate demand. Some would have been saved. On the other hand, the total of new public spending represents additional GDP. This means that under certain assumptions, total aggregate demand increases when a balanced budget increase in government spending occurs.[8] The relevant assumptions are that a) private investment is constant and does not increase when families save more, b) in the economy there is spare production capacity, and c) increased public spending does not entail higher interest rates, significant inflation or changes in productivity. If any of the above-mentioned conditions is not satisfied, the increase in public spending may not produce the expected desirable effects and could be counterproductive. Generally, the induced growth in GDP is equal to or less than that in public spending.[9]

14.2 Public procurement

Public procurement accounts for **a significant part of economies**: between 10 per cent and 25 per cent of gross domestic product (GDP). In the EU the public purchase of goods and services has been estimated as accounting for 16 per cent of GDP, while in OECD countries it accounts for 12 per cent. It is therefore important that governments spend this money well. Good procurement management can make a difference.

Public procurement is a key tool for increasing the capital of a country, i.e. for carrying out public investment in infrastructure (e.g. roads, railways, bridges, ports, airports), in hospitals, in schools, in museums and in R&D. All such investments increase business opportunities, reduce business costs and are complementary to private investment (Chapter 18).

Public procurement is **a tool that countries can also use to counter recession**.[10] When aggregated demand decreases, governments can increase the level of procurement and act against a recession. For long recessions this tool may work well, but for short recessions it has the limitation that it can only be made ready with some delay; it takes time to decide on new public works and carry out all the needed procurement procedures (definition of terms of reference, publication and tender, among other things). In some cases, when the public works finally start the recession is almost over and the public works may overheat an economy already working at full regime.

Procurement can also be used for other objectives. It can be a tool for fostering **nascent domestic industry**. Domestic firms may have lower productivity, produce worse quality goods and charge higher prices than foreign competitors. However, if they are never awarded public contracts, they have even fewer chances of achieving economies of scale (Section 5.2) and associated improvements. Governments do not face simple choices. What is most important: providing top-quality goods and services to citizens and domestic business or activating domestic firms and creating domestic jobs?

Procurement can also be used to enhance **human rights and social rights, protect the environment** and foster innovation. This can be done through clauses in the terms of reference. Under these clauses bidders for public procurement are accepted if they respect social clauses (*inter alia* conditions regarding avoidance of discrimination, child labour or forced labour; ensuring full inclusion of minorities or disadvantaged groups; and allowing trade union membership), green clauses (complying with certain environmental standards) or R&D clauses (adopting new technologies).

The opening of public procurement markets can be beneficial for the following reasons:[11]

1   It enhances government abilities to obtain better value for money and increases efficient use of public resources.
2   It is a powerful tool for fighting corrupt practices.
3   It increases transparency and legal certainty.

However, the opening of public procurement to international competition reduces its validity as a tool of economic policy. With a procurement market open to international competitors, governments spend money but are less confident of activating domestic demand or of encouraging local firms to make certain changes.

Read

Government spending as a way to avoid a recession

The recommended reading comes from Thailand. It shows the case of a government that wants to avoid a recession or a slowdown of the economy. The article clearly illustrates the main difficulties that they encounter in doing this.

Read

"Fast Track Budget Urged," Wichit Chantanusornsiri, *Bangkok Post*, 21 July 2015.

Questions

* What seems to be a problem with budget disbursements?
* Amid poor levels of exports, private investment and domestic consumption, what is the task given to public investment?
* Why does the Budget Bureau want to accelerate spending?

Analysis

The Thai Government faces a contraction of several components of demand: exports, private investment and domestic consumption, which could lead to lower growth, stagnation or recession. To avoid this, the government has decided to increase public investment and therefore public procurement. Public demand would compensate for the scarcity of private and foreign demand. However, it seems that there are some problems with the speed of disbursements. This is a standard problem when governments use procurement to provide a stimulus to the economy, and is particularly true when procedures are long and complicated. It is therefore understandable that government seeks to speed up the process so as to avoid public investment being undertaken when the economy is already recovering.

COMMENTS TO TABLE 14.1

France, UK, Estonia and Greece are those who spend the largest share of their GDP on defence. In the EU, those who spend more in public order and safety are mostly the lower-income countries (Hungary, Portugal, Greece, Croatia, Poland, Romania, Slovakia and Bulgaria). UK, Czech Republic, Belgium, The Netherlands, Austria, France, Norway and Denmark are the EU countries whose governments spend the largest share of GDP on health. Finland, Belgium, Sweden, Denmark and Iceland are the countries where public spending on education is higher, while in Spain, Italy, Bulgaria, Ireland and Romania, it is lower.

Health care: why is it publicly provided?

Places in a hospital are few and expensive to produce. If you are admitted, perhaps I will not be admitted (we are rivals for the use of the same bed). Once the ward is full, arranging for other beds means hiring new staff and finding new rooms. These things may be expensive. There is a high marginal cost (see Section 4.2) in health care. It would also be easy to say: "if you do not pay, you will not admitted to hospital and treated". Exclusion is technically possible and in some situations, actually occurs. So why, at least in some countries, is health care publicly provided? In the case of health care, there are not only distributional considerations, considerations of fairness and humanity (you cannot abandon a sick person), there are also other considerations. Health care is a field in which the provider (doctor) and the user (patient) have very different levels of information. This violates one of the basic assumptions of a competitive market economy. Buyers and sellers should have more or less the same information if we want markets to be efficient. When this does not happen, we say that there is **asymmetry of information**. Under such conditions the results achieved will not be efficient, and considerable waste can be expected. Finally, the health service creates important **externalities**, i.e. effects on those who neither use it nor work for it. Everybody derives benefits from the vaccination of people unable to pay or from the treatment of poor people with infectious diseases. In this way the spread of diseases diminishes.

In Figure 14.2 we compare health expenditure as a share of GDP in those countries which have high life expectancy (more than 79.9 years in 2013) and populations of more than 15m people. We may observe that the US spends an extremely high proportion of its GDP on health. In 2013, among the countries considered, the US was also the country with the lowest life expectancy. Such countries as the UK, Italy, France and Spain were able to achieve higher life expectancy with much lower expenditure. This is probably explicable by the fact that the US health system has a large private component whereas the other countries mentioned have mainly public health systems.

TABLE 14.1 Total general government expenditure by function in some European countries as a share of GDP

Year 2015	General public services	Defence	Public order and safety	Economic affairs	Environment protection	Housing and community amenities	Health	Recreation, culture and religion	Education	Social protection	Total
Austria	6.9	0.6	1.4	6.2	0.4	0.4	8.0	1.2	5.0	21.7	51.8
Belgium	8.1	0.8	1.8	6.5	0.9	0.3	7.7	1.2	6.4	20.2	53.9
Bulgaria	3.2	1.4	2.8	6.1	0.8	2.1	5.5	1.7	4.0	13.3	40.9
Croatia	9.1	1.3	2.2	5.0	0.5	0.8	6.6	1.5	4.7	15.1	46.8
Cyprus	10.2	1.4	1.7	3.5	0.4	1.8	2.6	0.9	5.7	12.0	40.2
Czech Republic	4.3	0.9	1.8	6.6	1.1	0.7	7.6	1.3	4.9	12.7	41.9
Denmark	7.4	1.1	1.0	3.7	0.4	0.2	8.6	1.8	7.0	23.6	54.8
Estonia	4.3	1.9	1.8	4.8	0.7	0.4	5.5	2.0	6.1	12.9	40.4
European Union	6.2	1.4	1.8	4.3	0.8	0.6	7.2	1.0	4.9	19.2	47.4
Finland	8.5	1.3	1.2	4.8	0.2	0.4	7.2	1.5	6.2	25.6	56.9
France	6.3	1.8	1.6	5.7	1.0	1.1	8.2	1.3	5.5	24.6	57.1
Germany	5.9	1.0	1.6	3.1	0.6	0.4	7.2	1.0	4.2	19.0	44.0
Greece	9.9	2.7	2.1	8.9	1.5	0.2	4.5	0.7	4.3	20.5	55.3
Hungary	8.9	0.5	2.1	8.6	1.2	1.1	5.3	2.1	5.2	15.0	50.0
Iceland	7.7	0.0	1.5	5.0	0.6	0.5	7.4	3.2	7.5	9.5	42.9
Ireland	4.1	0.4	1.1	3.4	0.4	0.6	5.7	0.6	3.7	9.6	29.6
Italy	8.4	1.2	1.9	4.1	1.0	0.6	7.1	0.7	4.0	21.5	50.5
Latvia	5.2	1.0	2.0	4.2	0.7	0.6	3.8	1.6	6.0	11.5	37.0
Lithuania	4.4	1.3	1.6	3.6	0.5	1.0	5.8	0.9	5.4	11.1	34.9
Luxembourg	4.4	0.3	1.0	5.0	1.1	0.3	4.6	1.2	5.2	18.9	42.2
Malta	6.8	0.8	1.2	5.1	2.0	0.5	5.8	1.2	5.5	12.4	41.2
Netherlands	5.0	1.1	1.8	4.0	1.4	0.3	8.0	1.4	5.4	16.6	45.0
Norway	4.7	1.5	1.1	5.1	0.9	0.8	8.4	1.5	5.5	19.4	48.9
Poland	4.9	1.6	2.2	4.6	0.6	0.7	4.7	1.1	5.2	15.9	41.5
Portugal	8.1	1.1	2.1	5.1	0.4	0.5	6.2	0.8	6.0	18.3	48.6
Romania	4.8	1.0	2.3	5.3	1.0	1.5	4.2	1.2	3.1	11.5	35.9
Slovakia	6.5	1.1	2.4	6.3	1.0	0.8	7.2	1.0	4.2	15.0	45.5
Slovenia	6.8	0.8	1.6	6.0	1.0	0.6	6.7	1.6	5.6	17.4	48.1
Spain	6.5	1.0	2.0	4.4	0.9	0.5	6.2	1.1	4.1	17.1	43.8
Sweden	7.1	1.1	1.3	4.2	0.3	0.7	6.9	1.1	6.5	20.9	50.1
Switzerland	4.3	0.9	1.7	3.7	0.7	0.2	2.2	0.8	5.8	13.5	33.8
United Kingdom	4.5	2.1	2.0	3.1	0.8	0.5	7.6	0.7	5.1	16.4	42.8

Source: Eurostat

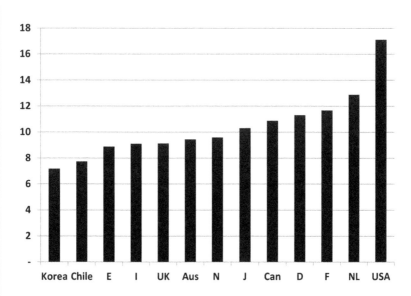

FIGURE 14.2 In 2013 the total health expenditure as a share of GDP in countries with life expectancy of at least 79.9 years and population of more than 15 million

The US with a health service largely privately supplied spends much more on health care than countries such as the UK, France, Spain and Italy, where the health services are mostly provided by a national health service. In the countries mentioned, health is good and life expectancy is very high.

Source: Elaboration of the author of World Bank and UNDESA data

Glossary

asymmetry of information Situation in which one party to a deal has much less information than the other, leading to inefficient results and wasted resources.

externality Effect of a production or leisure activity on a third party which has not carried out, purchased or invested in that activity.

government consumption The sum of the salaries of public employees (public value added) and of government intermediate consumption.

government outlays The sum of government purchases, payments of interest on the public debt and monetary transfers to families and firms. It is the money that government pays.

government spending (or government purchases) In macroeconomics this is the sum of the salaries of public employees (public value added) and of government procurement. Sometimes the sum of these two items is qualified as primary government expenditure. In public finance, although not in macroeconomic analysis, "government expenditure" (government outlay) also includes payments of interest on public debt and monetary transfers to families and firms.

green procurement Public procurement with the inclusion of environmental clauses.

green purchases Purchases, which occur through green procurement.

gross public value added Public value added plus depreciation of durable public goods.

nascent domestic industry An industry in the first phases of its development. A government may consider the possibility of protecting and supporting it for a certain period before it can become competitive.

public employment The employment generated and paid for by the public sector.

public intermediate consumption The purchases of non-durable goods and of external services by government bodies.

public procurement The purchase of goods and services by the public sector. It does not include the salaries of the public sector, but includes public intermediate consumption and the purchase of durable public goods, bridges, roads, ports, schools and hospitals, among other things.

public value added The sum of salaries paid to those in public employment. It cannot be calculated as a difference between total revenue and intermediate consumption, because the public sector does not sell its production, but imposes taxes on residents.

Notes

1 Defence is an example of so-called "public goods". Citizens do not compete to have these goods. Once a country is safe, the arrival of an additional citizen usually does not require additional defence costs. At the same time excluding some citizen from their benefits would be very difficult. You may contribute or not to the defence budget, but if the country is safe, it is safe also for you.

2 Abel et al. (2014:58).

3 United Nations Statistics Division (2009:96) http://unstats.un.org/unsd/nationalac count/docs/SNA2008.pdf and (European System of Accounts, 2010:433). The demand of government is considered final demand, but for government, the goods it buys to deliver its services are intermediate consumption as several documents confirm.

4 Government final consumption =

+ Government output
- sales of goods and services
+ social transfers in kind via market producers.

(European Commission, 2013:433)
The major item is usually government output.
Government Output =

+ compensation of employees
+ intermediate consumption
+ consumption of fixed capital
+ other taxes on production
- other subsidies on production,
+ operating surplus.

(European Commission, 2013:433).

5 Gross Fixed Capital Formation consists of resident producers' acquisitions, less disposals, of fixed assets during a given period plus certain additions to the value of non-produced assets realized by the productive activity of producer or institutional units. Fixed assets are produced assets used in production for more than one year. (European Commission, 2013:73). According to Eurostat (http://ec.europa.eu/eurostat/web/products-datasets/-/teina210), this definition also applies to investments done by the general government. The FED St Louis seems to indicate similar things https://fred.stlouisfed.org/series/I3GTOTLGES000.

According to the WB: "Gross capital formation (formerly gross domestic investment) consists of outlays on additions to the fixed assets of the economy plus net changes in the level of inventories. Fixed assets include land improvements (fences, ditches, drains, and so on); plant, machinery, and equipment purchases; and the construction of roads, railways, and the like, including schools, offices, hospitals, private residential dwellings, and commercial and industrial buildings. Inventories are stocks of goods held by firms to meet temporary or unexpected fluctuations in production or sales, and 'work in progress'. According to the 1993 SNA, net acquisitions of valuables are also considered capital formation." http://econ.worldbank.org/WBSITE/EXTERNAL/DATASTATISTICS/0,,print:Y~isCURL:Y~contentMDK:20451590~pagePK:641 33150~piPK:64133175~theSitePK:239419~isCURL:Y~isCURL:Y,00.html.

Some statistics do not distinguish the Gross Capital Formation paid with public resources from that which is carried out by private firms. This allows us to see the whole growth of the capital of the country but ignores the contribution, which the public sector provides.

6 This is the definition of the public net value added. The public gross value added is given by the sum of the salaries of public employees plus the consumption of public capital (depreciation in the public sector).

7 According to the European Commission: "Public procurement refers to the process by which public authorities, such as government departments or local authorities, purchase work, goods or services from companies. Examples include the building of a state school, purchasing furniture for a public prosecutor's office and contracting cleaning services for a public university." https://ec.europa.eu/growth/single-market/public-procurement_en.

According to OECD: "Public procurement refers to the purchase by governments and state-owned enterprises of goods, services and works." www.oecd.org/gov/ethics/public-procurement.htm.

8 www.jstor.org/stable/1906924?seq=1#page_scan_tab_contents.

9 For more advanced readers: Take the simple example of a closed economy. Then, $Y = C + I + G$. Let Consumption be given by disposable income in a linear fashion, i.e., $C = c + c (Y - T)$.

For investment exogenous, a change in government expenditure financed by an increase in taxes is given by: $\Delta Y = c (\Delta Y - \Delta T) + \Delta G$

However, $\Delta T) = \Delta G$

Hence, $\Delta Y = 1$ which is the balanced budget multiplier.

$$\frac{\Delta G}{\Delta Y}$$

Generally, if we allow investment to change due to changes in the interest rate, then, $\leq 1 \Delta G$

10 This is within the stabilization role of government: to act countercyclically. It pushes the economy, when it would not grow enough and it brakes it, when it would grow too much.

11 See http://ec.europa.eu/trade/policy/accessing-markets/public-procurement/

Bibliography

Abel, A. B., Bernanke, B. and Croushore, D. D. (2014). *Macroeconomics*. Boston: Addison-Wesley.

Chantanusornsiri, W. (2015). "Fast Track Budget Urged," *Bangkok Post*, 21 July.

European Commission. (2013). *European system of accounts — ESA 2010*, Luxembourg: Publications Office of the European Union.

United Nations Statistics Division. (2009). "System of National Account, 2008," European Commission, International Monetary Fund, Organisation for Economic Co-operation and Development, United Nations, World Bank. https://unstats.un.org/unsd/nationalaccount/sna2008.asp.

15

PUBLIC SPENDING ON EDUCATION, TRAINING, RESEARCH AND DEVELOPMENT (R&D)

Those interested in development, productivity and salaries must pay specific attention to the knowledge and skills available to the workforce of a country. In this field public expenditure plays a key role.

Public spending on education, training, and R&D therefore deserves special attention on account of its great impact on the economic development of a country. Section 15.1 addresses public spending on education, 15.2 public spending on R&D, and 15.3 their short-term and long-term effects on the economy.

15.1 Education and training[1]

In national accounts most of education expenditure is classified as public consumption. Many constitutions specify education as a right of citizens. It is therefore not so strange that we often think of education as a possible outcome of economic development or as a form of social expenditure. But this is not necessarily the case. The first questions could be: Why should government fund education? Why should government produce educational services? Is it not better to rely on market forces to handle it?

That great liberal economist, Adam Smith, long ago (1776) supported the idea that governments should help families with the purchase of education. This because probably some people, pressed by other needs or for limited information, would buy too little education for themselves or for their children, with heavy consequences for the latter in particular. The future of some children would depend too much on the wrong choices of their parents.

In some cases, parents understand that education would be a good investment for the future of their children, but the financial markets do not lend to them. This defect in the financial market would lead to a lower level of education and lower productivity in the economy.

Public funding of education is also a tool for fighting inequality. While it can be acceptable that there are different salaries for individuals with different levels of productivity (see Section 3.3), it is less acceptable that the productivity and therefore the salary of a person simply depends on the financial means of their parents. And worse, this is highly inefficient: we end up not rewarding those with the greatest abilities, but those with wealthier parents. This limits the possibilities in our economy, as it sweeps aside the abilities of some very capable people. In this sense, equality of opportunity underpins efficiency in the economy.

However, this is not the only reason for funding education: the education of a person benefits not only that person but the whole of society. In the US, those states that spend less on education per pupil tend to record lower performance as measured by earnings.[2] Each person lives better if they live in a society in which many people are educated; for example, crime is lower when education is higher.[3] Moreover education helps integrate immigrants into the society which receives them. This helps a nation grow. Education in science and technology provides society with those persons who are key to technological progress. These people, innovators, typically only capture a fraction of their overall contribution to the increase of productivity. Many benefits go to society at large.

Why should government produce or at least regulate education? People grow in one place and then often move somewhere else. If the educational standards within the country or the region are too different the mobility of people is seriously damaged and the labour market becomes less efficient.

Education increases the skills of individuals and therefore productivity, profits and wages. In this perspective, education should be considered as an investment. Education teaches people how to perform well in the workplace, by teaching them how to obey instructions, follow directions and work in teams. It leads to punctuality and reliability. Education is an activity which also provides benefits to those who do not provide or receive it. For this reason, we say that education generates "externalities". Externalities occur when a firm or individual imposes a cost on other firms or individuals, but does not compensate them – or alternatively when one firm or individual confers a benefit on other firms or individuals but does not reap a reward for providing it. When there are externalities there is strong justification for government intervention.[4]

Moreover, education helps identify the abilities of different individuals. It may be that schools do not greatly increase the productivity of individuals but help identify productive individuals and those with the necessary drive and ambition. In this sense, the school is a screening device which helps markets work better, bringing about a better match between individuals and jobs. This increases the productivity of the economy. In the field of education markets do not work very well. Parents, particularly less well-educated parents, are often not well-informed; they are ill-prepared to judge the effectiveness of schools in providing key skills. This argument supports the role of government in providing or regulating education.

Watch

http://heckmanequation.org/content/resource/early-childhood-education-has-high-rate-return.

Questions

* According to the research of the Nobel Laureate, Professor Heckman, what is the rate of return on early childhood education?
* In the case of early childhood education, is there a trade-off between efficiency and equality?
* What is the difference between investing in bridges and roads and investing in education?
* What is the view of the Boeing vice president on early childhood education?
* Is early childhood education "hard-headed" or "soft-hearted"?

Analysis

According to Professor James Heckman, the rate of return on early childhood education is one of the highest of any possible policy, around 7–10 per cent per annum. The case of early childhood education is the extreme case in the field of education because positive investment returns exist at every level of education, especially when money is spent on lower-income students and on those who would study much less if public help were not provided.

Early childhood education tackles inequality and at the same time fosters productivity; in this case therefore, there is no trade-off between equality and efficiency. Early childhood is no less an investment than the building of bridges and roads.

According to Diana Sands, Boeing vice-president for financial planning and investor relations, early childhood education is essential to providing corporations with those talents and skills they need to succeed. We can therefore say, as one of the persons interviewed for this video, David Pope, states, that a policy aimed at supporting early childhood education is both soft-hearted and hard-headed.

15.2 Public expenditure in R&D[5]

Governments play an important role in fostering innovation in at least two ways: regulating and financing. The regulation of innovation passes through the definition and protection of intellectual property rights. In providing this, governments should take into account two opposite interests and try to strike a balance:

1   The first is the immediate short-term interest of society in using as much innovation as possible, with as few constraints as possible. If a drug is available,

why not use it? We could treat as many patients as possible. In this sense, intellectual property rights encounter limitations when they go against economic efficiency[6] or human rights.[7]

2   The second is the medium-to-long term interest of society in having innovators and entrepreneurs interested in financing research. This would lead to granting intellectual property rights over very long periods. You finance research today and later derive benefits from this commitment.

A possible alternative to patents might consist of developing innovation within public institutions, as frequently occurs in practice. In that case, the community would pay for innovations in advance through financial support for research. Not by chance do many countries spend part of their public budget on R&D. The research that most of all needs public funding is basic or fundamental research. Research in theoretical physics, theoretical chemistry, mathematics or biology yields great returns to society but few benefits to those that carry it out. More controversial is government support for applied research and the development of new products. Those who oppose it say that governments are not good at picking winners. Those who support it say that this is not true and that governments have a remarkably good record in this regard. Countries which made choices recorded greater success. A possible solution might consist of forms of co-funding in which governments participate in applied research projects provided that some private firm puts up part of the money.

R&D is a semi-public good. This is because, when there is an invention, excluding somebody from its use is rather complicated and sometimes not possible (exclusion is difficult). Moreover, the fact that somebody makes use of an innovation does not limit the use made by other users (rivalry in use is low). If you cannot exclude someone from the use of a good and an additional user does not restrict the use of that good by other users (i,e, there is no rivalry), that good is called a "pure public good". Finally, there is a great degree of uncertainty associated with R&D. You may carry out research on projects with low returns. However, projects with high returns will benefit many people who did not pay for those projects (successful projects generate positive externalities). For these reasons, the private sector alone would carry out less research than we need, the so-called "social optimum", and therefore a public intervention in R&D is needed.

Watch

Mariana Mazzucato: "Government – investor, risk-taker, innovator." www.youtube.com/watch?v=3r1IPsldbBg.

Questions

- What is the secret behind the success of Silicon Valley?
- Why is the US so much more successful than Europe in making new IT innovations?
- How far is the private sector more innovative than the public sector?
- Who actually funded the most revolutionary objects that you have in your pockets or on your desk, e.g. internet, GPS and touchscreen display?
- Was the US government fixing market failures or shaping markets?
- Who obtains the rewards from innovation?
- Do high-tech companies pay many taxes to the US government?
- How can governments retain part of the profits from the innovations they have contributed to funding?

Analysis

Many countries admire the incredible US success in fostering innovation in IT and other technological fields. Silicon Valley has no real equivalent elsewhere in the world. The commonly held prejudice is that the US gave much more space to market forces, also represented by venture capital and angel investors, keeping government at bay and under control. This allowed the initiatives of revolutionary individuals to create exceptional innovations. The historic truth, according to the research of Professor Mazzuccato, is that all the innovations behind such innovative products as smartphones, the internet, GPS, the touchscreen display and much more, were heavily funded by the public sector. In this sense, we cannot say that the public sector was less innovative than the private sector.

According to Professor Mazzuccato, the US Government not only fixed market failures, i.e. situations in which markets do not lead to efficient results, but also shaped the market. However, she says the US Government receives very little reward for and acknowledgement of its successful investments. Indeed, the tax system allows large technological corporations to pay very low taxes on their huge profits. Professor Mazzuccato suggests that government should fund innovations, becoming shareholders of the companies they subsidize.

15.3 Government expenditure in education and R&D and its macroeconomic effects

During recessions, government may decide to spend more on education and R&D just as a way of creating additional demand and fostering short-term growth. Even if some economists[8] note that any long-run position of an economy is simply the result of a series of short-period positions, many economists would agree that the economy of a country grows for a limited number of reasons: the growth of the population and the workforce, the growth in the quantity of available equipment and of available buildings and infrastructures (the capital of a country), the growth in the skills of the population, improvements in technology, or a combination of these factors.

The first source of growth, population, may increase the GDP (see Section 8.1) of a country, but does not increase the *per capita* GDP of a country, which is the ratio between the GDP and the population of a country, a measure of welfare. Therefore, population growth increases the size of an economy, but does not improve the welfare of its inhabitants.

Equipment, buildings and infrastructures not only make the total GDP of a country grow, but also make *per capita* GDP grow; they enhance the productivity of workers and the welfare of citizens. The only problem with equipment and buildings is that when one is already well equipped with tools and infrastructure, any additional tool or infrastructure is less and less useful (i.e. the decreasing marginal productivity of capital, Section 8.1). Moreover, the more tools and infrastructure one has, the more one should pay to renovate existing tools and buildings when they become old. There is much depreciation (see Section 10.2) of the physical assets.

Education and training of people are further ways of increasing the welfare of a country. Better-educated people can better carry out more complex or productive operations; and the advantages are greater still when one provides education for all children than when one provides advanced university education to everyone of university age. In any event providing education and training increases skills and capabilities and improves the welfare of a country. Finally, technological progress is the best way of guaranteeing the continuous growth of a country. It allows production of new and better products, and production of more with the same resources or of the same with fewer resources. Since it allows production of the same or more with fewer employees, technological progress is accused of destroying jobs. Is this true? Yes and no. There are two effects of technological progress. The first concerns production processes and their productivity. Such progress increases the productivity of processes. This type of technological progress destroys jobs. The second type of technological progress concerns the development of new products, new needs and new jobs. This type of progress creates jobs. On balance, the latter effect usually wins over the former and innovative countries do not see their employment levels decrease.

Glossary

angel investor An investor who provides financial backing for small start-ups or entrepreneurs. Angel investors are usually found among an entrepreneur's family and friends. The capital they provide can be a one-time injection of seed money or ongoing support to carry the company through difficult times.[9]

externality The cost or benefit accruing to a party who did not choose to incur that cost or benefit. It is a case of market failure.[10]

market failure A situation in which markets produce inefficient results.

patent The exclusive right granted by a government to an inventor to manufacture, use or sell an invention for a certain number of years.[11]

per capita GDP   The ratio between the GDP and the population of a country. It is an indicator of the well-being of the inhabitants of a country. To have a precise idea of the wellbeing or welfare of a population, other indicators are necessary, for example, an indicator of inequality such as the Gini coefficient (see Section 20.1).

pure public goods   Goods with two properties: firstly, it costs nothing for an additional individual to enjoy their benefits; secondly, it is generally difficult or impossible to exclude individuals from the enjoyment of a pure public good.[12]

R&D   See *research and development*.

rate of return   The gain or loss made on an investment over a specified period, taking account both of the asset value at the end of the period and of its contributions in the course of the period. If the period lasts one year, we can build a ratio given by the total value of the asset (asset + its contributions) at the end of the year and its value at the beginning. If you subtract 1 from this ratio, you obtain the annual rate of return.

research and development (R&D)   Systematic activity combining both basic and applied research, aimed at discovering solutions to problems or at creating new goods and knowledge. R&D may result in ownership of intellectual property such as patents.[13]

semi-public good   A good which has several aspects of a pure public good, without completely matching the definition of the latter.

technological progress   An improvement in the state of technology. It may lead to producing the same as before but with fewer inputs; to producing more than before with the same inputs; or to producing completely new products. In the first two cases it can reduce employment, but in the third case it usually increases it. Its total effect on employment is usually not negative, as it implies additional demand for new products.

venture capital   Start-up companies with a potential to grow need a certain amount of investment. Wealthy investors like to invest their capital in such businesses with a long-term growth perspective. This capital is known as venture capital and the investors are known as venture capitalists.[14] Usually the sums provided by venture capitalists are greater than those provided by angel investors.

Notes

1 This sub-section widely makes reference to chapter 16 of Stiglitz (2000), which is the reading recommended on this topic.
2 Becker (1975) quoted by Stiglitz (2000).
3 See for example Moretti (2005), Lochner and Moretti (2003), or Machin et al., 2010.
4 See endnote 10.
5 This sub-section widely refers to Stiglitz (2000:342–350).
6 As early as 1986, empirical research into the effect of patent law on innovation found "its effects in this regard are very small in most of the industries we studied". Mansfield

(1986). Boldrin and Levine (2013) concluded that "while patents can have a partial equilibrium effect of improving incentives to invent, the general equilibrium effect on innovation can be negative." Other patent modelling research suggests that rather than encouraging innovation, patents can hinder development, lower R&D investments, and decrease overall economic output. Torrance and Tomlinson (2009).

7 The UN Special Rapporteur in the field of cultural rights, has written: "The right to protection of moral and material interests cannot be used to defend patent laws that inadequately respect the right to participate in cultural life, to enjoy the benefits of scientific progress and its applications, to scientific freedoms and the right to food and health and the rights of indigenous peoples and local communities. Patents, when properly structured, may expand the options and well-being of all people by making new possibilities available. Yet, they also give patent-holders the power to deny access to others, thereby limiting or denying the public's right of participation to science and culture. The human rights perspective demands that patents do not extend so far as to interfere with individuals' dignity and well-being. Where patent rights and human rights are in conflict, human rights must prevail. Whereas from the perspective of trade law, exclusions, exceptions and flexibilities under international intellectual property law, such as the World Trade Organization Agreement on Trade-Related Aspects of Intellectual Property Rights, remain optional, from the perspective of human rights, they are often to be considered as obligations" Shaheed (2015).

8 Kalecki (1971:165).

9 www.investopedia.com/terms/a/angelinvestor.asp#ixzz3iQvi8lIz.

10 See Buchanan and Stubblebine (1962) for a similar definition.

11 http://dictionary.reference.com/browse/patent.

12 See Stiglitz (2000:80).

13 www.businessdictionary.com/definition/research-and-development-R-D.html# ixzz3iR1aUKjk.

14 http://economictimes.indiatimes.com/definition/venture-capital.

Bibliography

Becker, G. (1975). *Human capital: A theoretical and empirical analysis with special reference to education*, 2nd ed. New York: NBER, Columbia University Press.

Boldrin, M. and Levine, D. K. (2013). "The Case Against Patents," *The Journal of Economic Perspectives*, 27(1): 3–22, 3. doi:10.1257/jep.27.1.3.

Buchanan, J. M. and Stubblebine, W. C. (1962). "Externality," *Economica*, 29(116) (November): 371–384.

Kalecki, M. (1971). *Selected essays on the dynamics of the capitalist economy*. Cambridge: Cambridge University Press.

Lochner, L. and Moretti, E. (2003). *The effect of education on crime: Evidence from prison inmates, arrests, and self-reports*. http://eml.berkeley.edu/~moretti/lm46.pdf.

Machin, S., Marie, O. and Vujic, S. (2010). "The Crime Reducing Effects of Education," IZA Discussion Paper No. 5000. IZA (Institute for the Study of Labor), Bonn, Germany.

Mansfield, E. (1986). "Patents and Innovation: An Empirical Study," *Management Science*, 32(2): 173–181, 180. doi:10.1287/mnsc.32.2.173. Archived (PDF) from the original on 10 May 2014.

Moretti, E. (2005). "Does Education Reduce Participation in Criminal Activities?" Department of Economics UC Berkeley, September. http://devweb.tc.columbia.edu/manager/symposium/Files/74_Moretti_Symp.pdf.

Shaheed, F. (2015). *Report of the special rapporteur in the field of cultural rights*. United Nations General Assembly.

Smith, A. (1776). *An inquiry into the nature and causes of the wealth of nations. London, Methuen, 1922.*

Stiglitz, J. (2000). *Economics of the public sector*, 3rd ed. New York: W. W. Norton & Company.

Torrance, A. and Tomlinson, W. (2009). "Patents and the Regress of Useful Arts," *Columbia Science and Technology Law Review*, 10: 130–168.

16

PUBLIC DEFICIT AND PUBLIC DEBT

The public policy debate often reaches a point at which policies cost too much and bring the public finances into deficit. In other cases, deficits have occurred in the past and a country has to handle the burden of public debt. But are they always an evil? How can countries handle them? Section 16.1 analyses the public budget and the public deficit, 16.2 presents public debt and sovereign bonds (Section 9.1), and 16.3 analyses the issue of the desirability and sustainability of debt.

16.1 The public budget and the public deficit

Governments receive and make monetary transfers (Chapter 13), and carry out government spending (Chapter 14). The difference between the net transfers from the private sector to the public sector (government revenue *minus* benefits to families and subsidies to firms), and government payments may be positive when government receives more than it spends, and in that case, there is a public surplus. At that point, the government is lending to the domestic private sector or to foreign economies, or to both.

In other instances, the difference between what the government receives in net transfers (net taxes) and what it spends on its outlays is a negative number, and then there is a public deficit and the government must borrow either from the private domestic sector or from abroad.

Among public payments one item deserves special attention: interest to holders of public debt. Many countries have a debt (see Section 16.2) and on this debt they pay interest to their creditors. These are often the holders of the bonds (promises of payment) issued by the country, even if governments can also receive credits which are not in the form of bonds. The bonds issued by governments are called sovereign bonds. The effects on the economy of interest on public debt change considerably, depending on who holds the debt.

If the debt is held by many domestic private savers or by domestic financial institutions which use most of their assets to lend to the domestic economy, payments of interest to bondholders go some way towards stimulating domestic demand. This assumes that domestic savers are numerous and include families of middle or low income, that is those with a higher propensity to consume. These are the families which, when they receive an additional dollar, will most probably spend most of it. If domestic savers are only wealthy families, this is much less true. Wealthy families can already satisfy most of their expenditure desires without receiving such interest. When they do receive interest payments, they probably save these sums and do not spend more. Their additional savings may or may not be used for new investments, this depends on the decisions of the financial system and of industrial firms. Let us therefore consider what happens when financial institutions receive private savings or interest on public debt which belongs to them. In some cases, domestic financial institutions may decide to make resources available for domestic firms and families. This may eventually lead to more investment and more consumption.

In other cases, financial institutions do not wish to do this, or cannot. They may use money to carry out some purely financial operation which does not entail the use (Section 8.2) of more domestic goods. In Section 9.3 is an explanation as to why money which enters the financial system may not affect the purchase of goods and services. Even when financial institutions fund domestic companies with credits or with the purchase of their corporate bonds or shares, firms may decide to use these additional resources to buy financial assets. For example, firms may buy their own shares without increasing their capital expenditure or the wages they pay.

When domestic savers are wealthy, when domestic banks do not lend to the domestic economy, or when firms borrow from banks but then use money for purely financial operations, interest payments to them may not stimulate demand for the goods of the borrowing country. Things are even worse when the holders of public debt are foreigners. In this case all interest which the domestic government pays them is probably lost. There is a reduction in the income that families can consume or save (disposable income, see Section 13.3). There is hardly any contribution to domestic demand. In all these cases, if governments raise taxes to pay the interest on their debt, they reduce disposable income and internal demand through taxes and barely contribute to it at all through their interest payments. In this way governments reduce the demand for domestic goods.

There is also a positive aspect. If this money does not contribute to domestic aggregate demand for goods, neither can it contribute greatly to inflation (see Section 9.3). This is the reason why when the central banks support governments in financing this expenditure, they do not necessarily generate inflation. This was the case with Japan, the UK and the US following the great recession of 2008–2009, at least up until 2017. Their central banks issued money[1] to buy government bonds from financial institutions. This purchase increased the price of bonds and the desire of the financial institutions for more government bonds. Even if governments were offering lower and lower yields, financial institutions were willing to buy government bonds. This *per se* reduced the public expenditure for interests. Add to this that in many cases the central banks were forwarding to their governments a large part of the profits they had made with these operations.[2] In this way governments paid less on interest and had more resources with which to reduce taxes or increase their expenditure. Therefore, even if central banks were not printing money to fund governments directly, they were doing so indirectly.

When the central bank supports the payment of interest, it can generate inflation if the payments contribute to the domestic demand for either national or foreign goods. If there is excessive demand for foreign goods, the country may have a deficit in its balance of payments (see Section 12.2). In such cases the risk of inflation is serious.

In public finance the government budget can be presented as in Table 16.1. We can observe a clear distinction between primary surplus (or deficit), which does not include expenditure on interest, and the government surplus or deficit which does include it. If a government has a primary surplus, we can say that it is highly probable that it reduces demand in the economy. If it has a primary deficit, it probably contributes positively to aggregate demand.

In countries with more than 10m people and in the absence of the production of some commodity (see Section 7.3) in great international demand, exports do not usually account for more than 35 per cent of GDP. In these countries a primary surplus of more than 3 per cent is not usually maintained for more than a few years. At least this is what we learn from IMF data in the 1980–2017 period. Countries which try to sustain large primary surpluses for many years, without being small or

TABLE 16.1 The government budget

ITEM	COMMENT	
+ Taxes from the private sector to the government		*Government Revenue*
+ Social contributions from the private sector to the government		
− Transfers to families	*Pensions, benefits and negative taxes*	*Primary Government Expenditure*
− Subsidies to companies		
− Salaries of public employees	*Government Spending*	
− Public Procurement	*in macroeconomic terms*	
= **Primary Surplus (+) or Primary Deficit (−)**	*General Government Primary Net Lending (+) or Borrowing (−)*	
− Interests on the Public Debt		
= **Government Surplus or Deficit**	*General Government Net Lending (+) or Net Borrowing (−)*	

without having substantial trade surpluses, usually end up in stagnation or recession. In theory, countries could compensate for scarce public demand with investment expenditure by the private sector. However, repeated substantial primary surpluses rarely fuel private sector investment sprees.

The primary budget deficit is a key variable. Those who are interested in development, wealth creation and job creation should always regard it with great care. Some governments sometimes offer a tax cut or spending increase but at the same time increase the primary surplus. These operations will hardly be expansionary,[3] and *vice versa*.

Read

Doctrinaire approach to primary surplus dangerous

The debate is on in earnest as to whether or not Jamaica can indeed sustain the 7.5% primary surplus target as agreed with the International Monetary Fund under the extended fund facility signed in 2013.

One set of persons call for a reduction of the target. They see it as too austere and choking the economy and inhibiting it from producing the much-needed growth to make lives and standard of living better off.

Similarly, another set of persons call for the target to be maintained at all cost since it is seen as a critical precondition to lay the foundations for the economic growth that the other side is saying that is so desperately required.

A number of persons who depend on the opinion leaders to help them make a decision are looking for an either-or answer (as the saying goes, black or white; no shades of grey) as the discussion sometimes sounds very credible from either side. Unfortunately, most of the persons who speak on the subject do not reveal their inherent epistemological biases toward a particular school of thought and thus give the impression that their analysis is objective and free from value judgement.

I prefer not to take this doctrinaire approach to the discussion but, instead, look closely at the extant contextual realities and propose ways to address the issues that are germane to the well-being of all citizens.

The reality

There is no doubt that since 2013 when Jamaica signed on to the extended fund facility with the IMF, the economy has shown improvements in key macroeconomic variables such as interest rate, inflation, doing-business scores, competitiveness scores, net international reserves, among others.

However, despite the strong performance in the macroeconomic numbers, the majority of citizens cannot say, with any confidence, that their quality of life has improved materially. This, I submit, stems from the severe lack of economic growth despite the macroeconomic stabilisation. Indeed, those persons who subscribe to the Ayn Rand views on economic management will argue that stabilisation is a precondition for growth and so there is no need to rush, as economic growth will come in the long run.

The reality, however, is that when hunger and poverty strike, humans do not have the patience to wait for the long run. It was Keynes who said, ". . . In the long run, we are all dead". It is imperative, therefore, that despite the stabilisation programme, the economic managers put projects in place so that growth can be generated in the short term.

I suggest that government play a strategic role in this regard, as growth cannot be left solely to the Invisible Hand, vis-à-vis the private sector. This is too risky, especially when persons are suffering daily.

Primary surplus and growth

The Gleaner continues to remind the nation that the primary surplus target did not come from a metaphysical place but instead, resulted from carefully studied empirical models on the economy.

While I have no doubt about the robustness of the econometric models that have been used to generate the primary surplus target, it must be noted that models generally take an atomistic view of the economy and, in most cases, cannot account for the vagaries of the political economy in which we operate.

Indeed, the outputs from models are generally a function of the assumptions underlying those models. If the assumptions are relaxed in one direction or another, different results will be generated. So, we cannot think that the results from a model are cast in stone and cannot be relaxed.

In the current environment, it is clear that running a primary surplus of 7.5% of GDP is taking a lot of money out of the economy and prevents investments in growth-inducing projects. In this environment where things are tough and economic growth has been elusive, especially in the short term, shaving off a portion of the primary surplus to invest in growth-inducement projects is a very viable option to pursue.

A primary surplus of 7.5% of GDP amounts to roughly J$122 billion at today's exchange rate, if we use a GDP of US$14 billion. A half a percentage-point reduction in this target will generate roughly J$8 billion in savings. Further, a one percentage-point reduction will generate roughly J$16 billion in savings.

There is no doubt that putting back J$8 billion–J$16 billion back into the economy will go a far way in generating much-needed economic growth once there is a strong growth strategy.

If we accept the PIOJ Growth Inducement Strategy of 2011, we can find more than enough projects to invest in that will generate jobs, valued added to GDP and tax revenues.

For example, initiatives such as rehabilitation of RADA farms roads, upgrading of sanitation facilities, implantation of youth literacy projects, implementation of community mobilisation and youth intervention programmes, among other things, are estimated by the PIOJ to cost J$14.4 billion.

Using the 2011 GDP as base year, the PIOJ estimated that this investment could stimulate economic growth in the region of 1.5–3.1%. In terms of dollar figures, this investment would generate about J$19 billion––J$37 billion in real value added to the economy.

Further, the impact on tax revenues would be in the region of J$4.4 billion–J$8.8 billion. Also, from the implementation of these various projects, at least 1,200 jobs should be generated. The economy is in dire need of this type of stimulus.

Shaving one percentage point off the primary surplus target and using those savings to invest in these critical projects is definitely an option that must be put on the table. We cannot be dogmatic about keeping the primary surplus at 7.5% when real suffering is taking place.

Concluding thoughts

Revising the primary surplus target without strong accountability as to how the funds will be used is not the way to go. The need for a revision is necessary, but it cannot be with the aim of paying salaries and funding opulent lifestyles.

The revision should be directed at investments in growth-inducement projects such as the ones outlined above. Indeed, the IMF, in its revision of the growth forecast for Latin America and the Caribbean on July 15, 2015, said, "Focusing government spending on infrastructure would enhance productivity, thus strengthening potential growth".

Cutting the primary surplus will provide the fiscal space so that this investment can take place in a framework of accountability and greater efficiency. Reducing the primary surplus target by one percentage point will pale in comparison to the social chaos that might arise if we do not tackle the high levels of poverty and inequality threatening the gains from the agreement thus far.

"Doctrinaire Approach to Primary Surplus Dangerous," Densil Williams, *The Jamaica Gleaner*, 26 July 2015.

Watch

"Why Greece Won't Ever Be Able to Pay Off Its Debts With Austerity" Brendan Greeley, *Bloomberg Businessweek*, 19 February 2015. www.bloomberg. com/news/articles/2015-02-19/why-greece-won-t-ever-be-able-to-pay-off-its-debts-with-austerity.

Questions

- What is the debate in Jamaica about?
- What is still lacking in Jamaica following the recommendations of the IMF, despite macroeconomic stabilization? Does this surprise you?
- In Jamaica, what is the problem with running a primary surplus of 7.5 per cent of GDP? From the video:
- How can you measure austerity?
- What is the primary surplus?
- Since 1974, which countries achieved a primary surplus greater than 5 per cent for more than ten years?
- According to the Centre for Economic Policy Research what are the conditions under which countries have durable primary surpluses?

Analysis

Austerity can be measured by the primary budget surplus, that is the difference between all government revenues and all government expenditure, excluding expenditure on interest on the public debt.

Since 1974, only three countries have achieved a primary surplus greater than 5 per cent for more than ten years: Singapore, Norway and Belgium. These are three small countries where exports account for most of GDP. This is not strange since, according to the Centre for Economic Policy Research, only countries with sustained growth and a positive current account balance in the balance of payments (see Section 12.3) can sustain primary surpluses for many years.

In Jamaica, the debate is about whether or not Jamaica can indeed sustain the 7.5 per cent primary surplus target, as agreed with the IMF, under the extended funding facility signed in 2013. According to Professor Williams, despite macroeconomic stabilization, economic growth is still lacking in Jamaica and the average Jamaican family does not live any better. This is not surprising because, as we see in Table 16.2, exports represent only about 30 per cent of Jamaican GDP. Therefore, the economy mainly relies on domestic demand for its growth, and a significant

TABLE 16.2 Percentage of exports as a share of GDP

	2010	2011	2012	2013
Greece	22.1	25.5	28.2	30.2
Jamaica	31.3	30.4	30.3	29.8

primary budget surplus entails a cut in public demand, one of the two components of domestic demand. As Professor Williams says, having such large primary surpluses means withholding resources from investment in growth-inducing projects.

The general lesson that one can draw is that countries where exports represent no more than 50 per cent of GDP should be aware of the recessive consequences of primary surpluses.

16.2 The public debt and the market for sovereign bonds

Public deficits are financed through monetization, i.e. when the central bank covers them by issuing new money (see Section 9.3) or through the creation of new debt. The former case today is extremely rare. In the latter case, governments may receive a credit from a financial firm or issue documents which promise to pay a certain sum in a certain currency at a certain date: namely sovereign bonds. The value of the promise written on the bond, its face value, may for example be $100, but the bond may be sold initially at a lower price or, more rarely, a higher price. $100 may be the sum promised by the bond at its maturity (Section 9.1) or redemption date. Bonds are issued by governments usually to a limited number of buyers which are generally important financial institutions, which may then resell them to retail savers.

The trading between the government which issues the bond and its initial buyers is known as the "primary market". This trading occurs only a few times a year, if at all. In some cases, governments organize auctions of their bonds. There is another form of trading which occurs every day between private buyers and private sellers of public debt. This is called the "secondary market". Secondary market bonds were originally acquired on the primary market. The distinction between the two markets is important. The price fixed in the secondary markets mainly affects the private traders who operate in them, even if it is an indicative value for the government and the few financial operators which buy on the primary market. The price defined on a specific day in the primary market defines the interest rate that the government offers to creditors on that part of its debt. For governments, primary markets are determinant since they determine the cost of their debt. Secondary markets however play an important role by influencing primary markets. The lower the price at which governments sell their bonds, the higher the interest rate they must pay on those bonds. If bonds are in great demand, their price is high and the interest on them is low.[4]

For these reasons, governments do their best to ensure strong demand for their bonds in the primary market. A possible way of ensuring strong demand for sovereign

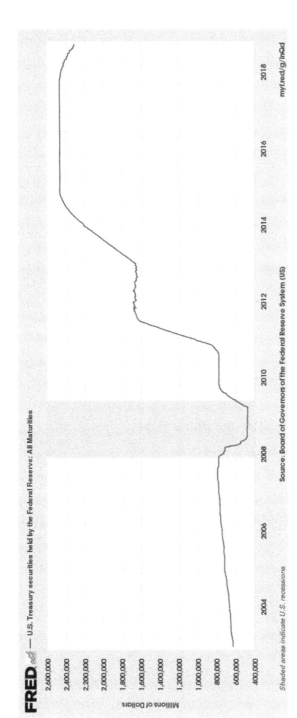

FIGURE 16.1 US Treasury securities held by the Federal Reserve

Source: Board of Governors of the Federal Reserve System (US), US Treasury securities held by the Federal Reserve: All Maturities [TREAST], retrieved from FRED, Federal Reserve Bank of St. Louis; https://fred.stlouisfed.org/series/TREAST, 27 September 2018.

bonds consists of having the national central bank among the buyers. Most present-day legislation allows the central bank to buy only in the secondary market (Figure 16.1 shows the US Treasury securities held by the Federal Reserve). In any case, purchases are much easier when bonds are issued in the national currency. The central bank is a potentially infinite producer of national currency, and should always be very careful, when buying government bonds, not to run the risk of issuing too much money and fuelling excessive inflation. This is usually the case when domestic production of goods can grow no further and money supply is already abundant. In that case, the purchase of bonds by the central bank may lead to excessive demand of goods, creating real inflationary pressures. Central banks should be particularly cautious when the balance of the current account of the balance of payments is negative; it means that the country is already paying the rest of the world more than the rest of the world is paying the country. A further injection of liquidity (money) can make things worse, creating further demand for foreign goods and new debts or sales of assets to foreigners.

It happened that, following the great 2008 financial recession, the US, UK and Japanese central banks intervened massively in their secondary markets, buying huge quantities of domestic bonds from financial institutions. They also bought stressed assets and mortgage-backed securities. This was called "quantitative easing" (see Section 9.3). In this way, they were able to guarantee that the prices of their domestic bonds were sufficiently high, and the rate of interest on them sufficiently low.

However, for countries which borrow in foreign currencies, the intervention of the national central bank is much more constrained, since it depends on the availability of foreign currency reserves.

16.3 The sustainability of a public debt

Is public debt a bad thing? A small public debt is certainly not so: it offers the government the possibility of playing an active role in the financial markets, influencing interest rates. Most economists would agree that if governments borrow for investment projects with high returns and pay interest rates well below those return levels, it should not be a bad thing. However, it is not always so. Governments often declare that they borrow to finance projects with very high returns and then spend money on low-return projects, merely to buy consensus and be re-elected.

Foreign debts can become very large and drain a considerable part of the resources of a country. Just the payments of interest on the debt can be burdensome. Even domestic debt can create distortions in the economy: holders of public debt tend to be older than the rest of the population and in many cases are retired people[5] who do not expect to live as long as younger citizens and are more interested in consuming than investing in the future. If the higher debt leads to higher incomes for these citizens, the economy of the country may tend more towards consumption than investment.[6] This may hinder the growth of a country. In general, if the debt finances growth-enhancing expenditure, then it pays for itself. If it does not, some future expenditure has to be cut or taxes raised to pay the debt – this affects disposable income adversely and in turn affects the motivation to work.

The absolute value of public debt mainly concerns the financial markets. As we have seen, larger debts are usually more liquid than smaller debts and, all things being equal, liquid debt (see Section 16.3) is more appreciated than illiquid debt. In economic terms, what really makes a debt sustainable at a specific moment is a country's ability to pay back the interest and the original principal (to service the debt).

Now if the debt belongs totally to domestic buyers, in a context of scarce capital mobility the ability of the country to service that debt is much higher. The government could tax bondholders or in extreme conditions print money to repay its debt.

In a context of great capital mobility, the government always runs the risk that domestic savers, if they are not satisfied, move their savings abroad and that foreign savers sell their part of the debt. In this context, if the country has substantial inbound payments and has no major outbound payments, creditors are reassured. If the country will have substantial net inbound payments in the future, it will probably have sufficient resources to service its debt. Therefore, investors will be willing to lend to it.

The current account of the balance of payments (see Section 12.1) describes the payments that a country makes to and receives from the rest of the world. A positive trade balance, positive net exports of services, positive net incomes from abroad and positive net transfers from abroad contribute to a positive current account balance. Of all the items that compose the current account, one is relatively easy to predict, namely net capital (or investment) income from abroad. In subsequent years a country that today has many assets (foreign bonds, foreign shares, foreign real estate, foreign firms, credits abroad and foreign currency) and few liabilities with the rest of the world will probably have positive net incomes from abroad. Foreign bonds will generate interest, foreign shares will produce dividends, foreign properties will generate rents, foreign firms will generate profits, foreign credits will be cashed and foreign currency will be available to pay debts. *Vice versa*, if foreigners own national bonds, interest must be paid to them, if they own shares in national firms, dividends must be paid to them, and so forth.

The assets and liabilities of a country with the rest of the world are well described by the net International Investment Position (net IIP, see Section 12.4) of the country. Therefore, we know that countries with positive Net IIP are probably going to have positive net investment income from abroad in the future. Those countries will usually be better prepared to service their foreign debt. Those countries with a negative net IIP will find servicing a debt much harder. Of course, a country with a large foreign debt will probably not have a positive net IIP.

The other major component of the current account is the trade balance in goods and services. A country with a structurally strong trade balance is better prepared to service its debts. Sometimes, however, the trade balance of a country is positive only because the main export of the country has a very high international price. Any change in that price can profoundly affect the trade balance of the country and its ability to honour its debts.

The sustainability of a public debt is often linked with the ratio between public debt and GDP. That measure is based on the notion that GDP is what a country produces and offers the means of paying public debts. However, this idea can sometimes be misleading. Such countries as Spain and Ireland in 2011 and 2012 were not considered very creditworthy, even if their public debt/GDP ratio was relatively small; at the same time Japan was considered as extremely creditworthy even though its public debt/GDP ratio was close to 200%. Careful consideration of the net IIP of these countries reveals that Spain and Ireland had very negative net IIP/GDP ratios and Japan a very positive ratio.

Financial operators consider the situation of a country and its debt and then decide the price they are ready to pay for the bonds of that country. The more creditworthy they consider the country, the more they are ready to buy its debt and the lower the interest rate they ask.

Frequently comparisons are made between different interest rates. Usually the interest on a bond, which pays back its face value in ten years (ten-year bond), is compared with the interest rate paid by the bond with the same maturity (duration), and which pays the lowest interest rate. This is called the benchmark bond. US, Japanese and German bonds are frequently used as benchmark bonds.

The difference between the interest paid by a country, for example Canada, and a benchmark bond, for example US bonds, is called "spread". The higher the spread, the riskier the country is considered. In some countries the spread of the national bonds is announced every day by the media as an indicator of the solidity of the national debt. This can be misleading if it is not interpreted correctly.

FEATURES OF SOVEREIGN BONDS

The debts of different countries are assessed and priced on the basis of different criteria:

1   Maturity: the time needed before bondholders receive all their money back.
2   Security: the risk that the government, which issued the bond, will not pay the money back at the agreed time (risk of default).
3   Currency: the risk that the currency of the bond will depreciate.
4   Liquidity: the ease of reselling the bond once you have purchased it.
5   Volatility: the variability of the value of the bond: the fact that the bond's price can change more or less freely.
6   Interest: the interest which bonds pay every six or twelve months to bondholders.

Creditors are less willing to lend for long periods than for short periods, therefore maturity is important. Fewer countries in the world can issue bonds for ten years or longer periods than those which can issue bonds for short periods, that is a few months or a year.

The security of a bond depends on many factors such as the solidity of the economy which issues the bonds, and the willingness of a country to honour its debt. Indeed, every country has defaulted at least once in its history and many have defaulted many times.

The currency risk is also linked with the risk of inflation. A country with high inflation often also experiences some depreciation of its currency. Following the depreciation bondholders may receive their money back, but that money has a much lower value in terms of foreign currency.

Liquidity means that even when all the other conditions (security, maturity and currency among others) are identical, a bond which is issued and traded in large volumes pays lower interest than do bonds which are traded in small quantities. Usually more liquid bonds are also less volatile. Since they are traded in large quantities, it is harder for a single trader to make their value increase or decrease. For this reason, countries with the same credit risk could save something on the bonds they issue if they issued a single multi-country bond rather than many different national bonds.

Finally, of course the annual payment of interest is also an important feature of a bond, particularly for small investors who expect an annual income from their investment. The higher it is, the higher the price of the bond.

Firstly, we should distinguish between countries which borrow in their own currency and those that borrow in a foreign currency.

The case of **a country borrowing in its own currency** is in some aspects similar to that of a private business. When business people take a credit in the national currency for a certain duration, they usually consider two things: the interest they will pay and their future revenues. If the interest is high, but they believe that their revenue will be very high, they are not afraid to borrow, while if the interest is low, but they expect low or decreasing income, they are probably unwilling to borrow. Their income may simply grow because of inflation, which does not matter, since if it grows it makes the burden of the debt smaller. This is the reason why business people look at interest rates (nominal interest rates) and inflation to determine whether they can sustain their debt. The real interest rate precisely describes this. Equation 1 can be very helpful.

Equation 1 Calculation of the Real Interest Rate

$$Real\ Interest\ Rate = \frac{\left(1\ +\ Nominal\ Interest\ Rate\right)}{\left(1\ +\ Inflation\ Rate\ \right)} - 1$$

The interest rate that a country pays on its debt must always be compared with the growth rate of the GDP of that country. In some cases, debts are updated for inflation with the use of inflation- indexed bonds. But often they are not. The debtor country owes a certain amount of currency at a certain date. Therefore, it does not matter whether the GDP of the country grows because the country produces more (i.e. real GDP growth) or because the prices of domestic goods grow (growth of nominal GDP, see Section 8.1). Inflation often contributes to reducing the debt- to-GDP ratio as much as economic growth does. Country with debts expressed in the national currency may benefit from some inflation provided that this does not lead to higher interest rates on the new emissions of debt. By the same token, deflation may be a serious problem for countries borrowing in domestic currency, in the absence of inflation-indexed bonds. Their nominal GDP shrinks, but their debt remains unchanged.

Let us consider the case of a country which has no primary deficit (Section 16.1), that is which collects in taxes and social contributions just as much as it spends on salaries of public employees, procurement and transfers to families and firms, without considering interest payments. It is a country with a primary balance. In that country the debt-to-GDP ratio grows only for the interest which the country pays and decreases thanks to inflation and GDP growth. Let us imagine that the country has issued bonds in the national currency with a (nominal) interest rate of 8 per cent. Let us also assume that in the country inflation is 5 per cent. Using Equation 1, we can calculate the real interest rate that this country pays:

$$\text{Real Interest rate} = [1.08 \ / \ 1.05] - 1 = 1.0286 - 1 = 0.0286 \text{ or } 2.86\%$$

If this country has an average annual growth of at least 2.86 per cent, its debt-to-GDP ratio will not increase or will decrease. If its average annual growth will be less than 2.86 per cent, the burden of its debt will grow.

The reduction in the nominal debt or spread of a country with a primary balance is not very important; what really matters is that the real GDP of the country is able to grow at a rate which is higher than the real interest rate that the country pays.

This is the reason why austerity policies which push a country to accumulate large primary surpluses to pay back a debt and lead that country into recession may be counterproductive. They may cause the sustainability of that debt to decrease. This is particularly so when austerity policies reduce the international competitiveness of a country, reducing what it spends on education, innovation, export promotion, and creation of high value-added (see Section 2.1) goods.

Everything becomes more complicated for **countries borrowing in foreign currency**. GDP growth and inflation may reduce their debt burden, but increases in interest rates on the foreign currency and reductions in the price of their national currency in terms of the foreign currency – the depreciation of their nominal exchange rate (Section 10.2) – may increase their debt-to-GDP ratio and make their debt less bearable. These countries should be careful not to generate inflation, as that may lead to the depreciation of their currency.

If the debt is held at least partially by foreign holders, it is also important that a country can generate non-negative current account balances.[7] In that way its net International Investment Position (IIP, see Section 12.4)[8] will not worsen and, if its GDP grows, its net IIP/GDP may even improve.

In open financial markets, the interest rate that a country pays depends not only on the total net foreign debt that the country has, but also on its total net foreign equity and its total reserves of foreign currency. These quantities are part of the Net International Investment Position of the country. The greater the net IIP of a country, the greater usually its future capital incomes (Section 12.1) from abroad will be. High capital incomes mean flows of foreign currency reaching the country. A country with a substantial level of income in foreign currency has a greater ability to pay its foreign debts.

Similarly, countries cannot always solve their foreign debt problems by selling assets to foreigners: that may not improve their net IIP. If they sell assets with higher returns than the interest they pay on foreign debt, the operation can be counterproductive. That country creates future substantial outbound financial flows in order to eliminate other, smaller outflows.

Very often developing countries borrow when the price of their key exports is high, their GDP is growing, foreign currency is relatively cheap and international interest rates are low. Then suddenly the prices of key exports decrease, economic growth slows down, the domestic currency depreciates, international interest rates increase and the country has difficulty paying the interest and capital of its debt. In some cases, the debtor needs new loans to pay back old loans. In an environment of higher international interest rates, the new loans will be at higher rates of interest. Some countries reach the point at which they are no more able to borrow in the financial markets and therefore apply to the IMF for help. The IMF provides help under strict conditionality; usually this implies worsening employment conditions and achieving large primary budget surpluses through cuts in social expenditure, that is on welfare, education and health care. These cuts induce reduced internal demand, emigration of the most skilled workforce members, and worse education and health for those remaining in the country. Under such conditions the productivity and the ability of countries to grow may be negatively affected.

In general, countries should be very careful when creating debt if they fund projects with low returns. The weight of that debt can become heavy and burdensome for future generations.

Read

Fragile Five ems redefined? ETFs to watch[9]

Taper[10] tantrums were heard all over the emerging markets in 2013, especially in the 'Fragile Five' countries. These countries – Brazil, Turkey, India,

Indonesia and South Africa – were then hugely reliant on foreign capital to finance their external deficits which put these at risk post-QE exit by the Fed. This was because the end of the cheap-dollar era had led to an uproar in these markets with their currencies plunging to multi-year lows. Widening current account deficit and worsening external debt conditions were the main headaches of the pack.

Moreover, most of these nations had some structural problems of their own which added to this turbulence. However, more than two years have passed since then and several changes – mainly political – have taken place in those countries. While a shift in political power and pro-growth reformative changes boosted India during the mean time, changes in Indonesia are yet to reap returns.

Meanwhile, India and Brazil managed to shrug off these risks to a large extent while Colombia and Mexico have entered this vulnerable bunch. These two have joined other three laggards, namely Indonesia, Turkey and South Africa to form a new Fragile Five emerging market bloc, per JP Morgan Asset Management.

What pushed India and Brazil out of Fragile League?

India has been able to reduce its current account deficit to 1.4% of GDP from 5% in 2013, the steepest cutback by any major emerging market, per Bloomberg. While Brazil has not been successful on this front as the commodity market crash restrained the economy to excel on this current account metric, Brazil offers foreign investors the highest interest rates.

Notably, foreign investors park their money in the riskier emerging market bloc for higher yields. Brazil's real cost of borrowing is the highest among the world's leading emerging markets. This might keep the flair for the Brazil investing still alive among some yield-hungry investors despite fast deteriorating fundamentals of the economy.

Coming to the ETF exposure, all Brazil ETFs were in deep red this year losing moreorless 30% each. Only one ETF – MSCI Brazil Hedged Equity Fund (DBBR) – lost 10% due to its currency-hedged technique. However, India ETFs appear steadier with exchange-traded products swinging between profits and losses. Highest gains of 7.6% were accumulated this year by India Consumer ETF (INCO) (read: India Small Cap ETFs: Best of Emerging Markets Now?).

DBBR has a Zacks ETF Rank 3 (Hold) while INCO has a Zacks ETF Rank #1 (Strong Buy).

What brought Mexico and Colombia in?

The second-largest economy of Latin America, Mexico, was fated for a down-trend mainly due to the oil price rout. Oil revenue makes up about a third of the Mexican government's revenues. This, coupled with the recent strength in the greenback, caused an extreme upheaval in Mexican peso recently and led the currency toward its lowest close on record in early August.

Mexican peso fell about 3.7% in the last one month (as of August 13, 2015). On August 12, Mexico's central bank lowered its 2015 economic growth outlook to the range of 1.7–2.5% from 2–3% to reflect lower-than-expected export and reduced oil output.

Due to the low inflation, Mexico's interest rate is also low at 3%, way low from an EM perspective. As per J.P. Morgan, the economy's real interest rate hovers around zero which leaves no way out for the government to the ease monetary policy further and quicken the economy. In short, low yield opportunity fails to lure investors towards Mexico (read: Which Country ETF Wins Cinco de Mayo 2015?). Mexico ETFs were moderately beaten up in the early part of this year, but crashed in the last one-month phase with Deutsche X-trackers MSCI Mexico Hedged Equity ETF (DBMX), iShares MSCI Mexico Capped ETF (EWW) and SPDR MSCI Mexico Quality Mix ETF (QMEX) all losing in the range of 3.5% to 6%. Thanks to the currency-hedged approach, DBMX lost the least. DBMX has a Zacks ETF Rank #2 (Buy) while EWW has Zacks ETF Rank #3.

Colombia was another victim of the oil crash. Oil accounts for more than half of Colombia's exports. As a result, Latin America's fourth-largest economy was hard hit by a drop in foreign direct investment in the oil sector, which continues to widen the current account deficit.

The country's currency tumbled 25% in the last one month against the greenback. The Colombian peso's 37% fall in the last one year was the third-worst performance among 151 currencies tracked by Bloomberg. The economy's 2015 growth will mark the most sluggish pace in six years and its current-account deficit will likely be the widest in three decades, per Bloomberg (read: Colombia ETFs in Focus after Incredible Crash).

Two Colombia ETFs Global X MSCI Colombia ETF (GXG) and MSCI Colombia Capped ETF (ICOL) have lost 30% so far this year while around 12% losses were incurred in the last one month. Both GXG and ICOL have a Zacks ETF Rank #5 (Strong Sell).

"Fragile Five Ems Redefined? ETFs to Watch," *Zacks Equity Research*.https://seekingalpha.com/article/3450066-fragile-five-ems-redefined-etfs-watch.

Questions

- What had the "fragile five" in common according to the author of this article?
- What happened to their currencies?
- What happened to their balance of payments?
- What happened to their ability to borrow?
- What did India and Brazil achieve in order to be able to leave the "fragile five"?
- Why was Mexico destined for a downtrend?
- What is at the same time good news for the sustainability of Mexican debt and a limitation on its monetary policy?
- What about Colombia?

Analysis

Tapering led to non- decreasing or increasing US interest rates. Therefore, the capital which for some years had left the US in search of higher returns in emerging economies started to flow back towards the US and other industrialized countries. According to the author, in 2013 the increase in US interest rates negatively affected Brazil, Turkey, India, Indonesia and South Africa, since these countries were heavily dependent on foreign money to finance their external deficits. The increase in US interest rates made financing of their debts more difficult. With capital flowing abroad, demand for the currencies of those countries diminished, reducing the value of the GDP of those countries in dollar terms. Depreciations also increased the cost of their imports and diminished the dollar value of their exports. Their trade balance and current account balances then worsened.

India is no longer considered a member of the "fragile five" group for two good reasons: it has increased its growth rate and improved its current account balance, which is now much less negative than it used to be. The greater the GDP of a country, the smaller its negative net IIP in comparison with its GDP. An improving current account balance offers some prospect of a net IIP that is deteriorating less than before or is improving. The net IIP is a key variable in determining the creditworthiness of a country.

The case of Brazil is different. Brazil is now paying creditors higher interest rates. While this encourages foreigners to keep investing in Brazilian bonds, it does not appear to be a sustainable strategy. It is leading Brazil to pay more for its debt. We know that a country borrowing in domestic currency should pursue high growth rates and low passive real interest rates, those interest rates that a country pays to its creditors.

Mexico has entered the "fragile five" group because its economy depends on oil and the price of this commodity has decreased. This reduces the value of Mexican exports, worsening its current account balance, increasing its liabilities with the rest of the world, worsening its net IIP, depreciating its currency and diminishing the ability of the country to service its debts. Real interest rates in Mexico are still low. This implies that Mexican debt in peso could be sustainable even in the presence of moderate growth in Mexican GDP, but this restricts the activities of the Mexican monetary authorities. Probably investors would not appreciate that some inflation could lead interest rates into negative territory.

The situation of Colombia is in some way similar to that of Mexico: the decreasing price of oil, one of its main exports, and decreasing economic growth make its balance of payments weaker and its foreign debt less sustainable. The general story that we learn from this article is that for many developing countries the sustainability of their debt depends on the prices of the commodities they export. Countries often borrow when those prices are high and international interest rates are low. Then, with falling commodity prices and high international interest rates, countries see their situation as much less sustainable.

The fiscal space approach does not explicitly take into account the balance of payments (Section 12.3) or the net IIP (Section 12.4) of a country. It is mainly concentrated on budget data. In reality, for many countries the foreign accounts are key elements in allowing them to increase their fiscal space. A government can spend more or tax less, if that does not entail increasing the dependency of the country on borrowed foreign resources. On the contrary a country runs serious risks if most of its additional expenditure is based on creating debt with foreign entities.

THE FISCAL SPACE[11]

The two major international financial organizations (the WB and the IMF) have developed a framework for analysing the situation of a country and its ability to create some fiscal space, i.e. undertake some fiscal policy: more government spending or lower taxes. According to them there are four major variables to take into account:

1 **Improving the efficiency of public expenditure**. Except for grants, all other options for creating fiscal space will ultimately involve a social cost in the form of higher taxation or reductions in other forms of productive expenditure, either now or in the future. Reducing wasteful public expenditure should be the first priority since the elimination of waste in the government's budget not only directly frees up resources that can be devoted to productive public expenditures, but may also do so indirectly by enhancing the government's credibility and thus its ability to borrow.

2 **Increasing revenue mobilization**. Governments can create fiscal space through increased revenue efforts, using tax and non-tax instruments. It would only be welfare-enhancing for governments to do so, however, if the collection costs and welfare costs of the distortions induced by higher levels of taxation or user charges are lower than the social benefits of the public spending. Thus, tax reforms that improve tax administration and reduce reliance on distortionary taxes will enhance the attractiveness of raising tax revenue as a way of generating fiscal space.

3 **Attracting Grant Aid**. From a purely solvency perspective, the receipt of grants is an attractive way of financing productive public expenditures as it permits new productive expenditure at no cost to government solvency. There are challenges, however. One problem arises from the possibility that the grants available may be insufficient (in a present value sense) to finance the desired public projects. Even where grant resources are available, the amount of effective fiscal space that can be created through grants will in general depend on the predictability of such grants and on whether such resources can be appropriately complemented with other sources of financing.

4 **New borrowing.** Governments can generate fiscal space by increasing their unutilized borrowing capacity. The maximum level of debt that a government can sustain can be increased by:

(i)   enhancing public sector fiscal credibility,
(ii) enhancing the growth of the revenue base, or
(iii) "locking-in" future fiscal resources. Given the rate at which the public sector can borrow, its borrowing capacity depends on the maximum resources – as a share of GDP – that it will be able to mobilize in the future to service debt. These four variables are represented in the so-called fiscal diamond, presented in Figure 16.2.

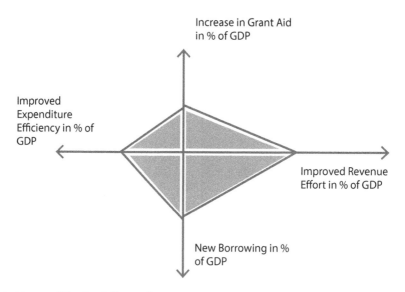

FIGURE 16.2 The fiscal diamond

A country has room to reduce taxes or increase government spending if it can achieve at least some of the following four objectives: increasing the efficiency of its public expenditure; increasing the amount of grants it receives; improving its ability to collect public revenue; or borrowing more.

Glossary

active interest rate   The interest rate that the lender receives on its credits.

austerity   A difficult economic situation caused by a government's reducing the amount of money it spends or increasing the taxes it imposes. It can be represented by the primary budget surplus or by a reduction in the primary budget deficit.

benchmark bond   A benchmark bond is a bond that provides a base of comparison for the performance of other bonds.

budget deficit   General government net borrowing.

budget surplus   General government net lending.

currency risk   The risk that the currency of a bond will depreciate, reducing the value of the bond, when that value is expressed in other currencies. High inflation may bring about a devaluation of the currency and therefore is linked with currency risk.

debt service   The amount or stream of money that is needed over a particular time period to pay interest and principal on a debt.

deficit   Generic word used to describe both the budget deficit and, more rarely, the deficit in the current account of the balance of payments.

ETF   An Exchange Traded Fund is a security whose value follows an index, a commodity, bonds, or a set of assets.

face value   The value of a security given by the issuer at its origin. For bonds, it is the sum paid to the owner at maturity.

general government net lending or borrowing   Total government revenue minus total government expenditure. It is called lending when revenue exceeds expenditure, or borrowing when expenditure exceeds revenue.

general government primary net lending (+) or borrowing (-)   Net lending/borrowing plus net interest payable/paid (interest payments minus interest revenue). It is the government equivalent of what in a business is the operating profit (see Section 1.3).

general government primary surplus or deficit   See *General government primary net lending or borrowing*.

government debt   The total financial obligations of a government outstanding at a moment in time. These typically take the form of government securities (bonds) held by e.g. the public, institutions such as banks and pension funds, the central bank or by foreign nationals.

IMF   International Monetary Fund, international financial organization which lends to countries which could only borrow with difficulty, if at all, or are completely excluded from financial markets. IMF loans usually come with strict conditions attached.

inflation-indexed bond   A bond that guarantees a return linked with the rate of inflation. Investors looking for returns with little to no inflation risk will often hold this type of securities.

interests   The cost incurred by an entity, e.g. a government or a business, for borrowed funds.

issuer Those parties (a corporation, investment trust, government, or government agency) who are entitled to develop, register and sell their securities usually to finance their activities.

liquidity of a bond The feature of those bonds that can be easily bought or sold without a significant discount on their market value. Liquid bonds are usually those traded in large volumes.

maturity The date at which the face value of a bond is expected to be paid in full.

maturity date The date on which a bond is due for redemption.

nominal interest rate The actual interest rate one pays, i.e. which has not been adjusted for inflation.

passive interest rate The interest rate that a borrower pays on debts.

primary market The market in which the issuer of a bond trades directly with those financial institutions which are the initial buyers of the bond.

primary surplus General government primary net lending.

real interest rate The interest rate which takes into account variations in prices (see Section 16.3).

redemption In bonds, the act of an issuer repurchasing a bond at or before maturity. Redemption is made at the face value of the bond, unless it occurs before maturity, in which case the bond is bought back at a premium to compensate for lost interest.[12] In order not to pay more than the face value, governments can buy back their bonds in the secondary markets, sometimes at prices much below face value.

rent The difference between the total return to a factor of production (land, labour, or capital) and its supply price – i.e., the minimum amount necessary to secure its services.[13] It is a synonym for income which does not arise from production.

secondary market The market on which securities are traded after being initially offered on the primary market. Most trading occurs on the secondary market.[14]

security Document giving title to property or claim on income. Income-yielding paper traded on the stock ex-change or secondary market.[15]

sovereign bond A bond issued by a government.

sovereign debt See *government debt*.

spread Difference between two rates or two prices. In the analysis of sovereign bonds is the difference between the yield offered by one bond and that offered by the benchmark bond.

tapering The reduction in the US Federal Reserve's (see Section 16.3) programme of purchases of bonds.

volatility Instability over time of the price of a security or commodity, or the level of a market, interest rate or currency. At high levels it implies rapid and large upward and downward changes over a relatively short period of time.

Notes

1 Technically this type of money is called "monetary base" (see Section 9.2) or M0. This is the main contribution that the central bank can give to the process of creation of money

supply. However, as we know, money supply is also heavily dependent on the decisions of the banking system and borrowers. Such decisions may go in the opposite direction. While the central bank issues new monetary base, the total money supply may not change or even shrink. See also: www.youtube.com/ watch?v=CvRAqR2pAgw. This was the case in the mentioned countries.

2 www.bbc.com/news/business-20268679. www.wsj.com/articles/fed-sent-record-97-7-billion-in-profits-to-u-s-treasury-in-2015-1452531787.

3 It is worth mentioning Income = Expenditure identity; by subtracting tax from both sides we obtain $Y - T = C + I + G - T + X - M$.

   In this, $(G - T)$ is the primary surplus if $G < T$. Thus, primary surpluses are contractionary in the short run.

   However, they allow the government to build up holding of financial assets that can be used in a recession to finance deficits that boost aggregate demand. Inter-temporal fiscal policy may require governments to build primary surpluses in booms so that they may handle recessions by primary deficits. Alternatively, governments can increase the Debt/GDP ratio during recessions years, which are supposed to be few, and can diminish it during expansionary years, which are supposed to be many. During economic expansions the GDP grows and therefore even with a primary balance, the Debt/GDP ratio decreases. If economic growth is strong enough, Debt/GDP may decrease in a substantial way. This was the successful path to debt reduction, which the US followed after World War II (IMF, 2012:112–114). About the negative effects of austerity on public debts see also Auerbach e Gorodnichenko (2017).

4 Let's assume that for simplicity we speak about annual bonds, which are sold on 1 January at price P, which is smaller than 100, for example $P = 90$. These bonds give right to the holders to be paid 100 after one year. After one year those who have invested 90, will receive 100. The gain is 100–90 or 100-P. In this case the gain is 10. How much is the yield or the return for those who bought the bond? $10/90 = 0{,}11$ or 11 per cent. In general terms, it is: $[(100\text{-}P) \,/\, P]$. Now let's assume that the same bonds are in greater demand. Its price P may rise to 95. A new investor would spend 95 and after one year obtain 100. Their return would be $(100–95) \,/100 = 5/100 = 0{,}05$ or 5 per cent.

5 For this argument see Fanizza and Tanzi (1995).

6 We should also notice that to buy public debt you must part with some of your income and that income comes from work. Considering this, the purchase of public debt can become a reward from previous work.

7 Catao and Milesi Ferretti (2013).

8 See Rinaldi (2012), Catao and Milesi Ferretti (2013) and Bianchi (2016).

9 An exchange traded fund (ETF is a marketable security (piece of paper representing financial wealth), the value of which is linked to that of other financial assets. ETFs have low management costs and so are liked by many investors. They can be used to track the trend in an economy.

10 Tapering is the name given to the reduction in expansive monetary policies which the US Federal Reserve carried out following the great recession of 2008–2009.

11 See IMF- World Bank (2006:14–18).

12 http://financial-dictionary.thefreedictionary.com/Redemption.

13 www.britannica.com/topic/rent-economics.

14 www.nasdaq.com/investing/glossary/s/secondary-market#ixzz3jU5SF1IX.

15 World Bank (1996).

Bibliography

Auerbach, A. J. and Gorodnichenko, Y. (2017). "Fiscal Stimulus and Fiscal Sustainability," September. NBER Working Paper No. w23789. Available at SSRN https://ssrn.com/abstract=3035137.

Bianchi, B. (2016). "Sovereign Risk Premia and the International Balance Sheet: Lessons from the European Crisis," *Open Economies Review*, 27: 471–493.

Catão, L.A.V. and Milesi-Ferretti, G. M. (2013). "External Liabilities and Crises," IMF Working Paper, IMF, Washington, DC.

Fanizza, D. and Vito Tanzi, V. (1995). "Fiscal Deficit and Public Debt in Industrial Countries, 1970–1994," IMF Working Papers, International Monetary Fund.

International Monetary Fund – World Bank. (2006). "Fiscal Policy for Growth and Development: An Interim Report," DC2006-0003, 6 April, Washington, DC.

International Monetary Fund. (2012). World Economic Outlook, Coping with High Debt and Sluggish Growth, Washington, DC, USA.

Rinaldi, G. (2012). "Cosa può spiegare lo Spread?" *Quadrante Futuro*, 26 June. www.quadrantefuturo.it/congiuntura/cosa-pu%C3%B2-spiegare-lo-spread.html.

Williams, D. (2015). "Doctrinaire Approach to Primary Surplus Dangerous," *The Jamaica Gleaner*, 26 July.

World Bank. (1996). *The World Bank Glossary*. Washington, DC: World Bank.

Zacks Equity Research. (2015). "Fragile Five Ems Redefined? ETFs to Watch," *Seeking Alpha*, 18 August. https://seekingalpha.com/article/3450066-fragile-five-ems-redefined-etfs-watch.

PART VII
Private demand

The private sector (families and firms) usually generates the major part of the demand for goods and services produced in a country. Countries usually grow and prosper, have strong firms and well-paid jobs, when private demand is strong. Purchases by families (consumption and residential investment) and by firms (fixed production investment and inventories) form private demand. In this sense, private demand is not under the immediate control of policy makers who, however, possess several tools to influence private demand: fiscal policy (taxes, benefits, subsidies, public salaries and public procurement), monetary policy, exchange rates and financial regulation.

Chapter 17 covers consumption and Chapter 18 private investments.

17

HOUSEHOLD CONSUMPTION

The main destination of goods and services

Most people work in order to consume, and consumption often represents the major objective of what we produce. Families decide consumption, but public and corporate policies may heavily affect families' choices. Section 17.1 describes the main features of consumption and 17.2 presents other important aspects of it.

17.1 The main features of household consumption

When families buy new goods, national accounts record their purchases as household consumption. The only exception concerns families' purchases of new buildings or parts of new buildings, for example apartments; this is the only instance of national accounts recording family outlays as investment (Chapter 18); only families consume.[1]

Consumption is probably the true objective of all economic activity: people produce, import, invest and export in order to be able to consume. A country which is very good at producing, investing and exporting but then has insufficient goods for consumption is a country which does not satisfy the needs of its inhabitants. For a time, countries may increase investment and reduce consumption in order to achieve higher future living standards, but this could not be a permanent strategy.

Consumption expenditures are grouped into three categories:

1 **consumer durables**, which are long-lived consumer items such as cars, televisions, furniture and major appliances (but not houses, which are classified under investment);
2 **non-durable goods**, which are shorter-lived items such as foods, clothing and fuel; *and*
3 **services**, such as education, health care, financial services, and transportation.[2]

CONSUMPTION IN THE US

Durable goods represent an important share of the total consumption of US families. They also represent an important portion of US GDP. However, they do not constitute the largest quota of expenditures. Personal consumption expenditures in 2017, including durable goods, non-durable goods and services, amounted to $13.32tn[3] out of a total GDP of $19.485tn, or 68 per cent of GDP. Of that total, consumers spent $1.41tn on durable goods (7.22 per cent of GDP), $2.75tn on non-durable goods (14.11 per cent of GDP), and $9.17tn on services (47.04 per cent of GDP). We should take into account that the US has exceptionally large expenditure on health care (17.9 per cent of GDP in 2016),[4] as their health-care system has low productivity in terms of health impact per dollar of expenditure. This contributes to making US expenditure on services as great as it is.

Changing furniture, the TV set, the refrigerator, the mobile phone or the PC are activities that can be postponed for some time and therefore are actually postponed whenever consumers perceive their future as less secure.[5] "The category of personal consumption expenditures for durable goods is (. . .) used as an economic indicator. Since the purchase of consumer durable goods can be postponed, the level of consumer expenditures tends to fluctuate a great deal from year to year. During a recession, consumer expenditures for durable goods tend to decline. Increases and decreases can be used as an indicator of consumer confidence and the direction of the economy. Increases in such consumer expenditures are usually interpreted as a sign of a recovering or strong economy."[6]

Among different types of consumption, we cannot forget a very special type of service, namely **housing services**. These services concern families' accommodation in houses and apartments. They are produced by the same families when they own their own accommodation, or by landlords when families rent their accommodation. Repairs to and cleaning of houses are not part of housing services, but are "other services". Housing services are the product of previous investment activity which takes place through the building industry. This employs many people for a short period, while housing services last longer but are not creators of jobs. Some countries experience economic booms when they build many houses but then experience severe difficulties when only housing services remain.

The fact that consumption usually represents the main use of goods in an economy explains its key importance in the policy debate. The government with its taxes, benefits (see Chapter 13) and salaries paid to public employees (Section 14.1) contributes directly to families' disposable income (see Section 13.3). Then through public procurement (Section 14.2) the government indirectly generates business for the private sector and therefore the consumption potential of private sector employees.

Private enterprises are also major players in influencing consumption. The standard situation in large non-oil-exporting economies is that exports account for less than half of GDP. In such countries the salaries that private businesses pay are a main component of disposable family income. Sometimes reducing the cost of labour is considered a key strategy in increasing the country's international competitiveness (see Appendix 1 Discussion). If the GDP of a country is mainly directed to exports and if the importing countries do not follow the same strategy, that is to say they do not reduce their salaries, then this strategy can be effective. We rely on foreign countries as providers of demand for the goods we produce. Sometimes this can be a dangerous strategy, because we then depend heavily on the policies of foreign governments.

In countries where domestic buyers account for most of GDP, salary reductions may profoundly affect domestic demand, making it hard for domestic firms to sell their goods. By the same token, if our commercial partners and competitors follow suit and reduce their salaries and therefore their consumption, they will import less, and in consequence we export less and become poorer. This implies that the social negotiators involved in setting salary levels should take particular care to strike a balance between making a country price-competitive while not diminishing internal consumption.

17.2 The determinants of consumption

In the long term, people consume a (large) share of their income. Those with no income in the long term cannot consume. However, matters are more complex. If the life of individuals is limited, that of families is much less so. Some individuals spend money which their parents accumulated or they leave wealth to their children. In some cases, policy makers should take into account the fact that, to a certain degree, individuals are ready to make sacrifices for their children and grandchildren; therefore people may save money that they will never spend or *vice versa*. People may spend money they never earned. Inheritance taxes enter into this story. On the one hand we may not approve of the fact that some people do not work and merely enjoy the fruits of their parents' work; on the other, we should not forget that some people also work hard to leave assets to their children. In the first case one could recommend high inheritance taxes and in the second, the opposite.

The disposable income (Section 13.3) of individuals is subdivided between consumption and saving. Saving implies planned future consumption. Hence consumption over time depends on the level of available income over time – from returns to past savings and from current incomes earned by working. Consumption today then is influenced by an average[7] of income over a period of time, which is not only by present income, but also by past income and income expected in the future.[8] In this perspective people may try to smooth their consumption levels in some way, so as to enjoy more or less the same level of consumption throughout their life. To this end they would borrow when they are poorer and save when they are richer.[9]

Such understandable requirements as smoothing out of consumption patterns throughout their life can be hampered by the financial system. Obtaining credit may be difficult, particularly for poor people. Sometimes even keeping savings presents risks, as they can be stolen. Economists say that many people are "financially constrained by imperfect financial markets". For this reason, at the end of the day a large part of consumption depends on the availability of money in cash or in the bank. Much consumption depends on disposable income (Section 13.3), which is the income that remains to consumers after paying taxes (Section 13.1) and receiving pensions or benefits (Section 13.2). The greater the disposable income of a family, the greater will be its consumption. When families receive an extra dollar, they consume a part and save the rest. Poorer families usually consume a larger proportion of their additional dollar and richer families a smaller part. We call the percentage of the additional dollar that families consume their **marginal propensity to consume**. Poor families still have to satisfy many basic needs and therefore have a higher marginal propensity to consume.

The mood of consumers is also very important. Economists say that "the expectations of consumers matter". Sometimes bad news is sufficient to put a brake on consumers. Few consumers own shares, but a major collapse in the stock market may lead many consumers to postpone the purchase of some durable goods or not take an important holiday. Similar effects stem from news that a war or an economic crisis is approaching. Even people with relatively safe jobs, such as civil servants, become much more cautious with their purchases when they hear bad news. Their income does not and probably will not change, but they reduce their consumption anyway. By the same token good news or new hope can lead consumers to consume more, even if their disposable income has not really changed. Such things occur because expectations of adverse or positive times ahead lead people to think that their future incomes will diminish or increase. These changes affect their average expected incomes during their lives and may lead them to change their consumption levels.

Moreover, banking regulations also play a major role in inducing or deterring consumption. Some regulations may foster credit to consumers and thereby consumption. In extreme cases, consumers lacking sufficient income to be able to afford certain consumption levels receive credit through credit cards and other forms of consumer credit. This increases the level of family debt and exposes them and the whole financial system to serious risk. As long as families' debts are modest, some credit to consumers may foster economic development, but when it becomes excessive it poses serious risks to the whole economic system.

Finally, we cannot forget that interest rates also influence consumption. Interest rates incentivise people to postpone consumption with a view to a higher level of future consumption. High interest rates reward savings and induce individuals to save more and consume less. Low interest rates provide little reward for saving but make payment for purchases in instalments cheaper.

In conclusion, most economists believe that in the short term, consumption depends only partially on the disposable income of families, which is the money they have in their pockets.

17.3 Disposable income which is not consumed: savings

Savings are that part of disposable income that families do not consume. They are an essential and positive part of the economy when they can be efficiently channelled to finance investment, principally, productive investment. Families can for example entrust their savings to banks or other financial institutions which in turn can finance companies planning to build new plants, buy new equipment, carry out research, or hire or train staff. When the available resources and production capacity are already fully utilized, the fact that somebody consumes less permits the use of resources to increase the capital of the nation, that is to invest. This is essential for the growth of the country.

Usually rich families save more than poor families, and therefore when most income is concentrated in a few rich families, consumption may decrease, reducing the total demand for goods and services. This lower consumption may or may not be compensated for by additional investment. Families who are saving, banks or financial firms may use money for purely financial operations. Otherwise they may transfer money to companies which, however, may use those resources to carry out purely financial operations, for example purchasing their own shares. In this way the value of their shares increases, as also do the returns to their managers. There is no production of new goods.

When there is bad news, consumers reduce their consumption and start saving more. However, these are usually moments when investments also decrease and savings are therefore less needed. People save to protect their future. Saving reduces demand and jeopardizes the future of the economy even more. Companies can sell neither to families (for consumption) nor to companies (for investment). They may go bankrupt and dismiss their employees. Then more families remain without income and reduce their consumption, and the environment becomes even more depressed.

Under such conditions the only actor which can reverse this negative trend is the public authority, with its fiscal and monetary policies. When savings are excessive only governments can rescue the market through expansionary policies.

As mentioned above, savings are influenced by interest rates. When interest rates are high there is a greater reward for those who save, and therefore an incentive to save more. When interest rates are low or even negative, people have little incentive to save.

Governments can play a key role in incentivising and protecting savings from depreciation, confiscation and from the improper behaviour of some financial operators who manage the savings of families. Financial regulation is also important as it is a tool to protect savings.

Glossary

durable consumption goods   Goods which are not consumed or destroyed in use and can be used over a period of time, usually for several years, for personal or family use. They include cars, vacuum cleaners, washing machines, TV sets, PCs, kitchen appliances, sports equipment among others.

expectations   What people or businesses expect to happen, especially in terms of markets and prices. Changes in expectations cause variations in the demand and supply of goods. Expectations are also important in understanding inflation.

financial constraints   "A Firm investment is financially constrained if a windfall increase in the availability of internal funds, results in higher investment spending."[10] By the same token, a consumer is financially constrained if a windfall increase in the availability of cash results in increased consumption. Financially constrained persons encounter difficulties in borrowing even when they would be able to pay back potential loans. This is the result of imperfect financial markets.

fiscal multiplier   The notion that a change in GDP is often greater than the change in government spending that originated it. This occurs because initial expenditure creates not only new GDP but also new income. New income induces new consumption and investment, creating additional GDP growth and new income. At each round the additional consumption is lower than in the previous round, because at each round, part of the disposable income of families is saved. The fiscal multiplier is usually greater than 1 if the economy has plenty of unused resources, that is unemployed people and unused equipment. It is smaller when the economy is already fully utilizing its production factors.

housing services   The service that houses provide or may provide, if occupied. Housing services are a component of personal consumption expenditure, and consequently part of GDP. The rental value of tenant-occupied housing and the imputed rental value of owner-occupied housing are both part of personal consumption expenditure on housing services, reflecting the amount of money tenants spend on shelter and the amount of money owner-occupants would have spent had they been renting.[11]

imperfect (or inefficient) financial markets   Financial markets which have a limited ability to assess the risk of lending and therefore give too much credit to some customers and too little to others. In such markets, information is not promptly disclosed to all stakeholders. There is not quick matching between sellers and buyers.

life cycle hypothesis   A notion according to which consumers aim at a relatively constant level of consumption throughout their life, notwithstanding the income level over the specific period.

non-durable goods   Goods used by consumers over relatively short periods, e.g. food, fuel, clothes.

permanent income   According to this notion consumers change their consumption levels only if they think the changes in their income are of a permanent nature. According to this theory, occasional changes in the income of families have modest effects on their consumption levels.

propensity to consume   The share of disposable income that a family utilizes for consumption. The marginal propensity to consume is the percentage of any additional dollar of disposable income that a family spends on consumption.

SAP   See *structural adjustment programme*.

savings   The part of disposable income that families do not consume. Savings may be efficiently channelled to finance investment and growth when firms desire to invest and additional consumption would make investment impossible. Savings may become a brake on the economy when firms do not wish to invest or when the financial system is unable to channel savings into investment projects.

service   An economic activity, which is often contrasted with the production of "goods", in that "goods", more precisely "merchandizes", are understood to be physical objects whereas "services" are the provision of intangible benefits to the recipient. Examples include medical services, transport services, teaching, accounting, hairdressing, legal services. When you rent a car, you are buying a service. When you purchase a car for your family, you are buying a durable consumption good.

structural adjustment programmes   Economic policies for developing countries promoted by the WB and IMF since the early 1980s through the provision of loans conditional on the adoption of such policies. (. . .) They are designed to encourage the structural adjustment of an economy by, for example, removing "excess" government controls and promoting market competition as part of the neo-liberal agenda followed by the Bank. SAP policies reflect the neo-liberal ideology that drives globalization. They aim to achieve long-term or accelerated economic growth in poorer countries by restructuring the economy and reducing government intervention. SAP policies include currency devaluation, managed balance of payments, reduction of government services through public spending cuts/budget deficit cuts, reduction of tax on high earners, reduction of inflation, wage suppression, privatization, lower tariffs on imports, tighter monetary policy, increased free trade, cuts in social spending, and business deregulation. Governments are also encouraged or forced to reduce their role in the economy by privatizing state-owned industries including the health sector, and opening their economies to foreign competition.[12]

Notes

1 Sometimes Government Expenditure is split between "public consumption" and "public investment", here we avoid this distinction to make things simpler. Companies and organizations carry out "intermediate consumption" (see section 2.1) of "intermediate goods" (see section 8.1).
2 Abel et al. (2014:57).
3 This and the following consumption data come from US Bureau of Economic Analysis, Personal Consumption Expenditures, retrieved from FRED, Federal Reserve Bank of St Louis; https://fred.stlouisfed.org/series/PCECA, August 13, 2018.
4 www.cms.gov/Research-Statistics-Data-and-Systems/Statistics-Trends-and-Reports/ NationalHealthExpendData/Downloads/highlights.pdf.
5 www.referenceforbusiness.com/encyclopedia/Dev-Eco/Durable-Goods.html#ixzz3 johlbZsd.
6 www.referenceforbusiness.com/encyclopedia/Dev-Eco/Durable-Goods.html# ixzz3johlbZsd.

7 Actually, this is a weighted average of the different incomes that the individual has during his life.

8 In some cases, people would not pay too much attention to temporary changes of their income, they would really increase or reduce their consumption only when they think that the changes are going to last.

9 Modigliani and Brumberg (1954).

10 www.nuffield.ox.ac.uk/teaching/economics/bond/financing%20constraints.pdf.

11 www.bea.gov/papers/pdf/RiPfactsheet.pdf.

12 See: www.who.int/trade/glossary/story084/en/.

Bibliography

Abel, A. B., Bernanke, B. and Croushore, D. D. (2014). *Macroeconomics*. Boston: Addison-Wesley.

Modigliani, F. and Brumberg, R. H. (1954). "Utility Analysis and the Consumption Function: An Interpretation of Cross-Section Data," in *Post-Keynesian economics*, edited by Kenneth K. Kurihara, pp. 388–436. New Brunswick, NJ: Rutgers University Press.

18

PRIVATE INVESTMENT

Supplying the private sector with new capital

While consumption is a relatively stable part of total demand, investment is its most variable component. Investment is also the process by which the capital of a nation increases, this being one of the main influences on growth of production in a country. Investment provides workers with better equipment and makes them more productive. Without investment employment usually does not grow. Investment fosters growth of workers' productivity (see Section 3.3), creating an opportunity for increasing their salaries. Thanks to investment, production can grow and prices can remain stable.

Firstly, we consider how firms decide on investment, and in particular the net present value (NPV) method. From there we can go on to explain the nation's investment as a whole.

18.1 The net present value (NPV) method for firms' investment decision[1]

Before speaking of NPV, we should explain what future value and **present value** are. For example, $100 of capital (the sum $A) can today be deposited in a bank and in a year's time its owner will receive $100 + interest, for example 5 per cent of $100, that is $5 (here we assume that the interest rate is 5 per cent, but you can assume any other interest rate); so in one year the value of the capital increases to $105. This sum is the future value in one year of $100 today. Let's use the letter $B to call this sum.

Then, if that capital of $105 is again deposited at the same rate, its value after a further year will be $110,25. That sum is the future value in two years of $100 today. Let's use the letter $C to call the future value in two years of the sum $A that we deposit today.

TABLE 18.1 The future value of an amount in successive years

The sum in year 0	The future value in year 1	The future value in year 2
$A	$A × (1+i) = $B	$A x (1+i) x (1+i) = $C
$100	$100 + (5% of $100)	$105 + (5% of $105)
$100	$105	$110,25

TABLE 18.2 The present value of future sums

Present value in year 0	A sum in year 1	A sum in year 2
$A = $B/(1+i)	$B	
$A= $C/[(1+i) × (1+i)]		$C

This calculation is illustrated in tabular form in Table 18.1, with the rate of interest represented by the letter "i". Expressed algebraically in row 1, "A" is your capital in Year 0, "B" its future value in Year 1 and "C" its future value in Year 2. Rows 2 and 3 illustrate the above numerical example with $100 as the value assigned to A, and 5 per cent the value assigned to "i".

If somebody promises a sum $B to you in one year, its present value $A is $B/(1+i). To calculate the present value of any sum available in one year, you should divide that sum by 1+i.

If somebody promises a sum $C to you in two years, its present value $A is $C/[(1+i) x (1+i)]. To calculate the present value of any sum available in two years, you should divide that sum by [(1+i)x(1+i)].

As you can see in Table 18.2 the present values of both B and C at rate of interest "i" are A.

On the above basis, the example below illustrates the meaning of **net** present value (NPV), in this case over a three-year period (such calculations can be extended over any number of years).

AN EXAMPLE OF A PROJECT

Consider the Table 18.3 below. As with most investments, outflows occur at the beginning of the period and inflows in later years. In this case the investment in a factory (outflow) is 1,000 in year 0, which is expected to generate revenues (inflows) of 300, 400 and 800 in the following three years 1, 2 and 3 respectively. The present values of those outflows in Years 1–3 depend on the rate of interest, and the NPV is the cumulative sum of all values from Year 0 to Year 3 in the extreme right-hand column, shown at different rates of interest. If the rate of interest is higher than about 19 per cent, the NPV becomes negative **and the factory is then not economically viable**.

TABLE 18.3 Net present value of a project with different interest rates

Interest rate	Year 0	Year 1	Year 2	Year 3	NPV
0%	−1,000.00	300.00	400.00	800.00	500.00
5%	−1,000.00	285.71	362.81	691.07	339.60
10%	−1,000.00	272.73	330.58	601.05	204.36
15%	−1,000.00	260.87	302.46	526.01	89.34
19.50%	−1,000.00	251.05	280.11	46880	0.05
20%	−1,000.00	250.00	277.78	462.96	−9.26
30%	−1,000.00	230.77	236.69	364.13	−168.41

Note that high interest rates affect the amounts received progressively in each subsequent year appreciably more than those received after only one year. Thus, in calculating present values the amounts received in the distant future are much more affected by interest rates than those received in the near future. This also explains why loans over long periods are usually considered riskier than loans over short periods, as they are more vulnerable to adverse interest rate changes. When interest rates are higher, firms are less willing to invest.

To conclude, (NPV) consists of expressing every annual cash flow in its present value and then totalling all such values.

18.2 The main features of investment

Investment consists of adding capital (equipment, buildings and intangible assets) to that already available in the country and is therefore also known as "Gross Capital Formation" or Gross Investment. This is the sum of the Gross Public Investment (Government Investment) and of the Gross Private Investment. Here we focus on investments made by private persons (Gross Private Investment), not those made by public authorities (Gross Government Investment or Public Investment). The latter type of investment also increases the total capital of the country but, being decided by the public authority, is analysed in the chapter on Government Spending (see Chapter 14).[2]

The value of the capital of a country, like that of a firm, continuously decreases due to wear, obsolescence and accidents – i.e., so-called depreciation (Section 10.2). When we subtract depreciation from gross investment, we obtain net investment (see Table 18.4).

We mentioned earlier that measurement of depreciation is a rather complex and imprecise business. For this reason, we often prefer to use data on gross investment rather than on net investment.

We have already seen the main types of investment (Section 8.2): **fixed productive** investments, changes in firms' **inventories** and purchases of new buildings by

TABLE 18.4 Net investment

+ Gross Capital Formation or Gross Investment
- Depreciation
= **Net Capital Formation or Net Investment**

families, residential investments. Only firms carry out private productive investment (fixed and inventories), while only families carry out private residential investment.

Firms undertake investment:

(i)   If they think it is going to generate profits.

(ii)   If those profits are likely to pay for the explicit or implicit cost of using capital (Section 1.1), and

(iii)   If firms have access to capital.

The NPV is relevant to the first two conditions. NPV links expected future **profits**, the rate of interest that the firm pays or considers as its opportunity cost (Section 1.1), and the current value of the project for the firm. This implies that firms are more willing to invest if they expect good profits, borrow at a low interest rate (or if the opportunity cost of capital is low) and can easily obtain financial resources.

Expected profits

Firms expect profits, if one or more of the following conditions is going to be fulfilled.

*   They are confident in handling their business, notwithstanding their environment.
*   They believe that their industry, sector or market is going to expand.
*   They believe that the economy as a whole is healthy and likely to expand.

The exceptions are those firms which can do well even when their industry, their market and the economy as a whole are going through difficult times. They are firms with exceptional managers who see opportunities where everybody else expects failures. They are leaders but they do not constitute the bulk of the industry. Firms usually expect profits if their sector, their market or the economy as a whole expect profits. Firms are therefore likely to invest when the foreign and the domestic economy are expected to grow, that is when there is real GDP (see Section 8.1) growth. External demand and the fiscal policy of a country may stimulate GDP growth and investment.

Expected profits are also higher when new technology makes equipment cheap. An example is solar panels, the decrease in the cost of which over time has increased their use. In this sense technological progress (Section 15.3) can bring about waves of investment.

Interest rates

This is the second key variable. High real interest rates (Section 16.3) can discourage private investment. The financial burden of borrowing becomes very heavy and the alternative of using money for some purely high-yield financial operation, for example purchase of bonds, becomes very tempting. This explains why monetary policy (see Section 9.2) may play an important role in supporting investment.

Access to finance

Firms may see great profit-making opportunities if interest rates are low, but they may also lack access to financial resources. This is often true of small and medium-sized enterprises; for some the stock market may be not an option and they cannot issue corporate bonds. From time to time banks may require considerable collateral, which some firms lack. In other cases, firms have previously had bad experiences with the financial system and consider borrowing a risky operation, and therefore prefer to avoid it. Economies need to strike a right balance between tight credit and too-easy credit. In the first case good projects do not receive funding, in the second, even poor unprofitable projects receive it, and the country wastes resources. For this reason, we cannot forget the key link between financial regulation and investment. Financial regulation plays a key role in determining who receives and who does not receive credit. The most serious investment mistakes are usually made with residential investment, loose financial policies and regulations sometimes leading to excessive levels of residential investment. Any minor shock (e.g. an increase or a decrease in the price of a raw material) can then expose the fragilities of these situations and lead to serial bankruptcies and major financial collapses.

When firms cannot or do not wish to borrow, they delay investment until those moments when they have sufficient cash flows to fund their projects with their own resources. This usually occurs during periods of real GDP growth, when total revenues (Section 6.3) are larger and cash is available.

There are two additional factors that on some occasions affect investment: high inflation and excessive public spending. High inflation may cause nominal interest rates (see Section 16.3) to grow, and since high inflation is often very variable (Section 9.4), it can lead to fluctuating real interest rates (Section 16.3). When real interest rates fluctuate over a very large range, investment planning may become too difficult or even impossible.

There are also instances when excessive public spending can hinder private investment. This may occur when countries are already fully utilizing their plants and have very low unemployment. Under such conditions public spending may lead to higher interest rates and higher prices, thereby hampering private investment.

On the basis of these considerations we can say that firms invest when they have positive expectations (see Glossary of Chapter 17) for their future, when they are already experiencing some positive growth and/or when real interest rates are not too high. Investment can therefore be affected by;

1 Fiscal policies which stimulate demand and improve the cash flows of firms.
2 Monetary policies which reduce the real interest rates that firms must pay,
3 Foreign trade (see Chapter 10) policies which increase foreign demand.
4 Financial regulation, which facilitates the access to credit.

Glossary

access to finance   The availability and affordability of financial services.[3] The ability of individuals or enterprises to obtain financial services, including credit, deposit, payment, insurance and other risk management services.[4]

cash flow   The difference between the cash that an organization or a family receives and that it pays. In the medium-long term, a positive net cash flow is essential for the survival of both families and organizations.

cash hoarding   The accumulation of large quantities of cash, usually in the expectation of future investments, future obligations or future risks.

net present value   A sum of the present values of all the positive and negative cash flows of a project.

present value   The amount of cash today that is equivalent in value to a payment, or to a stream of payments, to be received in the future. To determine the present value, each future cash flow is multiplied by a present value factor.[5]

present value factor   Factor used to calculate an estimate of the present value of an amount to be received in a future period. Thus if the opportunity cost of funds is 10 per cent over the next year, the factor is $[1/(1 + 0.10)]$.[6]

Notes

1 For a fast course on investment, the text part of 18.1 can be skipped.
2 Other presentations put on one side public consumption and on the other side private and public investment together. Our presentation puts together all the expenditure depending on the public choices and separates it from that expenditure depending on private decision makers.
3 See: www.ifc.org/wps/wcm/connect/region ext_content/regions/sub-saharan+africa/advisory+services/accessfinance/.
4 Demirgüç-Kunt et al. (2008).
5 http://financial-dictionary.thefreedictionary.com/present+value.
6 http://financial-dictionary.thefreedictionary.com/Present+value+factor.

Bibliography

Demirgüç-Kunt, A., Beck, T. and Honohan, P. (2008). *Finance for all? Policies and pitfalls in expanding access.* Washington, DC: World Bank.

PART VIII

The labour market and inequality

Last but not least, we present the labour market (Chapter 19), in which the influence of employers' organizations and trade unions is more direct. It is here that key social negotiations take place.

Firstly, we introduce the working of the labour market, how salaries are fixed, how growing GDP contributes to greater employment and the question of whether public policies can reduce unemployment. Then we consider how incomes and wealth are distributed, the effects of inequality and what one can do to prevent excessive inequality undermining economic growth (Chapter 20).

19

THE LABOUR MARKET

Those concerned with employment should know the key terms for describing the labour market. Not only do we have to know the key groups of people which make up the population, with reference to their working situation; it is also important that we understand who and why people move from one situation to another, for example from being unemployed to being employed. Firstly, we describe the main terms we use to describe the labour market. Then we try to understand the main elements in the setting of salaries. We continue by considering the relationship between economic growth and employment. If an economy grows does it mean that employment will also grow? Finally, we consider whether governments can do anything to increase employment or whether their actions are doomed only to produce inflation.

19.1 A basic description of labour market stocks and flows

Stocks and flows

In economics it is important to distinguish between stocks and flows (Table 19.1). Measuring a stock means measuring something at a precise instant. For example, if we measure the total quantity of water in a lake at noon on 31 December, we measure a stock. A flow refers to movements in a quantity between two moments in time. For example, a flow is the quantity of water that has entered a lake in one day. In economics, the equivalent is stocks: the capital of a company, its assets and its liabilities at a certain time on a specific day. In microeconomics we meet such flows as the output of a company over a period of a day, a week, a quarter or a year. Other flows include intermediate consumption, value added, economic profit, the wage bill, depreciation. All these things happen over a period between two moments in time. In macroeconomics we encounter stocks as the total capital of a country, its work force, the number of people who have a job (the employed) and the number of unemployed. The national debt and the net international investment position are also stocks. The expenses of a government, its revenue and the budget deficit are flows. Consumption, private investment, public spending, exports and imports are all flows, just as the GDP is a flow.

TABLE 19.1 Examples of stocks and flows

	Stocks	*Flows*
Microeconomics	Capital of a firm (Section 1.1)	Depreciation (Section 10.2)
		Cost of capital
	Workforce of a firm (Section 3.2)	Wage bill (Section 3.4)
		Sales/Total revenue (Section 6.3)
		Output (Section 3.2)
		Total costs
	Net Present Value (see Section 18.1)	Cash flow (see Glossary Ch 18)
		Debts of the firm
		Accounting profit (Section 1.3)
		Intermediate consumption (Section 2.1)
		Value added (Section 2.2)
	Debts	Financial costs (Section 1.1)
		Economic profit (Section 1.4)
Macroeconomics		GDP (see Section 8.1)
		Consumption (Ch 17)
	Capital of a country	Private investment (Ch 18)
	Labour force (see Glossary Ch 19)	National wage bill
	Employed people (see Glossary Ch 19)	People who found a job during a certain period
	Unemployed people (see Glossary Ch 19)	People who lost their job during a certain period
		Disposable income (Section 13.3)
		Total government outlays (see Glossary of Ch 14)
	The Public Debt (Section 16.2)	The public deficit. (Section 16.1)
		Payments for interests (Section 16.1)
		Total government revenue (Section 16.1)
		Government spending (see Ch 14)
	The N.IIP (Section 12.4)	The current account balance (Section 12.1)

The labour force (Table 19.2) is made up by those who are "Employed" (E), i.e. those who have a job, and those who are "Unemployed" (U), i.e. those without a job, actively seeking employment and available to work. Finally, there are those who do not have work and are recorded as not actively searching for a job, who are known as "non-participants" in the labour force (N). In reality the difference between the unemployed and non-participants is not clear-cut.[1] Many non-participants take up a job, for example through relatives and friends or because their former employer seeks them out. Moreover, many workers move from one job to another without experiencing unemployment.[2] The last-mentioned phenomenon is represented in Figure 19.1 by the curved arrow from employment back to employment, from E back to E.

The three sets of people represented by the circles in Figure 19.1 are complex entities.

Those who are unemployed (U) can be divided at least along the following lines:

- **Short-term**, those unemployed for short spells, *versus* **long-term**, those unemployed for long periods. For the first group, unemployment is a temporary condition, less dramatic than for the second group. Among the people in the first group there are those who are looking for the best job opportunities. This search requires some time. In some cases, there are short-term unemployed who are in that category because they have resigned from their job (moving from N to U) to look for better career opportunities. Long-term unemployed, since they remain for long periods far from their work, risk losing

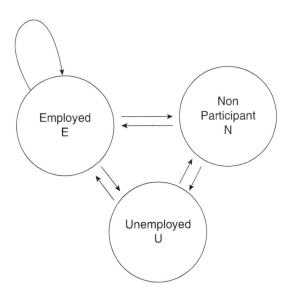

FIGURE 19.1 Major labour market groups and flows

their skills and eventually becoming discouraged, even leading them to stop their search and become non-participants (moving from E to N). However, in the US during the 1980s a consistent component of hiring concerned the long-term unemployed.

- **Attached,**[3] those who maintain links with a company and desire or expect to return to work there and who will eventually be recalled, as distinct from the unattached, that is those who do not expect or desire to go back to the company they left and will not be recalled.[4]

Some workers do not have a job and are job seeking, but are not really available for work. They may be registered as unemployed (U) and undertake some searching just so as not to lose unemployment benefits, but are not actually available for work. These are not truly unemployed. The majority of job-seekers are normally available for work.

Those "out of the labour force" (N) may also be divided between those who have been in this position for a long period and those in this position only for a short period, also in their case the length of the period affects their loss of skills. They can be divided between being available and unavailable for work.

Data show that a large proportion of new employees were previously "out of the workforce" (flow from N to E). The size of N is also sensitive to the business

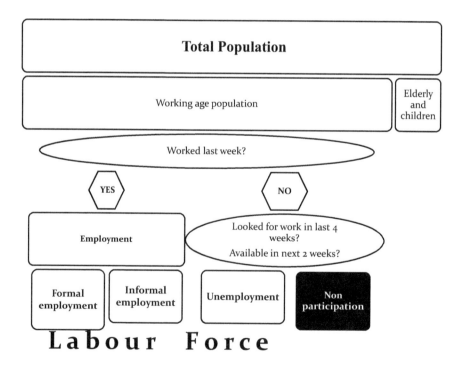

FIGURE 19.2 The total population and labour

The labour force is given by the sum of employment and unemployment.

environment. When the prospects for the unemployed become particularly bleak, many unemployed cease jobseeking to become non-participants (flow from U to N). On some occasions this leads to counter-intuitive effects: the deepening of a crisis may reduce the number of the unemployed; conversely an improvement in the business climate may lead discouraged workers in the "out of the labour force" category to restart jobseeking, thereby increasing the number of the unemployed (flow from N to U). When analysing data, these effects should be taken into due account.

The employed who leave their jobs may either do this on a voluntary basis because they want to improve their condition in some way, or because they are constrained to do so through being laid off by their employer. Of course, very often their subsequent actions may differ according to who took the original decision. Some of the employed leave the labour force and become "out of the labour force" (flow from E to N) in order to take care either of a relative or friend in need of assistance or of the family; or to restart studies; or simply to rest or take a break. Other employees leave their jobs to search for better jobs (flow from E to U) or because they have already found a new job (flow from E to E).

19.2 Key indicators of the labour market (KILM)[5]

1 Labour force participation rate

The labour force participation rate is a measure of the proportion of a country's working-age population that engages actively in the labour market, either by working or looking for work; it provides an indication of the relative magnitude of the supply of labour available to engage in the production of goods and services. In some poor countries this ratio is very high simply because the alternative to not working is starvation.

2 Employment-to-population ratio

The employment-to-population ratio is defined as the proportion of a country's working-age population that is employed. The employment-to-population ratio provides information on the ability of an economy to create employment; for many countries this indicator is often more insightful than the unemployment rate. Although a high overall ratio is typically considered as positive, the indicator alone is not sufficient for assessing the level of decent work or the level of a decent work deficit. In some poor countries this ratio is high even if the standard condition of people is poor.

3 Status in employment

Share of the employed population in the following categories:

1   Wage and salaried workers.
2   Employers.

3   Own-account workers, and
4   Contributing family workers.

4 Employment by sector

Three broad sectors: Agriculture, Industry, Services; an important factor in the analysis of productivity trends. The addition of further sectoral detail is useful.

5 Employment by occupation

Managers, professionals, technicians and associate professionals, clerical support workers, service and sales workers, skilled agricultural workers, forestry and fishery workers, craft and related trade workers, plant and machine operators and assemblers, elementary occupations, armed forces occupations.

6 Part-time workers

The indicator of part-time workers focusses on individuals whose working hours total less than "full time", as a proportion of total employment. The dividing line is determined either on a country-by-country basis or through special estimations. The key question is whether those in part-time work desire this or simply have no alternative.

7 Hours of work

The number of hours worked have an impact on the health and well-being of workers as well as on levels of productivity and the labour costs of establishments. Too few hours may indicate underemployment, too many hours may imply very stressful situations.

8 Employment in the informal economy

It is generally recognized as entailing a missing legal identity, poor working conditions, lack of membership of social protection systems, incidence of work-related accidents and ailments, and limited freedom of association.

9 Unemployment

It tells us the proportion of the labour force that does not have a job and is actively looking for work. It should not be misinterpreted as a measurement of economic hardship, however, although such a correlation often exists.

10 Youth unemployment

The term "youth" covers persons aged 15–24, although national variations in age definitions do occur.

11 Long-term unemployment

Unemployment tends to have more severe effects, the longer it lasts. It is not generally viewed as an important indicator for developing economies, where the duration of unemployment often tends to be short. Most of the available information on this indicator comes from the more developed economies.

12 Time-related underemployment

Underemployment reflects underutilization of the productive capacity of the labour force.

13 Inactivity (non-participation)

The percentage of the working-age population that is neither working nor seeking work (i.e., not in the labour force).

14 Educational attainment and illiteracy

Information on levels of educational attainment is currently the best available indicator of labour force skill levels.

15 Monthly wages and hourly compensation costs in the manufacturing sector

Wages are important from the workers' point of view and represent a measure of the level and trend of their purchasing power and an approximation of their standard of living. Hourly compensation cost provides an estimate of employers' expenditure on the employment of its workforce.

16 Labour productivity

Productivity, in combination with hourly compensation costs, can be used to assess the international competitiveness of a labour market. See also Section 3.3.

17 Poverty, income distribution and the working poor

The proportion of the population living below the international poverty line of US$1. The proportion of persons living with their families below the poverty line; the "working poor".[6]

19.3 The determinants of salaries

When is a salary high or low? How can we decide this? Salaries probably depend variously on the following factors:

- Productivity.
- Inflation.

- The salaries of other workers.
- Unemployment.
- Labour regulation.
- Bargaining power.

Different people will say that this element is more or less important than that element. They will now be considered in turn.

Productivity (Section 3.3)

Clearly what is not produced cannot be shared. If there is no production, income becomes unsustainable. In the medium term, only high productivity permits companies to pay high salaries. Low productivity necessarily condemns employees to low salaries. Does this mean that productivity can explain every wage differential? Can productivity explain why the CEO of a corporation today earns more than a thousand times the average wage in its company, whereas at the time of Henry Ford, the CEO of the same company used to earn less than forty times the average salary in the company? Is the CEO of today so much better than the one managing the company in the 1930s and 1940s? Have managerial skills suddenly become scarcer than they were in the past?

Inflation (Section 9.4)

People work mostly to earn a living for them and their families. It is obvious that they take into account the prices of goods when they make their wage requests. By the same token, employers understand that those who work for them need to survive. Therefore, employers consider price levels before making their salary offers. When salary levels are the outcome of a bargaining process or social negotiation, this does not take place continuously but only periodically. Every two or three, sometimes even five years, employers and employees discuss the new salary levels. The problem is that they must know not only the current prices, but also guess future prices, those covering the whole duration of the contract. This is more difficult. Maybe they will look at the recent past to predict the future, even if this is not always a perfect system. Different economists view this in different ways. Some economists say that people are good at knowing prices and quick to request salary increases; others raise doubts, saying that workers are not that good at knowing prices and not that quick to request adaptation of salaries to price levels. Consider also that different categories of workers update their contracts at different times. So even workers who are aware that prices have increased need to wait for a new round of negotiations for a salary increase.

The salaries of other workers (relative salaries)

"Keeping up with the Joneses" is certainly one of the objectives of many families. Individuals feel part of the same community and of the same group as long as they can afford the consumption level of that group. Studies show that this is one of the key determinants of human happiness. Therefore, it is not strange that workers take account of the salaries of their colleagues, their relatives, their friends and their neighbours and aim at keeping their salaries at least in a constant relationship with the salaries of those people. For workers, a comparison of their condition with that of their neighbours is probably easier than having an accurate idea of the level of prices in the country.

Unemployment

Workers understand that when unemployment is high, they have a higher risk of losing their own jobs. They see other people losing their jobs and this scares them. Higher unemployment will induce workers to limit their wage requests. In an environment in which many people are losing their jobs, keeping your own job, even with a low salary, looks like an achievement. High unemployment constrains the growth of salaries.

Labour regulation

Some legislation protects workers and makes them less exposed to the risk of unemployment and poverty. The right of association permits workers to have collective and stronger representation through trade unions. The right to abstain from work gives workers a bargaining chip. The existence of unemployment benefits makes the threat of unemployment less frightening. The existence of legislation regulating the dismissal of workers may reduce the risk of workers being dismissed. The existence of efficient job centres and public employment agencies may increase the possibilities of finding a new job. These and other types of labour protection will increase the bargaining power of workers and positively affect their salaries. Other legislation simply imposes a minimum salary, creating a floor on which other salaries are set.

Bargaining power

This includes many of the above-mentioned elements but also includes the political strength of the employees, the political support that they enjoy in the wider society and the support that they have in the media.

All these variables will play some role in the definition of salaries.

19.4 Economic growth and unemployment

How can we reduce unemployment? The optimum way of increasing employment and reducing unemployment is through economic growth. One can more or less say that the more economic growth there is, the more employment there will be. Economic growth is the outcome of private and public investment and of technological progress – albeit only up to a point, the reality being more complex.

For one thing, population may grow through the birth of new children or through the arrival of immigrants from other countries, When these new people start job seeking, unemployment automatically increases. If production (GDP, see Section 8.1) does not increase at least as much as the labour force, the unemployment rate will probably grow.

Unemployment also increases as a result of a certain type of technological progress (Section 15.3). When technological progress permits production of the same amount of product with fewer workers, unemployment may grow. Therefore a second reason why some GDP growth is necessary is to compensate for technological progress.

If the growth rate of GDP is insufficient to create enough jobs for the increasing number of people who want to work and for those who lose their job because of technological progress, the unemployment rate will grow. In a country where the workforce grows and there is technical progress, the unemployment rate will grow if economic growth is not strong enough. This is what economists call "The law of Okun" after the name of the US economist who defined it.[7]

Even assuming that there is neither growth of the population (or labour force, to be precise) nor technological progress, we should not expect that a 3 per cent growth in GDP should lead to a 3 per cent growth in employment. Firms do not hire and fire in strict proportion to the level of production.

In periods of crisis firms retain many workers even if they produce relatively little; in the jargon this is known as labour hoarding. On the one hand firms do not want to dismiss employees whom they have selected and trained at high cost, and on the other hand some employees carry out work (accounting, security and maintenance among other things – so-called indirect labour) which has to be carried out in any event, independently of the level of output. For these reasons, when production grows by 5 per cent firms do not necessarily hire 5 per cent more employees; they may simply make better use of those they already have.

We should also remember that a given contribution to GDP may be produced by different industries: some industries, for example the garment industry, require many workers, while others, for example the oil industry, require very few workers to produce the same level of output in value terms. Even a given industry may use a range of technologies and therefore employ different numbers of people to produce the same output. Some countries experience considerable growth in their GDP, but derive that growth from sectors – for example refineries and the chemical industry – which use very few workers and large quantities of capital. In some cases, countries are not even able to supply the few (highly specialized) employees that certain sectors, for example the oil industry, require. Therefore, those countries need to attract foreign workers to run such industries even if they have many unemployed people. In such cases GDP growth is perfectly compatible with zero-employment growth.

Finally, we should also remember that each country has a part of its population which works in the informal economy, this term being said to "refer to all economic activities by workers and economic units that are – in law or in practice – not covered or insufficiently covered by formal arrangements; and does not cover illicit activities".[8] The share of the informal economy varies from country to country, but in many developing countries the informal economy represents more than 50 per cent and even up to 90 per cent of total employment. The ability to calculate the number of workers in the informal economy varies from country to country. Sometimes economic growth in developing countries leads not to employment growth but to movements of workers between the formal and the informal economy. In some very poor countries the extension of the informal economy may contribute to very high participation rates. In those developing countries where, out of necessity, participation of the population in the labour force is very high, some economic growth may allow individuals to abandon the labour force, for example to study or to care for dependants. This confuses the picture, as in these countries economic growth may actually lead to decreasing employment levels.

In general, we can say that economic growth is a necessary, but not sufficient, condition for the creation of good new jobs.

FULL AND PRODUCTIVE EMPLOYMENT, AND DECENT WORK FOR ALL

The eighth goal of the 2030 agenda for sustainable development

The 2030 Agenda is a UN plan of action for people, planet and prosperity. It also seeks to strengthen universal peace in greater freedom. The UN recognizes that eradicating poverty in all its forms and dimensions, including extreme poverty, is the greatest global challenge and an indispensable requirement for sustainable development. All countries and all stakeholders, acting in collaborative partnership, will implement this plan. They are resolved to free the human race from the tyranny of poverty and to heal and secure our planet. The Agenda includes 17 Sustainable Development Goals and 169 targets. The eighth goal is: "Promote sustained, inclusive and sustainable economic growth, full and productive employment, and decent work for all".[9]

19.5 Unemployment and prices

Does unemployment reduce inflation? Does job creation cause inflation? Should we choose between inflation and unemployment? Can governments reduce unemployment by accepting more inflation? More generally, can governments do anything to reduce unemployment or will this only generate inflation?

When the unemployment level is very high, prices usually do not increase much. Some economists emphasize that unemployment is a threat to workers and that with high unemployment few workers dare demand salary increases. If a fall in unemployment makes workers able to obtain higher wages, then inflation rises. This occurs because firms pass on this cost increase.

Some economists (neoclassical monetarists) go further and also say that small reductions in unemployment should lead to some additional inflation. Other economists (those who follow Keynes) are more sceptical and think substantial salary increases will occur only when all productive workers are already employed and employers also start hiring less productive individuals or when they start poaching productive staff from their competitors. In order to attract staff, they are compelled to make better financial offers. The same economists (Keynesians) remind us that salaries are just one component of prices, and that profit margins also matter. Prices may grow because corporate margins and profits grow, not because salaries grow. In other cases, the state may increase taxes (Section 13.1) and social contributions (Section 13.1) and this may lead to higher prices. This can occur through different channels: for example, through increasing indirect taxes such as VAT, or increasing taxes on utilities which then raise their bills.

Everything in the end contributes to the level of prices. Wages are only one component of prices. In some cases, a reduction in sales compels companies to produce a less than optimal output. Companies then cannot fully exploit economies of scale (see Chapter 5) and reach the minimum efficient size (Section 5.4). Their fixed costs must be shared between a limited number of units, which must therefore be sold at a higher price. This explains why, at least in the initial phases of a crisis, prices may increase.

On the link between unemployment and prices there are basically three major positions:

1   Those who believe that with more inflation unemployment may decrease. These are those that believe in the so-called Phillips curve. Fostering demand generates some costs, but may be effective. They also believe that the only way to reduce inflation is by increasing unemployment.

2   Those who believe that in the medium term, about five years, any increase in the quantity of money (expansionary monetary policy), any increase in government spending, or any reduction of taxes (expansionary fiscal policy) will merely bring about inflation and no reduction in unemployment. Governments can only improve education and training and make the labour market efficient, no more than that. These are those who believe in the existence of a natural rate of unemployment; this is a rate of unemployment which, according to them, cannot be changed on a permanent basis. Greater government spending, lower taxation or lower interest rates (monetary policies, see Section 9.2) cannot change the natural rate of unemployment. According to them the only way to change the natural rate of unemployment consists of action on the labour market. Only better employment agencies, more flexible labour laws, fewer workers' rights, lower salaries and higher labour productivity (Section 3.3) i.e., only a lower unit labour cost (Section 3.4) will induce firms to hire more workers.

3   Those who believe that, up to a certain employment level, inflation and employment are scarcely related. Then, when resources are almost fully utilized, prices start to increase. This is the more Keynesian view of the issue. Fostering demand when it is weak makes sense according to this view.

Glossary

attached worker   Employee who maintains links with a company and desires/ expects to go back to work in it; they will eventually be recalled.

available for work   Those who are registered as unemployed or are outside the workforce (N) and are really interested in finding work.

capital-intensive   This term describes a business process or industry that requires large amounts of money and other financial resources but relatively few workers.

employed   A person who has a job.

frictional unemployment   Job seekers do not know where the available jobs are and firms do not know where the available workers are. So, labour demand and labour supply do not meet, some workers remain unemployed and some positions remain vacant. Such unemployment is associated with the search and matching of workers with jobs, which is standard in any dynamic economy.

informal economy   This refers to all economic activities by workers and economic units that are − in law or in practice − not covered or insufficiently covered by formal arrangements; it does not cover illicit activities. [10]

jobless growth   Economic growth which brings limited or no growth in employment. This can for example occur because the growth is based on capital-intensive industries or because it is insufficient to compensate for the growth in unemployment due to technological progress and a growing number of job seekers.

key indicators of the labour market (KILM)   This is a data-set produced by the ILO which has compiled and analysed country-level labour market information and produced comparable cross- country statistics for 178 countries.

Keynesian economists   Economists who follow the teaching of the British economist, John Maynard Keynes. These economists believe that markets are not perfectly self-regulating entities. Sometimes demand may be insufficient and in such cases government can and must intervene, increasing government spending, cutting taxes and increasing the money supply. The risk of generating inflation, according to them, is limited if the economy is not fully using its available resources (workers and capital).

KILM   See *key indicators of the labour market.*

labour force   The sum of those who are employed and those who are unemployed.

labour-intensive   This describes a business which requires relatively many workers and a lower quantity of capital.

long-term unemployment   This concerns workers who remain for long periods − a year or longer[11] − without work, and risk losing skills and eventually becoming discouraged, even leading them to stop their search and become "out of the labour force".

monetarist economists Economists who hold the strong belief that the economy's performance is determined almost entirely by changes in the money supply. Monetarists postulate that the economic health of an economy can be best controlled by changes in the money supply attributable to a governing body. The key driver behind this belief is the impact of inflation on an economy's growth or health and the belief that by controlling the money supply one can control the inflation rate. They believe in the self-regulating power of market forces.

natural rate of unemployment According to the neoclassical view there are two forms of unemployment: cyclical and natural. Cyclical unemployment is associated with the economic cycle of recession and boom. Natural unemployment is either frictional or structural. Frictional unemployment is that associated with the search and matching of workers with jobs, which is standard in any dynamic economy. Structural unemployment is more long term and occurs when workers' skills become defunct and do not meet the needs of modernizing workplaces.

neoclassical economist An economist who believe in the substantial ability of markets to self-regulate and therefore in limited government intervention.

non-available workers Those who either are registered as unemployed and undertake job searches only so as not to lose unemployment benefits, or else who are unwilling to go back to work.

non-participant An individual of working age who does not work and does not seek a new job.

outside the labour force See *non-participant*.

short-term unemployment A temporary unemployment condition (less than one year). Among people in this condition are those looking for the best job opportunities, a search that can require some time.

unattached worker Employee who does not expect/desire to go back to the company they left and will not be recalled.

unemployed Those who do not have a job, but in the last four weeks have carried out some job-seeking activity and are available for work.

Notes

1 Blanchard and Diamond (1989:15).
2 Ibid:3.
3 Blanchard and Diamond (1989) and Feldstein (1975).
4 "A worker who is laid off may remain attached to the firm in two distinct senses. One is that the worker is less available for employment elsewhere than the typical unemployed worker. The second is that the worker is available for recall by the firm without the need to post a vacancy. This practice is most common in manufacturing" (Blanchard and Diamond, 1989:18).
5 See: www.ilo.org/empelm/what/WCMS_114240/lang--en/index.htm.

6 These indicators are supplemented by other measures of economic well-being, including the employed population living in different economic class groups (denoted by different per capita household consumption thresholds), estimates of the population living below nationally defined poverty lines and the Gini index as a measure of the degree of inequality in income distribution.

7 In other terms, Okun's law is stating that each extra percentage point of cyclical unemployment rate is associated with about a 2-percentage point increase in the output gap measured as the percentage difference between GDP from its potential (that depends on the growth of the labour force and the rate of technological progress).

8 ILO, Recommendation 204, www.ilo.org/wcmsp5/groups/public/–ed_norm/–rel conf/documents/meetingdocument/ wcms_377774.pdf.

9 United Nations General Assembly (2015) www.un.org/ga/search/view_doc.asp?symbol= A/RES/70/1&Lang=E.

10 ILO, Recommendation 204, www.ilo.org/wcmsp5/groups/public/–ed_norm/–relconf/ documents/meetingdocument/ wcms_377774.pdf.

11 http://data.worldbank.org/indicator/SL.UEM.LTRM.ZS.

Bibliography

Blanchard, O. J. and Diamond, P. (1989). "The Beveridge Curve," *Brookings Papers on Economic Activity*, 1: 1–76.

Feldstein, M. S. (1975). "The Importance of Temporary Layoffs: An Empirical Analysis," *Brookings Papers on Economic Activity*, (3): 725. http://doi.org/10.2307/2534152.

International Labour Organization (ILO). (2015). "Recommendation No. 204 Concerning the Transition from the Informal to the Formal Economy," International Labour Organization, Geneva, CH.

Okun, A. (1963). *Potential GDP: Its Measurement and Significance*, Proceedings of the Business and Economic Statistic Section of the American Statistical Association.

United Nations, General Assembly. (2015). "Resolution 70/1 Transforming Our World: The 2030 Agenda for Sustainable Development," A/RES/70/1, adopted on 25 September.

20

INCOME DISTRIBUTION AND ITS EFFECTS

If I eat one chicken and you eat none, on average we eat half a chicken each, but you may starve and I will be overfed. When we consider the economy of a country, income distribution matters. Firstly, it is important to understand what inequality is, and secondly, to consider its effects on consumption and on the economy in general. Can we have a solid economy with poor income distribution? We shall go on to see how we can address inequality.

20.1 The nature of inequality

Essentially, income inequality is high when a few people earn a very large share of the total income of a country and the remainder of the population earns a very small share of the total. Inequality is low when everybody has roughly the same income. Wealth can also be distributed in a near uniform way or not. Some stress the importance of equality of opportunity: the opportunity of growing up healthy, of receiving an education, and using one's available skills and knowledge to the maximum possible extent. Inequality also relates to age, class and gender or exists between urban and rural dwellers.

Inequality negatively affects child mortality (Figure 20.1) and health: a rich country, for example the US probably has health levels worse than those of poorer countries such as Spain also because its levels of inequality are higher (0.415 in the US[2] vs. 0.362 in Spain). Inequality also affects education: with higher inequality, larger parts of the population receive insufficient education, preventing the development and accumulation of skills in the country. Skills and knowledge are the leading forces in the economic development of a country.

This is one of the reasons why a country with high inequality grows less than its potential. Moreover, inequality also fosters the development of violent crime.[3]

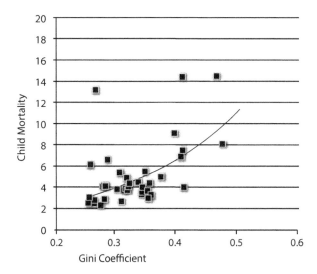

FIGURE 20.1   Income inequality and death in the first five years of life

It is possible to observe that countries with higher inequality tend to have higher child mortality.

Countries with per capita GDP above US$ 20,000, calculation in terms of purchasing power parity[1] (constant 2011 international $).

Source: elaboration by the author of World Bank data

National statistics usually include a measurement of income inequality, the so-called Gini index[4] (see Table 20.1). When the Gini index or Gini coefficient is high, it means that inequality is high. Comparing the income of the richest 10 per cent of the population with the income of the poorest ten per cent is an alternative measure of inequality.

The description of income distribution in a country: the Lorenz curve

The Lorenz curve (Figure 20.2) is a means of describing the income distribution of a country. At the base of the graph, the horizontal axis shows population shares (percentages), ordered with the poorest at the extreme left and the richest at the extreme right. From the left, the first quarter of the base of the graph represents the poorest quarter of the total population, the left half the poorer half of the population, the left three-quarters, the 75 per cent least well-off members of the population, and the whole of the base, the entire population, including the richest quarter. On the vertical axis, there is a measure of the share of the total income of the country, which is made up by the sum of incomes of the poorest x per cent of the population. At the extreme bottom left corner of the square there is 0 per cent

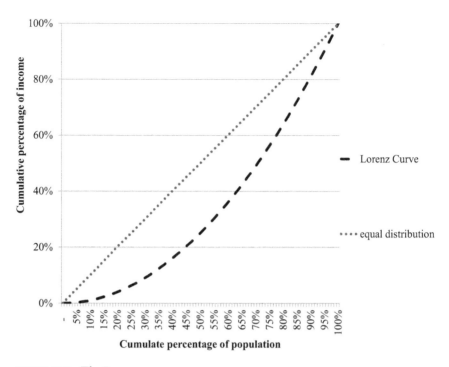

FIGURE 20.2 The Lorenz curve

The cumulate percentage of population is ordered from left to right according to their income, on the horizontal axis. The vertical axis indicates the cumulative percentage of income received by a certain share of population. In this example, the poorest 25 per cent of the population earns 6.25 per cent of the total income. The poorest half of the population earns 25 per cent of the total income and the poorest 75 per cent of the population earns only 56 per cent of the total income. This means that 44 per cent of the total income goes to the richest quarter of the population. An alternative Lorenz curve can be done to show the distribution of wealth.

of the population and 0 per cent of income. We may ask how much of the total income goes into the pockets of the poorest 25 per cent. If the poorest quarter of the country received a quarter of the total income, we would find a point on the diagonal straight line. However, as normally happens, the sum of the incomes of the poorest quarter of the population represents less than a quarter of the total income of the country, in this graph 6.25 per cent, on a point well below the diagonal. Then we total the incomes of the poorest half of the population and how much they have compared with the total income of the country, in this case 25 per cent; and in the same way, we observe that three-quarters of the population receive 56 per cent of total income. And of course, it need hardly be said that the total population of the country earns 100 per cent of total income. So, we have obtained five points, for zero, 25, 50, 75 and 100 per cent of the population. If we join these points, we obtain a curve. In a country where every individual earns the same income, the curve coincides with the diagonal straight line. In a very unequal country, the curve traces a very large crescent. In the case of extreme inequality, in which one extra rich person earns all the income, the crescent becomes a triangle, i.e. half of the square.

THE GINI COEFFICIENT

The Lorenz curve (figure 20.3) still does not provide us with a numerical measurement of inequality, whereas the Gini coefficient, does. The national statistical agencies and international organizations publish indexes for different countries, permitting comparison of income distribution in different countries. Gini has suggested calculating the area of the crescent of the Lorenz curve, then calculating the ratio between that number and the area of the triangle defined by the diagonal, i.e. half the square. The Gini index may vary between 0 (egalitarian society) and 1 (unequal society). It never reaches these two extreme values.

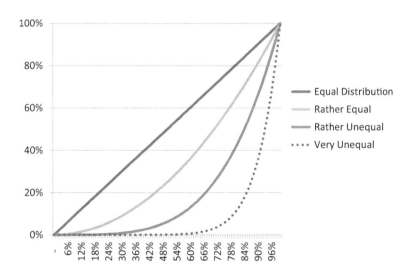

FIGURE 20.3   Different Lorenz curves

In the country with equal distribution, the Gini coefficient is 0, in the country with very unequal distribution, the Gini coefficient will be close to 1.

TABLE 20.1 Different degrees of inequality

Gini	Country	Year	Gini	Country	Year	Gini	Country	Year	Gini	Country	Year
25	Ukraine	2016	31.8	Poland	2016	36.2	Spain	2015	42.2	China	2012
25.4	Slovenia	2015	31.8	Egypt	2015	36.4	Fiji	2013	42.4	Argentina	2016
25.6	Iceland	2014	31.9	Montenegro	2014	36.4	Lao PDR	2012	42.4	Ghana	2012
25.9	Czech Rep.	2015	31.9	Ireland	2015	36.5	Georgia	2016	42.6	Madagascar	2012
26.3	Moldova	2016	32.3	Mongolia	2016	36.7	Yemen, Rep.	2014	43.1	Togo	2015
26.4	Kosovo	2015	32.4	Bangladesh	2016	37.1	Solomon Is.	2013	43.4	Mexico	2016
26.5	Slovak Rep.	2015	32.5	Armenia	2016	37.4	Lithuania	2015	43.8	Peru	2016
26.8	Kyrgyz Rep.	2016	32.5	Switzerland	2014	37.4	Bulgaria	2014	44.1	Djibouti	2013
26.9	Kazakhstan	2015	32.6	Mauritania	2014	37.7	Russian Fed.	2015	44.6	Bolivia	2016
27	Belarus	2016	32.7	France	2015	37.8	Thailand	2013	45	Ecuador	2016
27.1	Finland	2015	32.7	Estonia	2015	38.1	Myanmar	2015	45.3	Santo Domingo	2016
27.5	Norway	2015	32.7	Bosnia and Herz.	2015	38.6	Burundi	2013	45.3	Comoros	2013
27.7	Belgium	2015	33.2	UK	2015	38.8	Iran	2014	46.2	Nicaragua	2014
28.2	Denmark	2015	33.2	Liberia	2014	38.8	Bhutan	2012	46.6	Cameroon	2014
28.3	Romania	2016	33.7	Guinea	2016	39.1	Ethiopia	2015	46.8	Seychelles	2013
28.5	Serbia	2015	34	Cyprus	2015	39.5	Indonesia	2013	47.7	Chile	2015
28.7	Timor-Leste	2014	34	Tajikistan	2014	39.7	Uruguay	2016	47.8	Benin	2015
29	Malta	2014	34	Canada	2014	39.8	Sri Lanka	2013	47.9	Paraguay	2016
29	Albania	2012	34.2	Latvia	2012	40	El Salvador	2016	48.3	Guatemala	2014
29.2	Sweden	2015	34.3	Niger	2015	40.1	Philippines	2015	48.7	Costa Rica	2016
29.3	The Netherlands	2015	34.7	Italy	2015	40.1	Micronesia	2013	50	Honduras	2016
29.5	Iraq	2012	34.8	Vietnam	2012	41	Uganda	2012	50.4	Panama	2016
30.4	Hungary	2015	35.3	Burkina Faso	2015	41.1	Haiti	2012	50.4	Rwanda	2013
30.5	Austria	2015	35.5	Portugal	2015	41.4	Israel	2015	50.8	Colombia	2016
30.7	Pakistan	2013	35.6	North Macedonia	2013	41.5	US	2016	51.3	Brazil	2015
30.8	Croatia	2015	35.8	Mauritius	2015	41.5	Cote d'Ivoire	2015	54	Mozambique	2014
31.2	Luxembourg	2014	35.9	Gambia	2014	41.9	Turkey	2016	57.1	Zambia	2015
31.6	Korea, Rep.	2012	36	Greece	2015	42.1	Congo, Dem. Rep.	2012	63	South Africa	2014
31.7	Germany	2015									

Source: World Bank. See https://data.worldbank.org/indicator/si.pov.gini?end=2016&start=2016&view=bar.worldbank.org/indicator/SI.POV.GINI/

20.2 The change of inequality and its effects

When we consider world inequality, we can measure it in many ways. Here we limit our attention to just two. We can see, country by country, how inequality varies. In most OECD countries (Figure 20.4) the gap between rich and poor is at its highest level for 30 years.[5] Today, the richest 10 per cent of the population in the OECD area earn 9.5 times the income of the poorest 10 per cent; in the 1980s this ratio stood at 7:1 and it has been rising continuously ever since.

However, the rise in overall income inequality is not (only) about rich people becoming richer: often the incomes of poorer people grew much more slowly during years of prosperity and fell during downturns, putting relative – and in some countries, absolute – income poverty on the radar of policy concerns even in the rich OECD countries.

In these terms inequality in the world has probably increased in recent years. The Gini coefficient of China in 1982 was less than 0.3 and in 2008 was close to 0.50 (Li Shi, 2016). Inequality increased in the US (Figure 20.6), India (Figure 20.5), Indonesia (Figure 20.7), the United Kingdom, South Africa and Germany. It decreased in Brazil (Figure 20.8) and France. In Pakistan (Figure 20.9) and Nigeria (Figure 20.10) the identification of a clear trend is more difficult to determine.

The fact that inequality has grown both in such fast-growing large countries as China, India and Indonesia and in such leading industrialized countries as the US,

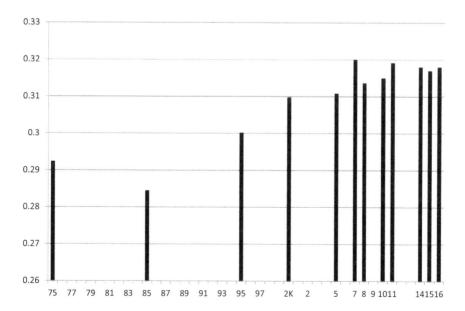

FIGURE 20.4 Average of Gini index in OECD countries

Source: Elaboration by the Author of OECD data[6]

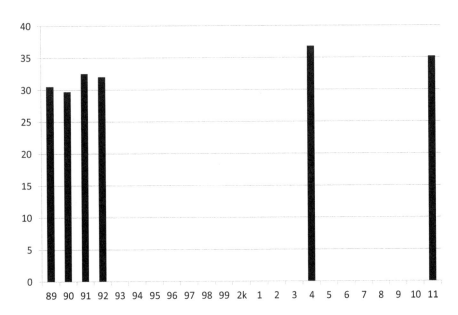

FIGURE 20.5 The Gini index in India

Source: World Bank elaboration by the author.

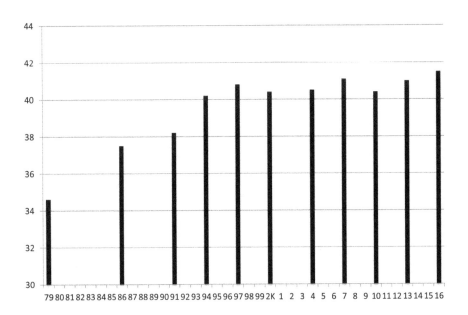

FIGURE 20.6 The Gini index in the US

Source: Data from World Bank https://data.worldbank.org/indicator/si.pov.gini

Elaboration by the author.

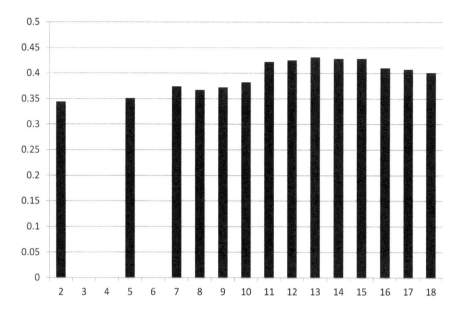

FIGURE 20.7 The Gini index in Indonesia

Source: Data from Badan Pusat Statistic www.bps.go.id/linkTableDinamis/view/id/1116

Elaboration by the author.

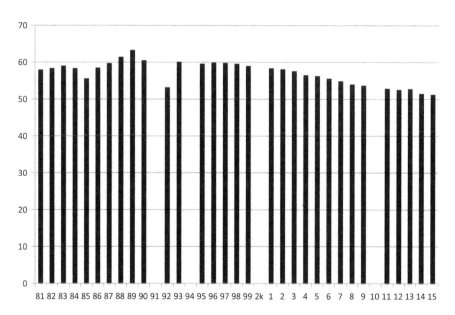

FIGURE 20.8 The Gini index in Brazil

The Anti-Poverty Policies Probably Bore Fruit.

Source: Data from World Bank https://data.worldbank.org/indicator/si.pov.gini

Elaboration by the author.

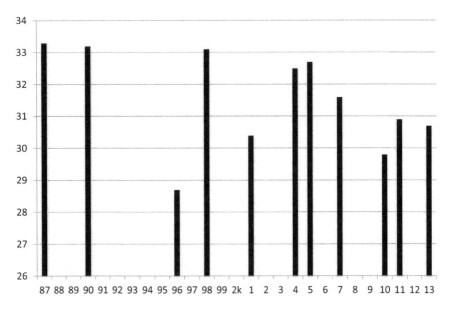

FIGURE 20.9   The Gini index in Pakistan

Source: Data from World Bank https://data.worldbank.org/indicator/si.pov.gini

Elaboration by the author.

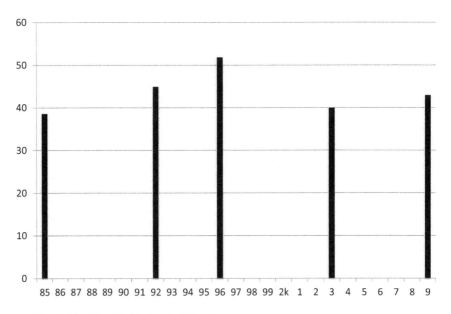

FIGURE 20.10   The Gini index in Nigeria

Source: Data from World Bank https://data.worldbank.org/indicator/si.pov.gini

Elaboration by the author.

the UK and Germany requires special consideration. These are countries which are or will probably become references for many other countries.

The other method of considering inequality at world level consists of considering the differences between the average incomes of different countries. In this perspective inequality has probably diminished.[7] Such large underprivileged countries as China and India have become richer, while many rich countries have grown relatively little and have not become much richer. What is the right method of measuring inequality in the world? What matters most? Each criterion has a specific purpose. The fact that the average incomes of different countries have drawn closer together is important in terms of development. There was a development process in very poor countries and they now are closer to rich countries than before. However, individuals do not organize their lives at world level, but at country level. The national dimension is still the prevalent one. Not only that, much of the loyalty of citizens is addressed to their country. There they pay their taxes, potentially do military service and maintain their loyalty to their country.

There is more. In large countries most production is usually for the internal market. Even if exports represent large shares of national GDPs, most production is still targeted on satisfying internal demand. Table 20.2 shows that for most of the large economies, exports do not account for the greater part of the output of a country: they represent 13 per cent of Brazilian GDP, 31 per cent of Canada's, 20 per cent of China's, 16 per cent of Egypt's, 20 per cent of Indonesia's, 19 per cent of India's, 16 per cent of Japan's and 12 per cent of the US's. Only in small economies such as those of the UAE and Luxembourg, in oil-exporting economies such as Saudi Arabia, and in exceptional cases in economies such as that of Germany, do exports account for 50 per cent of GDP or more. This is the reason why income distribution within countries is still so important.

What are the consequences of increasing inequality in several important economies? We have seen (see Section 17.2) that poorer people generally consume a larger share of their income than do richer people. Economists say that poor people

TABLE 20.2 Exports as a share of GDP in selected countries in 2017

Angola	30	China	20	Haiti	19	Mexico	38
UAE	100	Germany	47	Indonesia	20	Niger	17
Argentina	11	Algeria	24	India	19	New Zealand	26
Australia	21	Egypt	16	Italy	31	Philippines	31
Bangladesh	15	Spain	34	Japan	16	Russia	26
Brazil	13	France	31	Kenya	14	Saudi Arabia	34
Botswana	55	UK	31	Korea, Rep.	43	Venezuela	17
Canada	31	Ghana	40	Luxembourg	230	Vietnam	102
Chile	29	Guatemala	19	Morocco	37	US	12

Note: For Botswana, Japan and the US, data are about 2016. Data for Venezuela are about 2014.
Source: World Bank, https://data.worldbank.org/indicator/NE.EXP.GNFS.ZS

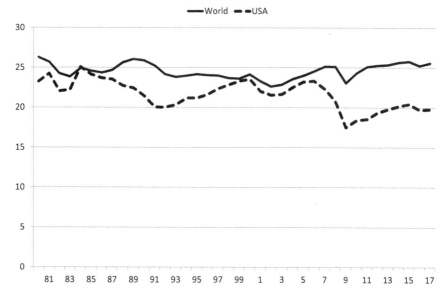

FIGURE 20.11 Investments as a percentage of GDP in the world and in the US between 1980 and 2014

Source: elaboration by the author of data from the IMF-WEO Database

have a higher propensity to consume (see Glossary of Chapter 17). When most of the new income goes to the richest part of society it also goes to people with low propensity to consume. This could reduce the average propensity to consume of a country.[8] The fact that rich people receive a wide share of the national income need be not a bad thing, as rich people save and invest more. Unfortunately, data both from the US (Figure 20.11) and from the whole world do not seem to confirm the hypothesis that there is substitution between consumption and investment.

In the US after 1980, while inequality was increasing, investment was not. This implies that there would be no additional investment to compensate for potentially lower consumption if this situation occurred. Consumption is one of the main outlets (see Section 8.2) for what is produced in a country. If it declines, many goods could remain without buyers. This would negatively affect the sales and profits of many firms. In most countries a fall in consumption did not occur, indeed in many industrialized countries a fall of consumption was avoided through more extensive credit to households.

US: INEQUALITY AND ITS EFFECTS ON ECONOMIC GROWTH

If US exports represented a larger share of US GDP, a stagnation or decline in the purchasing power of US consumers could be compensated for by the rising standards of life of the Chinese working class. Chinese workers, becoming richer, could buy those goods that US consumers could not buy. But this does not occur to a sufficient extent. In the US, inequality diminishes the income and wealth of lower- and middle-income citizens. The small proportion of the population that is becoming richer does not need many more goods and does not buy them. For this reason, US internal demand could not grow sufficiently. In theory it could be substituted by foreign demand. However, as seen above exports represent a small share of US GDP and therefore sales abroad could not compensate sufficiently for the shortfall in internal sales. Inequality in this way could become a brake on growth.[9] As we can see, credit booms and risky financial operations have prevented this from happening. The cure is however worse than the disease.

When people do not have the money to purchase goods, they receive credits to pay for them. Probably for this reason, in almost all the G7 countries (refer to figure 20.12) the debt-to-income ratio of households considerably increased after 1980.

This financial exposure of families brings risks. Any relatively small change in their disposable income (Section 13.3) may considerably reduce their ability to pay back debts. In 2007–8, for example, higher petrol prices contributed to putting low-income-and-high-debt US families under pressure, leading some of them not

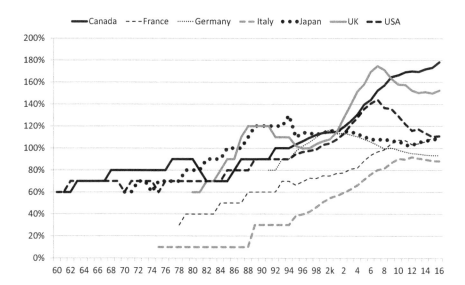

FIGURE 20.12   Households debt-income ratio in G7 countries between 1960 and 2016

Source: Elaboration by the author of data from Davies et al. 2012 for data until 1994 and from OECD (https://data.oecd.org/hha/household-debt.htm).

to repay their debts. This element, combined with weak regulation of the financial markets and the low reliability of corporate accounting data, increases the risk of financial crises, which in turn can have further heavy consequences for economic growth (and income distribution). In this way inequality is a serious threat to the stability of the economies.

Income inequality also has a negative impact on economic growth through a different channel: the education that poor young people receive.[10] In particular, what matters most is the gap between low-income households and the rest of the population. Moreover, human capital – the amount of education and skills that people acquire – is a channel through which inequality may affect growth. Increased income disparities depress skills development between individuals with poorer parental education background, in terms of both the quantity of education attained (e.g. years of schooling), and of its quality (i.e. skills proficiency). Last but not least, inequality fosters the development of violent crime,[11] making countries less pleasant places to live and less attractive destinations for investment.

20.3 Causes of and remedies for inequality

While we know that inequality has increased in different countries, there are different ways of explaining why this has occurred.

One explanation concerns technology. According to this explanation, the introduction of IT and the internet, of so-called ICT, and of automation in general, reduces the need for many routine and clerical jobs, leaving room only for jobs requiring very few skills and generating low salaries, or else for very sophisticated jobs requiring very advanced skills and generating high salaries for those few persons who have those skills. An example is in automobile production, where robots and computer-controlled machines have supplanted the simplest production jobs; that has increased auto-companies' demand for skilled operatives who know how to work with this new equipment. For this reason, middle-income jobs would disappear and there would be a scarcity of highly skilled workers.[12] This is the explanation preferred by neo-classical economists. It leads to the conclusion that we can do relatively little to reduce inequality apart from improving the efficiency and the effectiveness of the educational system. The only thing that we can do is to increase the number of people with the advanced skills required by the new technologies.

A second explanation relates to trade. Some workers are exposed to the effects of trade because they produce traded goods, other workers are not. Those workers exposed to trade will have a wage tending towards the world level in that field. Conversely, in low-wage countries trade will bring benefits if those countries specialize in labour-intensive production, thereby raising the wages of workers.

The third explanation refers to increased capital mobility. If workers or capital cannot move, they can at best receive the return available in the local market. If they can move freely around the world, they can obtain the best available return at world level, for that type of labour or for that type of capital. The freedom of movement of many workers is limited by the cost of moving their families, by the cost of finding rented accommodation or obtaining a mortgage, by language barriers, or by possible non-recognition of their educational titles, of their credit ratings or of their experience. For many workers these barriers can be very high. Therefore, the mobility of most workers is quite limited. Similar problems may affect small businesses, but do not affect top managers and financial capital wherever legislation allows free movement. The cost of moving financial capital is quite low. If they see their prospects in one country reduced by the high salaries or taxes of that country, they can potentially move elsewhere.

This threat can be enough to induce countries to keep salaries low and offer corporations the best tax arrangements. This starts a race in which every country competes with lower taxation of financial assets. Some small countries with very small populations and low running costs can meet the needs of their state just through commission charges on their financial assets. They can afford not to impose taxes. They can become tax havens. They do not need to provide large infrastructures to host capitals. Some bank branches are sufficient. The assets that they hold produce results elsewhere, usually where public investments have been made, to provide those countries with ports, roads, schools, R&D and hospitals that make the use of capital effective. Competition with tax havens impels many countries to reduce their taxation on financial assets as much as possible. Perfectly movable capital will be moved elsewhere if its after-tax yield falls below a certain threshold. The reward should also materialize rapidly otherwise the capital will move elsewhere. In this framework we can also include the trend, at corporate level, towards paying more attention to short-term than to long-term objectives.

Capital mobility increased after 1970, after having been constrained for 50 years.[13] That probably increased the downward pressure on salaries with a smaller share of total US income going to them (Figure 20.13) and on tax rates on financial assets. Governments had to redirect their tax pressure towards other targets or to cut their spending in such fields as education, health care, R&D, infrastructures or social security. The most successful US investor ever, Warren Buffett, offered his view of events: "Actually, there's been class warfare going on for the last 20 years, and my class has won. We're the ones that have gotten our tax rates reduced dramatically".[14]

Policies to reduce income inequalities should be pursued not only to improve social outcomes but also to sustain long-term growth. Inequality has more negative effects on growth when it increases the gap between low-income households and the rest of the population. Human capital (education) is a channel through which inequality may affect growth. Increased income disparities depress skills development among individuals with poorer parents, in terms both of the quantity of education attained (e.g. years of schooling) and of its quality (i.e. skills proficiency).[15] A country with many poorly educated people can hardly increase its productivity and its salaries. These poorly educated people cannot handle new more productive technologies. With an uneducated workforce, the benefits of investments even in new modern equipment are scarce.

Redistribution policies via taxes and transfers are a key tool for ensuring that the benefits of growth are more widely distributed, and experience suggests that they

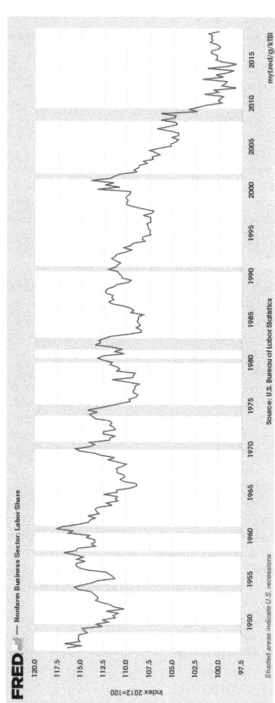

FIGURE 20.13 The share of total US income going to labour

After the Financial Crisis the Share of Income Going to Labour has Remained Smaller.

Source: US Bureau of Labor Statistics, Nonfarm Business Sector: Labor Share [PRS85006173], retrieved from FRED, Federal Reserve Bank of St Louis; https://fred.stlouisfed.org/series/PRS85006173, September 11, 2018.

need not be expected to undermine growth.[16] But it is also important to promote equality of opportunity in access to, and the quality of, education. This implies a focus on families with children and youths – as this is where decisions about human capital accumulation are made – promoting employment for disadvantaged groups through active labour market policies, childcare support and in-work benefits.[17] The possibility of implementing these policies depends on the possibility of coordinating at international level the taxation of financial assets (an idea of Professor Piketty's) or, in the absence of such coordination, on the regulation of capital mobility. While this can look counterintuitive, it is probably a necessary tool for preventing falls in the free-market economy in periods of slow growth and frequent financial crises, and for guaranteeing long-term prosperity.

Glossary

equality of opportunity According to this principle every individual or citizen should be offered the same opportunities in terms of safety, nutrition, health care, education and access to quality jobs, but not the same job, income, consumption, standard of life or wealth at the end of their life, which depend instead on their effort and skills.

equality of outcomes or results Individuals achieve the same ends, for example the same incomes, levels of consumption, standards of life and wealth. This is the outcome of extreme egalitarian policies.

Gini index or coefficient An indicator of inequality. Its values range between the extremes of 0, when all incomes or the wealth of all individuals are equal (fully egalitarian society) and 1 when one individual receives all the income or owns all the wealth and the remaining individuals earn and have nothing (totally non-egalitarian society). Sometimes the range is multiplied by 100 and is then between 0 and 100.[18]

households A family or a group of people living together in one house.

ICT (information and communication technologies) It refers to technologies that provide access to information through telecommunications. It is similar to Information Technology (IT) but focusses primarily on communications technologies.

inequality of opportunity Individuals are denied access to institutions or employment, limiting their ability to benefit from living in a market economy. For example, children from poor homes may be denied access to high-quality education, which limits their ability to achieve high levels of income in the future.[19]

inequality of outcome Measuring the actual differences of income, wealth, consumption or something else between people at adult age, without taking into account if they were or were not offered the same opportunities at the start of their life.

IT (information technology) This term refers to anything relating to computing technology, such as networking, hardware, software, the internet, or the people that work with these technologies.[20]

Lorenz curve It plots the cumulative shares of total income against the cumulative share of the population. It is a graphical representation of wealth or income distribution. It was developed by the American economist, Max Lorenz in 1905.

Notes

1 The Purchasing Power Parity (PPP) methodology consists of dividing the per capita GDP of a country by the value in that country of a basket of goods, which are substantially the same in every considered country. In this way the average standard of life of the population is better described than simply converting every per capita income in the same currency.
2 The US Gini coefficient concerns the year 2016 and the Spanish one, 2015. The per-capita PPP GDP 2014 was for Spain $31,195 and for the US, was $51,922.
3 Laderman et al. (2002).
4 Technically the Gini index is a measurement of concentration. Here we consider the concentration of income and wealth, and therefore we use it as an index of inequality.
5 Cingano (2014).
6 For the years 2014–15–16 www.oecd.org/social/income-distribution-database.htm. For the years 1975–2008 www.oecd.org/els/soc/dividedwestandwhyinequalitykeepsrising. htm. All data retrieved on 1 October 2018.
7 Milanovic (2012).
8 See also Asian Development Bank (2014) and Stiglitz (2012:106) "When money is concentrated at the top of society, the average American's spending is limited, or at least that would be the case in the absence of some artificial prop, which, in the years before the crisis, came in the form of a housing bubble fuelled by FED policies. The housing bubble created a consumption boom that gave the appearance that everything was fine. (. . .) Moving money from the bottom to the top lowers consumption because higher-income individuals consume a smaller proportion of their income than do lower-income individuals. (. . .) The result: until and unless something else happens (. . .) total demand in the economy will be less than what the economy is capable of supplying – and that means that there will be unemployment." Stiglitz (2012) provides references to Jayadev (2013) and Dynan et al. (2004).
9 See also: http://ged-project.de/2015/07/16/growing-income-inequality-in-germany-a-brake-on-economic-growth/ with an analysis of the German situation.
10 Cingano (2014).
11 Fajnzylber et al. (2002).
12 This is referred to in the literature as skill-biased technological change, i.e., a condition of technological change that favours the marginal productivity of more skilled and educated workers over lower-skilled workers.
13 Taylor (1996).
14 www.washingtonpost.com/blogs/plum-line/post/theres-been-class-warfare-for-the-last-20-years-and-my-class-has- won/2011/03/03/gIQApaFbAL_blog.html.
15 Cingano (2014) and "inequality can undermine progress in health and education, cause investment-reducing political and economic instability, and undercut the social consensus required to adjust in the face of shocks, and thus that it tends to reduce the pace and durability of growth" (Ostry et al., 2014:4).
16 Cingano (2014); "Equality-enhancing interventions could actually help growth: think of taxes on activities with negative externalities paid mostly by the rich (perhaps excessive risk-taking in the financial sector) or cash transfers aimed at encouraging better attendance at primary schools in developing countries, as examples" (Ostry et al., 2014:4).
17 Cingano (2014).

18 Gini index measures the extent to which the distribution of income (or, in some cases, consumption expenditure) among individuals or households within an economy deviates from a perfectly equal distribution. A Lorenz curve plots the cumulative percentages of total income received against the cumulative number of recipients, starting with the poorest individual or household. The Gini index measures the area between the Lorenz curve and a hypothetical line of absolute equality, expressed as a percentage of the maximum area under the line. Thus, a Gini index of 0 represents perfect equality, while an index of 100 implies perfect inequality. http://data.worldbank.org/indicator/SI.POV.GINI.

19 www.economicsonline.co.uk/Managing_the_economy/Inequality_and_equity.html.

20 http://techterms.com/definition/it.

Bibliography

Asian Development Bank. (2014). *Inequality in Asia and the Pacific: Trends, drivers, and policy implications*, edited by Changyong Rhee, Juzhong Zhuang and Ravi Kanbur. Philippines: Asian Development Bank, Mandaluyong City.

Cingano, F. (2014). "Trends in Income Inequality and Its Impact on Economic Growth," OECD Social, Employment and migration Working Papers, No. 163, OECD, Paris.

Davies, J., Lluberas, R. and Shorrocks, A. (2012). *Credit Suisse global wealth data book*. Zurich: Credit Suisse.

Dynan, K. E., Skinner, J. and Zeldes, S. P. (2004). "Do the Rich Save More?" *Journal of Political Economy*, 112(2): 397–444.

Fajnzylber, P., Lederman, D. and Loayza, N. (2002). "Inequality and Violent Crime," *Journal of Law and Economics*, 45(1): 1–40.

Jayadev, A. (2013). "Distribution and Crisis: Reviewing Some of the Linkages," in *The Handbook of the political economy of financial crises*, edited by Martin H. Wolfson and Gerald A. Epstein. Oxford: Oxford University Press.

Laderman, D., Fajnzylber, P. and Loayza, N. (2002). "Inequality and Violent Crime," *Journal of Law and Economics*, 45(1), Part 1.

Milanovic, B. (2012). "Global Income Inequality by the Numbers: In History and Now," Policy Research Working Paper 6259, World Bank Development Research Group Poverty and Inequality Team, November.

OECD. (2013). *Crisis squeezes income and puts pressure on inequality and poverty*. OECD.

Ostry, J. D., Berg, A. and Tsangarides, C. G. (2014). *Redistribution, inequality, growth*, IMF, April.

Shi Li. (2016). *Recent changes in income inequality in China, in world social science report 2016: Challenging inequalities: Pathways to a just world*. Paris, France: UNESCO Publishing.

Stiglitz, J. E. (2012). *The price of inequality: How today's divided society endangers our future*. London: Penguin Books.

Taylor, A. M. (1996). "International Capital Mobility in History: The Saving-Investment Relationship," NBER Working Paper No. 5743.

APPENDIX – INDEXES OF COMPETITIVENESS

During the last four decades, different organizations have developed so-called competitiveness indexes. Some groups of people accord them real authoritative status. In other cases, indexes become crucial elements in evaluations by government.[1] This section first presents three of the most famous competitiveness indexes, then offers reflections on the contemporary use of indicators – on composite indicators which combine the data from several simple indicators – and continues with consideration of the economic debate on competitiveness indexes. Finally, some conclusions follow.

Even if today the available indicators are many, here we concentrate our attention on three of them:

1   The GCI, from the WEF (World Economic Forum).
2   World Competitiveness Ranking, from the IMD business school.
3   The Doing Business Indicator (DBI), from the WB (World Bank).

The first two, by WEF and IMD, aim specifically at measuring country competitiveness, while the index produced by the WB tries to measure one of the possible determinants of competitiveness, the ease of doing business – or having a good business environment in one country – using some "proxy" indicators. Investors frequently consider all three.

A) Global Competitiveness Index (GCI)

www.weforum.org/reports/global-competitiveness-report-2014-2015

The WEF, until 1987 known as the European Management Forum, has produced this index since 2005; WEF is a private no-profit organization based in Switzerland

and chaired by Professor Klaus Schwab. The GCI is a complement and a development of the Global Competitiveness Report, which the WEF has produced since 1979. The index and report are based on the experience of the WEF, which has been convening top economic players since 1971 in Davos, in what is probably the top business-networking event of the world. WEF introduced its Sustainable Development Index in 2011.

The GCI was developed by Sala y Martin (Columbia) and Elsa Arvadi (Bocconi). Their work has followed the ideas of Michael Porter (Harvard). Until 1996 the report was produced in cooperation with the IMD business school of Geneva.

WEF defines "competitiveness as the set of institutions, policies, and factors that determine the level of the productivity of a country. The level of productivity, in turn, sets the level of prosperity that can be reached by an economy. The productivity level also determines the rates of return obtained by investments in an economy, which in turn are the fundamental drivers of its growth rates. In other words, a more competitive economy is one that is likely to grow faster over time."[2]

The GCI compares 144 economies and uses 100 indicators. The index is a weighted average of many different components, each measuring a different aspect of competitiveness. The components are grouped into 12 pillars of competitiveness:

1   Institutions.
2   Infrastructures.
3   Macroeconomic environment.
4   Health and primary education.
5   Higher education and training.
6   Goods markets efficiency.
7   Labour market efficiency.
8   Financial market development.
9   Technological readiness.
10 Market size.
11 Business sophistication.
12 Innovation.

Pillars 1–4 represent, according to the WEF, "basic requirements" and play a key role in initial phases of development. Pillars 5–10 constitute "efficiency enhancers" and play a greater role in countries at more advanced stages of development. Pillars 11 and 12 are defined as "innovation and sophistication factors" and are particularly important for the more advanced economies.

The GCI is produced with the support of a network of over 160 partner institutes worldwide. The partner institutes are instrumental in carrying out the Executive Opinion Survey, an inquiry into the opinions of 14,000 business leaders around the world. This survey provides a large part of the data in the report, which includes the index. This survey is then quoted by other organizations, for example Transparency International, OECD and the IMF.

From the outset its declared goal has been to provide insights and stimulate discussion between all stakeholders on the best strategies and policies to help countries overcome the obstacles to improving competitiveness.

In more recent times, the WEF has also begun exploring the complex relationship between competitiveness and sustainability as measured by its social and environmental dimension.

The final objective of WEF's work is to inform a series of meetings to raise awareness and rally support geared to the transformation of countries, to help them become more competitive, and increase prosperity.

The most recent version warns of the risks from inequality, but its major recommendations concern enhancement of productivity and do not address inequality or lack of demand in economies at risk of deflation.

Considering the 12 pillars of competitiveness, some considerations arise.

Pillar 1: Institutions

According to Lall (2001) "WEF indexes assign uniformly higher values to freer trade, stronger intellectual property protection and more liberal capital accounts across countries. This ignores valid arguments for interventions in all three, at least for developing countries with fledgling industrial sectors, weak capabilities and backward institutions."[3]

The concept of corruption itself is usually considered in a narrow sense. However, while illegal monetary payments to public officials are not rare in developing countries, it is frequent that these payments originate in industrialized countries.

Finally, we should note that some countries which have grown more in recent years are also countries in which many indicators of freedom and transparency have not been particularly high.

Pillar 3: Macroeconomic environment

This pillar gives a higher rank to countries with a balanced budget and low inflation. Some economists argue that under certain conditions deficit spending and inflation at 5 per cent or 11 per cent may be useful or even necessary to foster economic development.[4] Neither the balance of payments nor the N.IIP of the country is included among the variables used to build this pillar. These variables indicate the ability of a country to accumulate wealth with the rest of the world.

Pillar 6: Goods markets efficiency

"The best possible environment for the exchange of goods requires a minimum of government intervention that impedes business activity. For example, competitiveness is hindered by distortionary or burdensome taxes and by restrictive and discriminatory rules on foreign direct investment (FDI) – which limit foreign ownership – as well as on international trade".[5] WEF supports the thesis that limited government intervention is beneficial to development and competitiveness. Such very highly productive and competitive countries as Scandinavian countries do not seem to confirm this thesis.

Pillar 7: Labour market efficiency

The variables contributing to this pillar imply that the more flexible a labour market, the better it is. Moreover, in this case the empirical evidence is not as clear as this pillar would suggest.[6]

Pillar 8: Financial market development

While finance is an essential element of a developed market economy, it becomes more and more evident that countries need financial development, but may suffer when finance occupies too large a part of the economy.[7]

Additionally, financial development is often achieved through deregulation. "After the Asian crisis, the dangers of premature liberalization of the capital account hardly need to be argued."[8]

Some deregulation in the financial sector probably also contributed to the devastating 2008 financial crisis and the subsequent global recession.

Pillar 9: Technological readiness

"It measures the agility with which an economy adopts existing technologies to enhance the productivity of its industries, with specific emphasis on its capacity to fully leverage information and communication technologies (ICTs) in daily activities and production processes for increased efficiency and enabling innovation for competitiveness."[9]

According to Lall "Strong intellectual property protection by non-innovating countries can lead to higher costs of importing technology and products embodying new technology. It can also constrict a valuable avenue for learning, copying and reverse engineering".[10] However WEF also strongly supports the defence of intellectual property in developing countries.

Pillar 11: Business sophistication

Business sophistication concerns two elements that are intricately linked: the quality of a country's overall business networks and the quality of individual firms' operations and strategies.[11] This pillar is built on the opinions of managers, which are certainly important, but the absence of objective measurements can be perceived as a limitation.

TABLE A The global competitiveness index

Pros	Cons
It presents several valuable data	The criteria of data aggregation are not strongly motivated
Summarizes the opinions of several managers	The use of survey data can sometimes be considered excessive, especially when alternative objective data are available
It is supported by Porter (Harvard), Sala i Martin (Columbia) and Artadi (Bocconi)	It is criticized by Krugman (MIT), Lall (Oxford)
Identifies the problem of competitiveness of countries	Underestimate the issue of market failures
Generates a debate	It explains just 2/3 of the determinants of productivity
Is accepted by many managers	Underestimates the differences between large and small countries
It explains the determinants of productivity.	

Pillar 12: Innovation

This pillar is mostly concerned with technological innovation as a tool for enhancing productivity. In this case most of the data also derives from the opinions of managers, even when hard data is available.

The GCI is probably the best known and most-used index of competitiveness. Its strength is based on the large amount of data attached to it and on the acceptance and recognition it has in a wide network of companies and in the business community as a whole. Its major limitations derive from the soundness of the methodology used, on the validity of its theoretical assumptions and on the quality of the survey data (see the Table A).

Not everybody shares the opinion of John Thornhill, but it is worth mentioning it: "The World Economic Forum does a remarkable job of forging the conventional wisdom among the global elite. The trouble is that conventional wisdom is invariably wrong."[12]

B) World Competitiveness Ranking (WCR)[13]

In 1990, the merger of the training centres of Alcan and Nestlé created the Institute for Management Development (IMD) business school based in Lausanne (Switzerland). Since 1989 one of its founding members has been producing the World Competitiveness Yearbook, which until 1996 was co-published with the WEF. In 1994, IMD developed the World Competitiveness Ranking, which ranks and analyses the ability of 66 nations to create and maintain an environment in which enterprises can compete. It is based on the work of Michael Porter (Harvard). Stephane Garelli (IMD) and Arturo Bris (IMD) have since developed it. It assumes that wealth creation takes place **primarily at enterprise level**, whether private or state-owned. IMD calls this field of research "competitiveness of enterprises". However, according to IMD enterprises operate in a national environment which enhances or hinders their ability to compete domestically or internationally.

IMD calls this field of research: "competitiveness of nations".[14]

> Competitiveness of Nations is a field of economic theory, which analyzes the facts and policies that shape the ability of a nation to create and maintain an environment that sustains more value creation for its enterprises and more prosperity for its people.[15]

> The IMD World Competitiveness Yearbook (WCY) looks at the relationship between a country's national environment (where the State plays a key role) and the wealth creation process (assumed by enterprises and individuals). The WCY focuses on the outcome of the interaction of four competitiveness factors, which generally define a country's national environment.[16]

Its methodology divides the national environment into four main factors:

1   Economic performance.
2   Government efficiency.
3   Business efficiency.
4   Infrastructure.

Each of these factors in turn is divided into five sub-factors which highlight every facet of the areas analysed. Altogether the World Competitiveness Yearbook features 20 such sub-factors, which comprise more than 300 criteria, although each sub-factor does not necessarily have the same number of criteria (for example, it takes more criteria to assess Education than to evaluate Prices). Each sub-factor, independently of the number of criteria it contains, has the same weight in the overall consolidation of results, which is 5 per cent ($20 \times 5 = 100$).

Criteria can be hard data which analyse competitiveness, as far as it can be measured (e.g. GDP), or soft data, which analyse competitiveness as far as it can be perceived (e.g. availability of competent managers). Hard criteria represent a weighting of two-thirds in the overall ranking, whereas the survey data represent a weight of one-third. In addition, some criteria are for background information only, which means that they are not used in calculating the overall competitiveness ranking (e.g. population under 15). Finally, aggregating the results of the 20 sub-factors creates the total consolidation which leads to the overall ranking in the WCY.

Hard data including statistics are taken from international organizations (IMF, WB, OECD, ILO, etc), private institutions (CB Richard Ellis, Mercer HR Consulting, PwC, etc) and national sources through their network of partner institutes. Each year, IMD conducts a survey; 6,100 business executives in top or middle management are asked to assess the situation in their own country in response to a questionnaire.

Read

IMD economic assumptions for world competitiveness factors

I Economic performance

1 Competitiveness of a country heavily relies on past economic performance
2 Competition governed by market forces improves the economic performance of a country
3 The more competition there is in the domestic economy the more competitive the domestic firms are likely to be abroad
4 A country's success in international trade and/or investments reflects competitiveness of its domestic companies
5 Openness for international economic activities increases a country's economic performance
6 International investment allocates economic resources more efficiently worldwide
7 Export-led competitiveness is often associated with growth-orientation in the domestic economy

II Government efficiency

1 State intervention in business activities should be minimized, apart from creating competitive conditions for enterprises
2 Government should, however, provide macroeconomic and social conditions that are predictable and thus minimize the external risks for economic enterprise
3 Government should be flexible in adapting its economic policies to a changing international environment
4 Government should provide a societal framework, which promotes fairness, equality and justice while ensuring the security of the population

III Business efficiency

1 Efficiency and the ability to adapt to changes in the competitive environment are managerial attributes crucial for enterprise competitiveness
2 Responsible finance support value-adding activities in business
3 A well-developed, internationally integrated financial sector in a country supports its international competitiveness

4   Maintaining a high standard of living requires integration with the international economy

5   Entrepreneurship is crucial for economic activity in its start-up phase

6   A skilled labour force increases a country's competitiveness

7   High productivity reflects an optimum utilization of resources

8   The attitude of the workforce affects the competitiveness of a country

IV Infrastructure

1   Traditional infrastructure – energy, transport, etc – is fundamental for economic development

2   Advanced infrastructure – information technology, environment sciences, health sciences, etc – are nonetheless essential and can provide "leap frog" development

3   Competitive advantage can also be built on efficient and innovative application of existing technologies

4   Investment in basic research and innovative activity creating new knowledge is crucial for a country in a more mature stage of economic development

5   Long-term investment in R&D is likely to increase the competitiveness of enterprises

6   The quality of life is part of the attractiveness of a country

7   Adequate and accessible educational resources help develop a knowledge-driven economy

Questions

- What is the IMD approach to market openness?
- What type of attitude has IMD towards FDIs?
- How extensive should state intervention in business activities be?
- Do you know of any successful country with extensive state intervention in the economy?
- Do IMD assumptions ever refer to possible market failures (e.g. pollution, insufficient amount of education, monopolies, difficulty of relying on privately paid armies and privately funded lighthouses)?
- Is there any reference to different types of market environment, where market forces operate?
- Does IMD make any distinction between large and small countries?
- What are the main references to risks similar to those which brought on the 2008 financial crisis?

- Does assumption II4 "Government should provide a societal framework which promotes fairness, equality and justice while ensuring the security of the population" imply that countries with less inequality are better than countries with higher inequality?
- Is there any reference to the role of military spending and geo-strategic power of countries?

Analysis

IMD considers market openness as clearly good; this is probably true with perfectly working and perfectly competitive markets, in the absence of monopolies and pollution, and in the absence of political considerations and the politically motivated behaviour of countries. In the real world, countries are as much motivated by economic considerations as by considerations pertaining to their ideology, their culture and their political and military power. Military expenditure in some cases represents a major component of total public spending of countries. The suspicion that this has consistent implications for their economies is legitimate. Military spending drains resources, but in some cases constitutes an investment. Countries with similar economic and financial parameters may experience quite different conditions, depending on their strategic relevance.

Some economists raise some doubts about the undiversified net effect of market openness.[17]

Something similar occurs with FDIs (see Section 11.3). More generally IMD assumptions make no direct reference to such market failures as oligopolistic markets (see Section 7.3), the market environment in which the majority of the firms which are partners and clients of IMD operate, asymmetrical information, moral hazards, pollution and public goods. Oligopolies and monopolies are more the rule than the exception. Under such assumptions, competition is best, but the reality could be different.

In the same context we can understand why state intervention is assumed to be minimal: in a perfectly working market there is not much room for state intervention, there is just room for some income and wealth redistribution, which however the IMD assumptions do not mention.

IMD AND WEF ABOUT SOUTH AFRICAN COMPETITIVE POSITION

The work of Kaplan (2003) has analysed the IMD and WEF rankings for South Africa. "It has a country focus – South Africa's overall competitive position, South Africa's competitive position with regard to technology, and the contribution of technology to South Africa's overall competitive position. In particular, the IMD and WEF measures were investigated to see if they could provide a clear guide as to South Africa's relative competitiveness ranking and the manner in which this ranking has altered over time. The clear conclusion is that, neither individually nor collectively can the indexes generated by the IMD and the WEF be utilized to give consistent and unambiguous answers to these questions."[18] "Neither provides a clear and persuasive guide to South Africa's overall competitiveness ranking, nor how this has altered over time. The problem resides principally in the assessment of technological capacities and the contribution that technology makes to overall competitiveness. The IMD and the WEF approaches to technology diverge significantly, but both are inadequate. As a consequence, there is a substantial discrepancy between the two as regards South Africa's current overall competitiveness ranking. Neither individually, nor collectively, are these competitiveness indicators – as they are currently constituted – useful as a guide to policy."[19]

Assumptions do refer to the need for fairness and equality even if inequality does not seem to be at the centre of the IMD evaluation of a country. The case of very fast growing China or that of highly productive France may eventually not fit perfectly into a framework of minimal state intervention. The case for state intervention is particularly strong in the financial sector where the simple actions of market players may create quite considerable risks. Finally, these assumptions do not mention the differences between large and small countries. Such small countries as Singapore, Ireland, Dubai, Iceland and Hong Kong may often be presented as examples for other countries, even if the economies of small countries operate under substantially different conditions: their internal demand is often a small part of their total demand and from the fiscal point of view they can employ certain strategies, for example low taxation of capital which generates revenues abroad, which are not available to large countries (see Table B).

TABLE B The world competitiveness report

Pros	Cons
It includes several valuable data	The criteria of data aggregation are not strongly motivated
Summarizes the opinions of several managers	It is criticized by Krugman (MIT), Lall (Oxford)
It is supported by Garelli (IMD), and Bris (IMD)	It underestimates the issue of market failures
Identifies the problem of competitiveness of countries	No China until 1994
Generates a debate	Shares much of the criticism addressed to the GCI
Is used by foreign investors to take investment decisions	

C) Doing Business Indicators (DBIs)[20]

The International Finance Corporation (IFC), a part of the WB Group, has produced the Doing Business Indicators (DBIs) since 2003. They are based on the work of Djankov and are supported by many published articles. Such economists as Djankov, Shleifer, Alesina and Perotti have written in favour of these indicators. IFC has also produced an aggregate indicator, the "Ease of doing business ranking", since 2005. More recently IFC has also measured the distance of a country from the "frontier", that is from the optimality represented by the best-performing country. In this way it offers a measure of the distance of a country from best practice.

The indicators measure the quality of business laws and related legal institutions across 189 countries. They concern the regulations that affect domestic small and medium-size enterprises, operating in the largest business city of an economy. For economies with more than 100 million people, they also consider the second largest business city. The Doing Business team, with a large group of partners, compiles the raw data by reading laws and regulations, asking 10,700 respondents mostly lawyers, from all over the world to report on the steps that a hypothetical firm would have to undertake in order to perform various tasks, including starting a business, hiring and firing workers, and enforcing a contract. Other sources of information are local governments and WB staff in the country. The indicators generally reflect the time, cost and number of procedures associated with each task. The considered tasks are the following:

- Starting a business.
- Dealing with construction permits.
- Getting electricity.
- Registering property.
- Getting credit.
- Protecting minority investors.
- Paying taxes.
- Trading across borders.
- Enforcing contracts.
- Resolving insolvency.

They also collect data on labour and market regulation, but these data do not contribute any more to the ease of business ranking, which a country obtains.

The creators of the DBIs are very explicit about their theoretical presumptions:

> A fundamental premise of Doing Business is that economic activity requires good rules – rules that establish and clarify property rights and reduce the cost of resolving disputes; rules that increase the predictability of economic interactions and provide contractual partners with certainty and protection against abuse. The objective is regulations designed to be efficient, accessible to all and simple in their implementation.[21]

These presumptions as to the relationship between law and economic development inform every aspect of the construction of the DBIs. To begin with, the very existence of the indicators – which are not very costly to create by the standards of a large global organization – reflects a presumption that **rules and regulations are important**. Secondly, the fact that the indicators focus exclusively on rules embodied in the **formal legal system** reflects a presumption that it is those rules, as opposed to rules reflected in informal practices, that influence economic activity. Thirdly, the idea that regulations that make transactions such as starting a business or firing a worker fast, cheap and simple are automatically desirable clearly informs the choice of **time, cost, and simplicity as metrics**. The Doing Business project's empirical methodology implicitly presumes that **elite lawyers are reliable sources of information on how small and medium-size enterprises** navigate the formal legal system. The project's proponents tend to gloss over the fact that all of these claims are in fact contestable. The specific theoretical claims embodied in the DBIs reflect ideas disseminated through networks linking elite academic economists to the WB.

At the same time, there is no mention of competition policy and provision of education, if only to mention topics that economics (e.g. Smith, 1776) has stressed from its very beginning.

The DBIs are tremendously influential and exemplify the range of mechanisms through which power can be exercised beyond the state. To begin with, the DBIs are used, in combination with other indicators, to guide the allocation of foreign aid by multilateral development banks and USAID in the US.

The DBIs also appear to be successful in attracting the attention of senior policy makers, government officials, and business leaders in many of the WB's client countries, as well as potential foreign investors in those countries, thus prompting significant amounts of benchmarking, dialogue and reform. Even critics of the DBIs seem to agree that their promulgation has prompted many countries to reform their legal systems.

The Doing Business indicators also shed light on how governance through indicators can be contested and regulated. A transnational group of workers' representatives (spearheaded by the International Trade Union Confederation), together with the International Labour Organization (ILO, several key figures in the US Congress, and a range of academics and NGOs, campaigned to achieve significant change in the use of the WB's Employing Workers Indicator (EWI). The activists complained that the indicator was biased in favour of labour market deregulation and so was being used by international financial institutions to pressurise developing countries to dismantle protections for workers. In April 2009, the WB agreed that it would stop using the controversial indicator in decisions about the allocation of funds; that it would begin revising the EWI so as to give more favourable scores to certain worker-protection policies aligned with ILO Conventions; and that it would establish a consultative group to formulate a new worker-protection indicator.[22]

The campaign against the labour indicators was aided by the release in 2008 of a report by the WB's Independent Evaluation Group (IEG), which endorsed

TABLE C Findings of the Independent Review Panel appointed by the WB president

Major concerns	Some recommendations
The report may be misinterpreted	Retain the Doing Business Report
It relies on a narrow information source	Remove the aggregate rankings
It only measures regulations applicable to certain business	Group by topic or shift to categories as an alternative to ranking
Its data-collection can be improved	Change the report's title
It is not designed to help countries respond appropriately	Implement a peer-review process
Paying taxes and employing workers topics require additional consideration	Increase the report's level of transparency
The governance of the project is insufficient	Reform the report's methodology.
The use of aggregate rankings is problematic	Align the report with the WB's mandate and other flagship publications
	Relocate the report in the WB
	Improve the report's governance framework

complaints that the indicators were inconsistent with the spirit of key ILO Conventions. The IEG's evaluation represents the kind of accountability mechanism that might serve as a model for future efforts to regulate the production of indicators. The IEG report does not, however, consider or propose mechanisms that might be used to monitor and control future uses of indicators such as the DBIs. While no special purpose control mechanism exists, concerns about the DBIs have prompted some WB personnel and outside commentators to express private or public scepticism about relying (or overly relying) on the indicators to make policy (see Table C).[23]

In conclusion the DBI are examples of very important indicators which officially constitute a basis for important public decisions. We could note that these indicators have attracted criticism, which, in several respects, is similar to that addressed to the GCI. We can appreciate that there is a form of dialogue between the IFC, which produces these indexes, and its critics. We also appreciate the recent choices of the WB's management.

D) Discussion[24]

"The use of indicators is a prominent feature of contemporary global governance. Indicators are used to compare and rank states for purposes as varied as deciding how to allocate foreign aid or investment and determining whether states have complied with their treaty obligations."[25]

"As tools of governance, indicators are commonly developed by powerful bodies seeking to manage and control populations or allocate resources. They may also be used to rank countries or organizations or to determine eligibility for a benefit. Indicators are directed not only at helping decision makers decide where to build a railroad or in what country to invest, but also at promoting self-governance among the governed. By establishing standards according to which individuals, organizations, or nations should behave, indicators should inspire those who are measured to perform better and improve their ranking."[26]

"Simplification, or reductionism, is central to the appeal (and probably the impact) of indicators."[27]

"Indicators are a **political technology** that can be used for many different purposes, including advocacy, reform, control, and management."[28]

"A composite indicator is formed when individual indicators are compiled into a single index on the basis of an underlying model. The composite indicator should ideally measure **multi-dimensional concepts** which cannot be captured by a single indicator, e.g. competitiveness, industrialization, sustainability, single market integration, knowledge-based society, etc."[29]

"Composite indicators (CIs) which compare country performance are increasingly recognized as a useful tool in policy analysis and public communication. [. . .] Such composite indicators provide simple comparisons of countries that can be used to illustrate complex and sometimes elusive issues in wide-ranging fields, e.g., environment, economy, society or technological development. It often seems **easier for the general public** to interpret composite indicators than to identify common trends across many separate indicators, and they have also proven useful in benchmarking country performance [.]. Their 'big picture' results may invite users (especially policy-makers) to draw **simplistic analytical or policy conclusions**. In fact, composite indicators must be seen as a **means of initiating discussion and stimulating public interest**."[30]

Table D presents the main pros and cons of using composite indicators according to OECD (2008), a text published in cooperation with the EU Commission.

"The quality of a composite indicator as well as the soundness of the messages it conveys depend not only on the methodology used in its construction but primarily on the quality of the framework and the data used. A composite indicator based on a weak theoretical background or on soft data containing large measurement errors can lead to disputable policy messages, in spite of the use of state-of-the-art methodology in its construction. [. . .] Whichever framework is used, transparency must be the guiding principle of the entire exercise."[31]

More specifically on competitiveness indexes "most analysts, however, use a broader definition of competitiveness and focus on structural factors affecting medium to long-term economic performance: productivity, innovation, skills and so on". You are concerned with these issues only if you assume that markets may fail. There are three ways to approaching the issue of market failures:

1   The first assumes that basically free markets work and all institutions are in place. Relatively few people take this approach. It must be said that if it is true, then there is no room for policies to enhance competitiveness. The market takes care of itself.

2   The second "accepts that some markets and institutions are deficient". It advocates interventions to remedy market failures, as long as these are "functional" and do not favour selected activities over others (the "market friendly" approach).

COMPETITIVENESS IN ECONOMICS

For economists there are three key measures of competitiveness:

> Unit labour cost (see Section 3.4)
> Real exchange rate (see Section 10.3).
> The terms of trade.

The **Unit Labour Cost** does not include compensation of capital. Precisely for this reason it is of considerable interest to employers. If they deduce unit labour cost from price, they obtain their margin. In an international comparison, a product's unit labour cost is only one of the factors determining its competitiveness. A country may have a very low unit labour cost, but its companies have high profit margins, landlords receive high rents and there is very low capital productivity, and therefore this country may not be able to sell its product in the world (it is not competitive).

The **real exchange rate** (Section 10.3) takes into account the productivity and cost of both capital and labour. However, in addition, the real exchange rate has a limitation: it includes the prices of all goods: those which are traded and those which are not traded (barbers, personal services in general, shopkeepers and accommodation, among others).

There are three reasons why a commodity might not be traded internationally: [1] some are simply not transportable (housing for instance); they are non-tradable (see Section 10.2); [2] others may be transportable and hence tradable but are not traded as it is unprofitable to do so due to the high costs of transportation or tariffs; [3] products may be tradable but trade in them may be illegal. The alternative could consist of using the **terms of trade**: the prices of exported goods *vis-à-vis* the prices of imported goods. However, even terms of trade have a problem: they include the prices of traded goods, but they ignore tradable goods, that is those which are not traded but potentially could be. Some countries like the US trade relatively few goods but have a great quantity of tradable goods. The optimal measure should include traded and tradable goods. Unfortunately, we usually do not have reliable data on tradable goods. So, what can be done? The right solution could be as follows: if the majority of non-traded goods are tradable, then use the real exchange rate, and although you commit a mistake, it is small. If the majority of the non-traded goods are non-tradable, then use the terms of trade, and again although you commit a mistake, it is small.

3   The third also includes selective interventions where market failures require this.

The difference between the second and the third approach is critical to competitiveness analysis.

> It takes the analysis beyond the existence of market imperfections to the nature of those imperfections [.]. In theory, however, it is clear that conditions that call for selectivity are common in developing countries: diffuse information market failures, costs of mastering tacit technology, existence of widespread externalities and linkages, and pervasive weaknesses in factor markets and institutions. This brings us to the second issue: when selective interventions are theoretically justifiable, whether it is feasible in practice for governments to mount selective "strategy." Krugman opposes competitiveness analysis mainly on this point: accepting the validity of strategy, he is deeply sceptical of its practical utility.[32]

Krugman is therefore generally sceptical about competition between countries, about indexes for measuring it and about government policies to increase competitiveness. According to Lall (2001) the study of such a subject as competitiveness makes sense, because markets are not perfect and countries should try to overcome market failures. For him the development of competitiveness indexes makes sense too. According to him the WEF and the IMD indexes have two major problems:

1   untested theoretical assumptions, e.g. the idea that free trade is always better and that government intervention should be minimal and,
2   weak methodology (quality of the data and methods of their aggregation). On this basis, he considers that the importance given to the WEF index is not fully deserved.

Garelli,[33] an IMD professor and creator of the IMD index, stresses that the traditional emphasis of economists on trade, when they speak about international competition, is misplaced. According to him, FDIs (Section 11.3) matter too; probably for him they are the true cornerstone. To support his point, he stresses that the amount of FDI grew considerably after 1980. With the liberalization of capital movements (Section 11.4), countries compete not only for trade but also for receiving FDI.

In recent years the use of indicators for policy purposes has considerably increased. Among indicators, composite indicators play a special role, because they synthesise much data into a single number. Competitiveness indexes are simple or composite indicators. They play an important role in the choices of private and public decision makers. The WEF, the IMD and the WB have developed indexes which are at the centre of many important debates and are recognized as sources of information by many key stakeholders. They come together with well-written reports which include much useful data. The analysis presented in this chapter

TABLE D Pros and cons of composite Indicators according to OECD

Pros	Cons
Can summarize complex, multi-dimensional realities with a view to supporting decisionmakers	May send misleading policy messages if poorly constructed or misinterpreted
Are easier to interpret than a battery of many separate indicators	May invite simplistic policy conclusions
Can assess progress of countries over time	May be misused, e.g. to support a desired policy, if the construction process is not transparent and/or lacks sound statistical or conceptual principles
Reduce the visible size of a set of indicators without dropping the underlying information base. Thus make it possible to include more information within the existing size limit	The selection of indicators and weights could be the subject of political dispute
Place issues of country performance and progress at the centre of the policy arena	May disguise serious failings in some dimensions and increase the difficulty of identifying proper remedial action, if the construction process is not transparent
Facilitate communication with general public (i.e. citizens, media, etc) and promote accountability	May lead to inappropriate policies if dimensions of performance that are difficult to measure are ignored
Help to construct/underpin narratives for lay and literate audiences	
Enable users to compare complex dimensions effectively	

Source: OECD (2008:13–14)

presents as evidence not only the advantages of these indexes (synthesis, easiness of utilization, recognition in a community and ability to stimulate debate) but also their limitations: theoretical assumptions, quality of the data and methodology of their aggregation. We can conclude that while competitiveness indexes maybe useful information tools, their present roles in decision making should at least be further critically discussed.

Glossary

CIs See *composite indicators*.

composite indicators A composite indicator is formed when individual indicators are compiled into a single index on the basis of an underlying model. The composite indicator should ideally measure multi-dimensional concepts which cannot be captured by a single indicator, e.g. competitiveness, industrialization, sustainability, single market integration, knowledge-based society, etc. [34]

country policy and institutional assessment   The primary determinant of WB aid allocations.

CPIA   See country policy and institutional assessment.

DBIs   See *doing business indicators*.

doing business indicators (DBIs)   They measure the quality of business laws and related legal institutions across 183 countries and are produced by IFC.

employing workers indicator   Formerly one of the DBIs. It addresses hiring conditions.

executive opinion survey   An inquiry into the opinions of top managers around the world. This survey provides a large part of the data of the GCI.

EWI   See *employing workers indicator*.

GCI   See *Global Competitiveness Index*.

Global Competitiveness Index   A composite indicator produced by the WEF, a private no-profit organization based in Switzerland since 2005. It is based on the experience of the WEF, which has been convening top economic players since 1971 in Davos, in what is probably the top business-networking event of the world.

IFC   See *International Financial Corporation*.

ILO   See *International Labour Organization*.

International Financial Corporation   A part of the WB group which encourages private sector development in developing countries.

IMD   See *Institute for Management Development*.

Institute for Management Development (IMD)   A major business school, which is based in Lausanne (CH); it produces the WCY.

International Labour Organization   The UN agency concerned with labour issues.

USAID US   Agency for International Development.

WCI   See *World Competitiveness Index*.

WCR   See *World Competitiveness Ranking*.

WCY   See *World Competitiveness Yearbook*.

WEF   See *World Economic Forum*.

World Competitiveness Index   An annual index produced by WEF.

World Competitiveness Ranking   An index produced by the IMD in Lausanne.

World Competitiveness Report   An annual report produced by WEF.

World Competitiveness Yearbook   An annual report on the competitiveness of nations published annually by IMD since 1989.

World Economic Forum   Private no-profit organization which organizes a meeting of chiefs of major companies and politicians in Davos (CH) every year. It also produces the GCI.

Notes

1   Lall (2001).
2   WEF (2015:4).

3 Lall (2001:1506). Lall (ibidem) continues so: "There is a good economic case for infant industry protection in developing countries, particularly in overcoming the initial costs of tacit learning and building new skills and networks. The evidence also bears out the vital contribution that well-managed industrial policy can make to rapid technology upgrading and competitiveness building."

4 Islam (2014).

5 WEF (2015:7).

6 IMF (2015:104–107).

7 Wolf, Martin, 2015, Why finance is too much of a good thing, *Financial Times*, 27/05/2015.

8 Lall (2001:1506).

9 WEF (2015:7–8).

10 Lall (2001:1506).

11 WEF (2015:8).

12 John Thornhill, review of the book: *The Fourth Industrial Revolution*, by Klaus Schwab, January 17, 2016.

13 The IMD website www.imd.org/wcc/research-methodology/ is acknowledged as source of information for this sub-section.

14 Garelli (2014:493).

15 Garelli (2014:493).

16 Garelli (2014:494).

17 E.g. Rodriguez and Rodrik (2001) or Baldwin and Robert Nicoud (2008).

18 Kaplan (2003:88).

19 Kaplan (2003:87–88).

20 This section is largely based on the work of Davis et al. (2012).

21 Doing Business, 2011: Making a Difference for Entrepreneurs. (2010:v).

22 In the 2011 Doing Business report, the International Finance Corporation (the entity in the WB group that produces the indicators) ceased to give any weight to the EWI, while preparations were made for a replacement indicator much more closely aligned with ILO conventions.

23 More formally, reports suggest that at the October 2010 meeting of the WB's executive board, executive directors representing Brazil and China were among those expressing opposition to the bank's continued use of rankings in this area. In t2012, the WB president appointed an independent review panel to conduct a review of the Doing Business project. The major conclusions of the panel are exposed in the Table C.

24 The first part of this section largely follows Davis et al. (2012).

25 Davis et al. (2012).

26 Engle Merry (2011:S89)

27 Davis et al. (2012:77) They continue so: "Yet, the transformation of particularistic knowledge into numerical representations, which are readily comparable, strips meaning and context from the phenomenon. [. . .] They take flawed and incomplete data that may have been collected for other purposes and merge them together to produce an apparently coherent and complete picture. Indicators often have embedded within them, or are placeholders for, a much further-reaching theory – which some might call an ideology – of what a good society is, or how governance should ideally be conducted to achieve the best possible approximation of a good society or a good policy. At a minimum they are produced as, or used as, markers for larger policy ideas. [. . .] Often the theory or policy idea is not spelled out at all in the indicator but remains implicit".

28 Engle Merry (2011:92–93). This text continues so: "In some ways, indicators are like witchcraft. [. . .] And like witchcraft, indicators presume a system of knowledge and a theory of how things happen that are hegemonic and rarely subjected to scrutiny, despite their critical role in the allocation of power".

29 OECD (2008:13).

30 OECD (2008:13).

31 OECD (2008:17).

32 285 Lall (2001:1504) cites Krugman (1996, p. 24). Lall (2001:1504) continues so: "He [Krugman] divides analysts into 'realists' and 'strategists'. Realists (as he considers himself) are sceptical of government abilities to mount effective selective interventions. Strategists are naive about strategy, believing that interventions can work and yield significant benefits. Krugman uses the unsuccessful US government intervention in semiconductors to argue that 'it is very difficult to formulate strategic trade policies, and even if you could, it would not be worth much to the economy.'"
33 Garelli (2014).
34 OECD (2008:13).

Bibliography

Baldwin, R. E. and Robert-Nicoud, F. (2008). "Trade and Growth with Heterogeneous Firms," *Journal of International Economics*, 74(1) (January): 21–34.

Davis, K., Kingsbury, B. and Engle Merry, S. (2012). "Indicators as a Technology of Global Governance," *Law & Society Review*, 46(1): 71–104.

Engle Merry, S. (2011). "Measuring the World: Indicators, Human Rights, and Global Governance," *Current Anthropology*, 52(S3).

Garelli, Stéphane. (2014). "The Fundamentals and History of Competitiveness," IMD World Competitiveness Yearbook 2014, IMD, Lausanne, CH.

International Monetary Fund. (2015). *World economic outlook*. International Monetary Fund. Washington, DC.

Islam, I. (2014). "Macroeconomic Policy After the Global Recession of 2008–2009: A Development Perspective." in *The twin challenges of reducing poverty and creating employment*, pp. 123–139. New York, NY: United Nations.

Kaplan, D. E. (2003). "Measuring Our Competitiveness: A Critical Examination of the IMD and WEF Competitiveness Indicators for South Africa," *Development Southern Africa*, 20(1): 75–88.

Krugman, P. R. (1996). "Making Sense of the Competitiveness Debate," *Oxford Review of Economic Policy*, 12(3): 17–25.

Lall, S. (2001). "Competitiveness Indices and Developing Countries: An Economic Evaluation of the Global Competitiveness Report," *World Development*, 29(9): 1501–1525. http://doi.org/10.1016/s0305-750x(01)00051-1.

OECD. (2008). *Handbook on constructing composite indicators: Methodology and user guide*. Paris: Organization for Economic Co-operation and Development.

Rodriguez, Francisco and Rodrik, Dani. (2001). "Trade Policy and Economic Growth: A Skeptic's Guide to the Cross-National Evidence," in *NBER Macroeconomics Annual 2000*, vol. 15, edited by Ben S. Bernanke and Kenneth Rogoff. MIT Press.

Smith, A. (1776). *An inquiry into the nature and causes of the wealth of nations. London, Methuen, 1922.*

Stiglitz, J. (2000). *Economics of the public sector*, 3rd ed. New York: W. W. Norton & Company.

Thornhill, J. (2016). "Review of the Book: *The Fourth Industrial Revolution*, by Klaus Schwab," *Financial Times*, 17 January.

Wolf, M. (2015). "Why Finance Is Too Much of a Good Thing," *Financial Times*, 27 May.

World Bank (2011) Doing business: Making a difference for entrepreneurs. (2010). Washington, DC: World Bank

World Economic Forum. (2015). *The global competitiveness report 2014–2015: Full data edition*. Geneva, CH: World Economic Forum-The Global Competitiveness and Benchmarking Network.

INDEX